Gerard Hardy's Misfortune

A SEA-CHANGE MYSTERY

DOROTHY JOHNSTON

The mystery is not the way we die, it's the way we live.

Martin Cruz Smith

Cover design by John Cozzi – jjcozzi@bigpond.com
Some cover images are based on the Rider-Waite tarot deck.
Internal design by Barbie Robinson – Writing with Light

Ms. Johnston's portrait by Lindsay Kelley –
www.lindsaykelleyphotography.com.au
Printed in Australia by IngramSpark

Gerard Hardy's Misfortune / Dorothy Johnston
9780648416579 (paperback)
9780648416586 (ebook)

Also by Dorothy Johnston

Sea-change Mysteries:

Through a Camel's Eye
The Swan Island Connection

The Sandra Mahoney Quartet:

The Trojan Dog
The White Tower
Eden
The Fourth Season

*****

Tunnel Vision
Ruth
Maralinga My Love
One for the Master
The House at Number 10
Eight Pieces on Prostitution (short story collection)

Praise for *The Sandra Mahoney Quartet*

'Detective Sergeant Brook, making cheerful capital out of terminal illness to fast-track police department procedure, is one of the most unusual and attractive characters to hit the Australian crime scene in years.'
The Adelaide Advertiser

'An artfully seductive crime story with a denouement which is chilling, fast and furious.'
The Age

'A class act.'
The Weekend Australian

'A realistic setting, a strong storyline, plausible and affecting characters and writing of sensitivity and strength.'
The Sunday Age

Praise for Dorothy Johnston's literary fiction

'An awesome talent.'
The Australian

'What I like most about *One for the Master* is its passion and its mystery.'
Australian Book Review

'Johnston achieves the difficult double feat: she creates and maintains a convincing physical world, and yet transcends it through a lovely and original imagination.'
The Sydney Morning Herald

For Jen McDonald

With grateful thanks to all those who have supported me in the writing of this novel, including members of the Queenscliffe Historical Museum and the Henry Handel Richardson Society, especially Janey Runci and Barbara Findlayson. Thanks to Mathew and Lisa Jose from The Bookshop at Queenscliff, who have been a great support. Congratulations to John Cozzi for his cover design. Finally, to my family and the team at For Pity Sake Publishing: to editor David Burton; Barbie Robinson for her internal design, Sara Dowse for proof-reading; and in particular Jen McDonald, to whom this book is dedicated.

ONE

Sarah Kent, who had found the body, sat shaking, shoulders hunched, in the early morning shadows behind the *Royal's* reception counter. This counter stood in an alcove some ten metres from the hotel's huge front doors; the terrazzo floor that led to it would once have made the entrance grand. The counter with its phone, computer, brochures and its vase of flowers fitted the alcove snugly; the shadows were caused partly by an elaborate spiral staircase rising above it.

As Chris Blackie stepped inside out of the pearly autumn light, he understood that Matthew, the hotel manager, had been holding Sarah in his arms and that the two had moved apart when they heard him coming.

Chris observed as well that it would always be dim in that corner, that whoever worked there would always need artificial light.

Sarah's face was red and swollen with crying, but underneath this she was an attractive young woman, her fair hair cut just above her shoulders, her features clean and finely-made.

Matthew turned to Chris and spoke gravely. 'The basement door's locked. Here's the key.' In the shadows, the young man's teeth shone unnaturally white. He made a complex movement of his right hand that might have included an apology. 'You'll see there's renovations being done.'

'Who used the key this morning?'

'I did, and Sarah – oh, I'm sorry. I didn't think of that.'

Chris used his handkerchief to take the key from Matthew, then folded it carefully and put it in a plastic bag.

He explained that his job was to secure the area and that detectives from Geelong CIU would be there within the hour. He repeated what he'd said on the phone. It was important that no one in the building should leave, and that no one else should be allowed to enter.

Matthew nodded. Few of the rooms were occupied, he said. The night before there'd been only four guests. He named them quickly, the last one, Gerard Hardy, at that moment lying underneath their feet.

Matthew's expression indicated that he was waiting for confirmation as to the cause of death, hoping against hope that there was some other explanation for what he'd seen. But Sarah, by the look of her, had no doubts.

Chris wondered why she'd gone down to the basement.

'What about security cameras?' he asked.

Matthew looked blank for a moment, then he shook his head.

'I raised that with the owner, but he said to wait.'

The phone rang and Matthew reached across to answer it. Chris was struck by how young they looked, and guilty, like two children caught trespassing perhaps.

It was a short walk from reception along a corridor leading to an old, heavy door.

Chris slipped his hand into his jacket pocket and fingered the key in its double folds of cotton and plastic. After a moment's hesitation, he took it out and, still using his handkerchief and holding the key by its tip, inserted it in the lock. His curiosity had got the better of him. He had to see the body for himself.

He'd never liked the *Royal*, with its turreted tower, reputed to be haunted, and its general air of gloom. As a child the place had given him the creeps.

He took a deep breath and began his descent. Overhead lights picked out the crumbling edges of the stairwell and brick walkways branching out on either side. One led to an underground bar that looked as though it had not been used in decades. Chris shuddered to think of people actually choosing to spend time drinking down there.

Wine racks along one wall indicated that the space was being used for some practical purpose. He went closer and peered at the labels. The wines were expensive. Perhaps the new owner, or Matthew as manager, hoped to attract a rich clientele?

Making his way in the opposite direction to the wine racks, Chris recalled the few facts Matthew had told him on the phone, the barely contained panic in his voice.

'Something terrible has happened. There's a – one of our guests is dead.'

It seemed strange to Chris that, with more than half the hotel in a state of dilapidation, there were any guests at all.

Gerard Hardy was lying on his back, at the end of the brick passage, in an area that, in Queenscliff's early days, had once done duty as the morgue. He was lying on a sandpit, in his pyjamas and dressing-gown, with his hands in prayer position at right-angles to his chest.

Chris went close, but didn't touch the body. Hardy's dressing-gown cord – at least Chris assumed it was his – was folded neatly beside him. A clear red line around his throat, lividity under the skin and bulging eyes indicated that he had been strangled.

The dressing-gown was good quality, made of fine wool, with a tartan pattern in blue, green and dark brown. The pockets looked heavy. Perhaps one held a torch. Sand spattered the dead man's clothing and bare feet. It was grey and damp, not at all like the clean yellow sand to be found on the beach. It smelt sour and mouldy, and it was this, rather than the sight of the body, that made Chris step back and catch his breath.

It looked as though someone had been interrupted in the act of burial. Was it rigor mortis holding the hands upright like that? How long would they stay that way?

After Queenscliff had grown big enough to boast a proper morgue, the area around the sandpit had been transformed into a cell, in the days when the *Royal's* basement had doubled as a mental asylum. The windows were still barred, though the door that separated this end cell from the next one had long since been removed. It was very cold, cold enough, Chris guessed, to delay the onset of rigor by an hour or more.

Measuring with his eye, he noted that the pit was just long enough to take the body; its depth he couldn't guess. Had Hardy known his killer? Had they descended the stairs together, or had the murderer followed his victim in silence?

All sounds from above were blocked off in the basement, which made any noise down there stand out. Chris scraped his foot against the stone floor. The sound was magnified, as he'd expected it to be. It was hard to imagine the killer stalking his victim without making some kind of noise.

Chris made a circuit of the body. The light was good, if, that is, Hardy had switched on the lights. Did the fact that he'd apparently come down without his slippers suggest that he'd left his bedroom in a hurry? Would the search team find them there?

On his way back to the ground floor, a new question occurred to Chris – what if Matthew or Sarah had arranged Hardy's body like that, after someone else had strangled him? Thankfully, this was not a question it fell to him to answer, but he couldn't help wondering about it. He figured that, even if they made good time, there was still half an hour until the investigative team arrived.

Matthew had said that there was only one entrance to the basement. When the hotel was built in the 1850s, there would have been access from outside for coal deliveries. Perhaps, while he was waiting, he could check this detail.

Chris fetched a roll of police tape from his car and stretched it across the entrance. There was nowhere suitable to fix it to, but he did his best. He made sure that the guests, including Charles Nevis, whom Matthew had described as Hardy's friend, were in their rooms. The male half of a honeymoon couple was slow to answer the door and opened it no further than a crack. He assured Chris that his wife was in bed and Chris had no reason to doubt him.

Matthew and Sarah were waiting in a small courtyard café at the back of the hotel. It was attractive, with a tiled floor and potted plants. Chris looked out through glass doors to a low stone wall.

Matthew asked if he would like a coffee. He and Sarah moved like one person, though they barely touched; it was as though each wore another layer of skin with which to make contact and reassure.

Chris tried to rid his nostrils of the smell of mouldy sand.

The chef, Manoli, came out with the coffee. When Matthew introduced them, Chris noticed that Manoli kept his head down and did not make eye contact with anyone. His fear was like a fifth person in the room.

When Manoli asked if he could prepare some trays for the guests, Chris said yes, but that he would carry and deliver them himself. The cook had the dark Greek looks of his forebears and a flat Australian accent. When he finally looked up, his eyes were an unusual light brown, not the greeny-brown normally called hazel, but a colour that looked as though it had been faded by the sun.

Chris drank his coffee, which was very good. Bridget, the only other staff member, wasn't rostered on that day. Chris spoke briefly to her on the phone, confirming that the police would want to interview her.

Bridget's response to this surprised Chris. She asked no questions, but said bitterly, 'I'm not going anywhere.'

When Chris asked how long Mr Hardy had booked for, Matthew said, 'Two nights.' He seemed about to add something, but when Chris looked at him inquiringly, he shook his head.

Chris glanced at his watch, checked with Manoli as to how long it would be before the trays were ready, then said he'd take a walk outside.

He wished that his assistant, Anthea Merritt, was with him, but Anthea had taken leave to go bushwalking with her husband. When he'd tried her mobile straight after receiving Matthew's call, it had been switched off.

He could hardly blame Anthea for that. She and Olly were probably still curled up in bed.

There was no coal hole, or none that remained visible to the naked eye. It was probably somewhere under the fancy pavers that had recently been laid. A beer garden appeared to be part of the new owner's plans. Chris wondered if the owner had taken into account how long winter could last at the end of the Bellarine Peninsula.

He approached a bluestone wall dividing the hotel from the property next door. Climbing it would be no problem. A wooden paling fence, a gate with an ordinary padlock, would present no problem either.

There was no fence at the front; wide stone steps curved straight up from the footpath. But the front door had been locked the night before, Matthew had assured him, and the back one which Manoli used. Manoli had arrived first that morning, to take in the deliveries and prepare the breakfast. Matthew and Sarah did not live on the premises, but in a flat close to the harbour.

Neither door showed signs of forced entry. The front door had a deadlock, but the back just an ordinary Yale. It could be opened from the inside without a key.

Chris was sure – the conviction was sudden and absolute – that Matthew had taken his time to study the death scene, learn all he could from it, before picking up the phone.

When Chris knocked on Charles Nevis's door, the young man opened it immediately, demanding to know what was going on and how long he was going to be kept a prisoner.

Chris made no attempt to answer either of these questions. He handed over the breakfast tray with a brief 'Good morning'.

When he knocked on the honeymoon couple's door, a woman's voice called, 'Come in.'

He introduced himself and the woman said her name was Isobel. Her husband's name was Tony. Isobel was sitting up in bed with a rug around her shoulders. Chris acknowledged her thanks for the breakfast with a small smile and inclination of the head. She told him Tony was in the bathroom and wanted to know when they could leave. He said he was afraid he couldn't answer that.

TWO

Chris took up a position at the top of the steps, where he could see the inspector's car and the forensic van arriving.

He could not recall ever having had a meal at the *Royal* and wondered how much Hardy's killer knew of its history and the town's. He felt conspicuous standing in front of the enormous double doors, as he'd known he would. The doors had recently been painted green and decorated with a gold, ornamental knocker. Chris thought the knocker ugly and impractical. He hadn't asked Matthew who the new owner was, or where he was – Chris assumed it was a he – perhaps he didn't even live in Australia.

Chris stepped back, though the street in front of him was empty. It would take a while before curious onlookers started to arrive.

His phone rang. Anthea sounded happy, her voice full of the glitter of morning sun on eucalyptus leaves. Chris imagined her smile, her nod at Olly's sleepy but inquiring face.

When he told her she would have to come back, there was a brief pause before Anthea said in a different voice, 'Okay.'

As soon as he'd said goodbye, his phone rang again, the *Geelong Advertiser* this time. How had they got to hear so soon? Chris said he had no comment to make, and sighed to think of the messages waiting on the station's landline.

Matthew walked up behind him, looking grim and pale, asking what to do about the media. Chris was beginning to feel apprehensive about the delay of the CIU, but he didn't want Matthew to see that. One uniformed constable wouldn't be much good against a horde of journalists. He advised Matthew not to answer any questions.

Matthew nodded, then said with a catch in his voice, 'I've put off the carpenters. They were due to start on the second floor today.'

He turned to stare behind him at the bulk of the hotel.

'Gerard Hardy was twenty-nine. I remember his date of birth from his driver's licence. He told me when I booked him in that he'd come to Queenscliff to research some famous novelist.'

'Henry Handel Richardson,' Chris said.

Matthew frowned. Chris asked if that was all Hardy had said.

'To me, yes. He talked a bit to Sarah. I think there was some kind of meeting he was looking forward to. But you'd have to ask Sarah about that. Be careful with her. Please.'

Chris didn't say that it wouldn't be his job to question Sarah. Instead he asked why she'd gone down to the basement.

'She wanted to check the wine.'

'At seven in the morning?'

Matthew bit his lip. 'I know it seems an odd thing to do.'

'Why did she go all the way to the sandpit?'

'I don't know.'

There was something calculating in Matthew's expression. He was keeping his responses to a minimum. That was understandable, Chris thought. On the other hand, he reflected that you didn't need to be a detective to recognise a lie.

Sarah came to the door. Matthew walked quickly over to her and put his arm around her. The gesture, the way their two bodies leant together, suggested to Chris that they'd tested each other's capacity for endurance before.

Chris's phone rang again. There'd been a three-car pile-up on the highway, but the team was on its way and shouldn't be more than twenty minutes.

Unwilling to go on standing on the steps, Chris climbed

the spiral stairs into the hotel's tower, having first carefully stepped around the 'No access. Staff only' notice, and the barrier made of a single fraying rope.

Threadbare carpet was littered with shards of fallen plaster, and dust covered every surface. Chris trod warily up the last few steps to a small rectangular landing with large windows looking directly out over the heads to Point Nepean.

His stomach turning over, he placed both hands on the window ledge and then stood perfectly still. He seldom looked directly at the sea, only rarely and as some kind of test. He didn't know why he was forcing this test on himself now.

Before long, Chris supposed, someone would write a social history of Queenscliff and include the *Royal*. The murder in the basement would become part of the town's folklore, joining the story of the woman who'd jumped in despair from the window he was standing in front of now.

Every day for weeks, this woman – Chris had no name for her, but no doubt the historian would dig it up – had climbed these stairs to watch for the ship bringing her husband back to Australia.

It was before the days of steam. According to the versions Chris had heard – they differed in detail while remaining essentially the same – the woman had been allowed into the tower to watch. Apparently the staff had taken pity on her. But then she'd decided to stay there; she'd refused to move. The staff had tried to coax her down, then tried to feed her, make sure she had enough to drink. And one night, perhaps spent and exhausted, perhaps driven past the last threads of self-control by worry and frustration, perhaps at last seeing the ship she'd been waiting for and understanding that her husband wasn't on it, she'd thrown herself from the window and smashed her body on the street below.

Chris checked his watch again. He decided that he

liked this story; he liked the fact that he knew only the bare bones of it, and how there was probably a similar story for every on-the-surface-dull Australian country town. He liked how the nameless woman might have been a mental patient, kept in the basement behind barred windows; yet she hadn't been. She'd climbed the tower of her own free will. The staff had let her keep her vigil and they'd tried to help.

He thought it said something about a frontier town, and also about kindliness.

THREE

Inspector Masterson began asking questions before he was out of the car.

'How many entrances? How many ways could someone get in?'

Chris answered promptly, glad he'd walked around the outside and checked for himself.

Masterson was a tall man with a rugby player's bulk and thick, rough-looking skin. His sergeant, shorter and more finely built, moved beside him with what looked to Chris to be controlled impatience.

The staff were in the courtyard café waiting to be interviewed, he said, except for Bridget McGuire, who was at home. The three guests were in their rooms.

Masterson indicated with a sideways movement of his head that DS Thomas should go straight inside. The sergeant looked Chris up and down and frowned as he briefly met his eye. Impatience, Chris thought again. Well, they'd been held up.

The inspector asked about the front and back doors and who had keys to them. Again Chris answered quickly, saying that Sarah Kent had locked up before leaving for the night at around 10 PM.

'She's the manager's girlfriend?'

Chris hesitated before replying. He finally settled on, 'It seems they share the work.'

'But they don't live here?'

'No.'

Chris wondered if he should explain about the hotel being more or less a building site, but Masterson would see this for himself soon enough.

He said the guests had individual room keys, naturally.

Other keys, including those to the basement, were kept under the reception counter.

He took the plastic bag from his pocket and explained that Sarah and Matthew had both used the basement key that morning. He wondered whether to mention the coal hole. Since he hadn't found it, he decided that he'd better not.

The inspector's phone rang. He listened then said, 'There can't be accidents on every frigging highway.'

He frowned, turning back to Chris. 'Was the deceased's bedroom locked when you got here?'

'Matthew locked it this morning before he phoned me. He says he found Hardy's door shut but not locked. He opened the door, looked around, saw that Hardy's key was on the bedside table and locked up behind him.'

'And claims not to have touched anything? Well, we'll see about that.'

Chris wondered if this was meant not only as a criticism of Matthew, but himself. He listened while he was given his instructions. As soon as the van arrived, he was to prepare an incident room at the station. He was to get Constable Merritt back pronto.

Chris said that she was on her way.

Masterson answered another phone call. Chris watched him, glad he didn't have to face those shoulders and that bull-neck in a rugby scrum.

A car arrived and he watched a man get out of it, recognising the doctor who'd attended an accidental drowning the previous December.

Chris showed the way to the basement, his footsteps sounding unnaturally loud on the stone floor. He left the inspector and the doctor at the top of the basement stairs, heard a noise and turned to see Matthew walking towards him.

The only natural light came from high leaded windows.

Matthew appeared in silhouette. He looked at Chris with worried eyes and said he was going to phone for a solicitor.

Chris returned to the front of the hotel, thinking about the words 'manager' and 'manage'. No doubt Matthew had done courses. He wasn't at all what Chris imagined a hotel manager to be like, but then he'd had a dreadful shock. Had the staffing been left up to him? Had the owner trusted him for that?

Computers were installed and a wall display of photographs set up, delivered by a member of the scene-of-crime team who shook her head at the nightmare of searching a huge, old ramshackle hotel. Chris printed and pinned up the photos, pausing to study Hardy's body, the two hands in prayer position looking even larger than he remembered. He got the whiteboard out of the cupboard in the back office and cleaned it.

He'd missed breakfast, but he wasn't hungry. He and Anthea usually kept the small fridge in the kitchen stocked well enough for two. Chris wondered if he should go out and buy more, then recalled that the detectives had food and drink laid on at the hotel.

FOUR

Hardy's travelling companion, Charles Nevis, was to be brought to the station to be interviewed on tape. Chris tested the recording equipment and rearranged the chairs.

He'd been keeping watch for Anthea, and went outside to greet her. His assistant's uniform was neat, as always. Her freshly washed hair smelt faintly of lemon.

Anthea's eyes clouded when Chris apologised for ruining her holiday; then she shrugged and said not to worry.

Her healthy skin reflected the sun off the rain forest – an autumn glow with the light behind it – but something wasn't right. It could just be that the drive from the Otways on her own had tired her. Olly was an even-tempered man, but maybe he'd been angry that her leave had been cut short.

Chris wasn't able to stop himself from glancing down at her abdomen. Anthea shook her head. Of course he wouldn't say anything unless she wanted him to.

Charles Nevis was freshly-shaven and his hair was damp. A much slighter, thinner man than the inspector, he appeared to Chris abnormally small, sitting opposite Masterson at the interviewing table. After switching on the tape, Chris took up a position at the far side of the room.

Masterson went through the preliminaries, giving the date and time and naming everybody present. Then he said, 'I want you to tell me everything that happened since you arrived here yesterday. What time was it? We'll start with that.'

They'd arrived in the middle of the afternoon, having driven down from Melbourne. Hardy didn't own a car.

Chris watched Nevis, who kept his eyes fixed on the inspector. The dead man's friend, if friend he had been, did not appear to be shocked or sad. He held his lips together when not speaking, but Chris didn't miss the hint of mischief in his eyes, as though this interview was part of an elaborate game for which the police were necessary, but which they could not possibly hope to understand.

He said, 'Gerry *did* have a laptop. He made some concessions to the modern world.'

Matthew had checked them in and they'd gone up to their rooms. They'd understood that the hotel was undergoing renovations and was far from fully functional, but Hardy had wanted to stay there because it was actually in Mercer Street.

'Once Gerry found that out, there was no deterring him.'

Again, Chris heard veiled amusement, but not so veiled that Nevis did not expect it to be heard.

'And the significance of that?'

'Henry Handel Richardson lived in Mercer Street,' Nevis said. He sounded pleased, as though he'd expected Masterson to be ignorant of the fact, and had had his expectation confirmed.

His and Hardy's rooms were next door to one another. The inspector asked at whose request.

'No one's,' Nevis said, and repeated his point about there only being a few rooms fit for guests.

'Have you ever been to Queenscliff before?'

'For day trips only.'

'When was the last time?'

'About six months ago.'

'Was the deceased with you then?'

Nevis shook his head. He'd felt tired after the drive and had lain down for a rest. He'd only meant to shut his eyes for a few minutes, but had ended up sleeping for an hour.

In response to Masterson's next question, Nevis said that after he'd freshened up he found Gerry in the lobby, talking to Sarah at the reception desk. She'd introduced herself and the three of them had chatted for a few minutes.

'I did wonder if he told that girl he was on his way to an appointment with a spirit medium.'

Chris expected Masterson to ask what spirit medium. Instead, he asked why Nevis had agreed to the trip, it being obvious that it was in Hardy's interest to have someone to drive him, but not what Nevis hoped to gain by it.

The question could have been interpreted as insulting and for a moment it seemed as though Nevis was going to take offence. But he replied mildly that some of his forebears had settled in Queenscliff. His great-uncle still lived there, in a cottage by the boat harbour, and he'd wanted to pay him a visit.

'What about Mr Hardy's parents?'

'His father died when Gerry was thirteen. His mother re-married a couple of years later. Gerry didn't get on with his stepfather. The usual story. His Mum sends him a Christmas card. I don't think they've really talked in years.'

Masterson went on asking questions, sitting solid and foursquare, his expression alternating between neutral and mildly speculative. It could be a tactic; if so, not a bad one.

Hardy had insisted on walking to the psychic's – not that Nevis had objected; he'd been happy to stretch his legs – and Hardy had also insisted on detouring past the author's house. There'd been no car out the front and no lights on inside.

'Had the deceased met the present owner?'

'I don't know. He didn't tell me if he had.'

Chris glanced up sharply, thinking surely Hardy would have mentioned it, especially since he'd wanted to walk past.

Hardy became excited as they turned into Bridge Street, where the medium lived. His appointment had lasted for a little over an hour, time Nevis had spent having a cup of tea with his great-uncle.

Hardy had desired, passionately desired, to make contact with the spirit of Henry Handel Richardson.

'Ever since I met him,' Nevis said.

This had been at university, where they'd been post-graduate students. 'Well, I still am.' For a moment Nevis looked confused.

Hardy had been working on manifestations of the paranormal in Richardson's novels and short stories. Nevis described himself as having 'a rather more hard-headed approach to scholarship.'

'You were against what the deceased was doing?'

'Not *against*, inspector. Gerry and I are – were – academic colleagues. Differences of opinion and approach – well, that's normal in our field.'

Hardy had wanted to ask the novelist about her childhood. He was convinced that being in Queenscliff – 'I mean *physically*,' Nevis emphasised – was important.

'What did you think about that?'

'I thought he was likely to be disappointed.'

'Disappointed?'

'Yes. I foresaw no danger, or else I would have tried to talk him out of it.'

'Did the deceased think that what he was doing might be dangerous?'

'I doubt it.'

Chris thought it odd that Hardy had waited so long if his desire was as strong as Nevis claimed.

After the session, Nevis had met Hardy on the medium's front porch; Hardy had looked pleased and happy.

They'd walked towards the pier. The tide had been out, then the moon came out as well, a full moon. Nevis's way of speaking indicated that this fact was somehow relevant. Perhaps Hardy had timed his visit to Queenscliff to coincide with a full moon? When they turned back towards the centre of town, Hardy had insisted on detouring via Mercer Street again and they'd stopped briefly outside the house, which was still in darkness.

Nevis was beginning to feel cold by then, and hungry.

There'd been a couple of restaurants open in the main street and they'd chosen one. Hardy had said he didn't feel like eating at the *Royal*.

'It was Gerry's call. I was along to assist, plus I had an interest of my own, as I've already said.'

Over dinner, Hardy had talked about the reading and his hopes for the next day.

Ethel Richardson had sent him a message through the cards. She was content in the spirit world, and she was watching over him. She took her own name there.

'A more specific message?' the inspector asked.

After hesitating for a moment, Nevis said, 'Gerry had high hopes that she would speak to him directly. A channel had been opened, and that was the first step.'

'Why wait all this time for a tarot reading? He could have had one done at any time.'

'I've – I mean, I had – I'm sorry, it's hard for me to think in the past tense. Gerry didn't talk about himself much. He was used to being misunderstood. And he knew I was a sceptic, though I didn't openly scoff at his ideas like others did. But I do know he'd been preparing himself for the attempt for quite a while, and that the physical place, the energies and spirits gathered here, were important to him.'

It sounded to Chris as though this speech had been rehearsed. He wished he had a chance to ask some questions of his own.

There was a short silence, then Nevis continued, as though it was his duty to inform the police concerning matters about which they were most likely to be ignorant. 'Ethel Richardson was a committed spiritualist, as was her father, Walter. As were Arthur Conan Doyle and Abraham Lincoln.'

Masterson frowned, as though the idea of having a discussion about spiritualism bothered him; but perhaps, Chris thought, he was simply aware that Nevis was trying to lead him off on a tangent.

One difference between Ethel and her father was that while Walter had been open about his spiritualist beliefs, Ethel had kept hers private. Had Hardy really believed that she'd speak to him frankly, from the spirit world, concerning matters about which she'd been secretive during her life?

'Look,' Nevis said in a different voice, the voice of someone who expected to be able to state his case once and for all. 'Gerry and I got on okay. He was an odd man. You never met him, but if you had, you'd have come to that conclusion in less than a minute. I didn't share Gerry's belief in paranormal phenomena, but it didn't worry me that he held such beliefs. They were his affair. And my – agnosticism, if you like – didn't worry Gerry. He told me once that he'd been born in the wrong century. I think he genuinely felt that. But he accepted me.'

'Did you and the deceased have a physical relationship?'

'I find that question offensive after what I've just been trying to explain.'

'Answer it, please.'

'No.'

For a moment, Masterson looked as though the idea of any homosexual relationship was abhorrent to him. Then he recovered his composure.

Hardy and Nevis had had dinner at *The Chandler*. The food had been borderline inedible, but Hardy hadn't noticed.

Nevis spoke as though it was his right to expect the best, even in a small seaside town in the off-season. Chris felt indignant on the restaurant's behalf, and on behalf of the men and women who worked there. He wondered if Nevis was lying about having been Gerard Hardy's lover, and if the inspector thought so too.

They'd walked back to the hotel where they'd separated, Hardy going straight up to his room. Nevis ordered a brandy which he drank in front of the fire. The cook had served him. The honeymoon couple had been there; they'd had dinner in the dining-room and pronounced it excellent. The couple had taken their coffee to the armchairs by the fireplace, and the three had chatted pleasantly for fifteen or twenty minutes.

'Did he tell you he was going to the *Royal's* basement?'

'No, no,' Nevis said.

'What *did* Mr Hardy tell you?'

'I wasn't so much told as – look, I don't know if this means anything, but as I was heading for the stairs I heard voices in the corridor. I turned to look, and Gerry and Sarah Kent were talking by the basement door.'

'Did you hear what they were saying?'

'They were speaking in low voices and I didn't want to eavesdrop.' Chris picked up a hint of jealousy in Nevis's voice.

'Did you talk to Hardy about it when he came upstairs?'

Nevis raised his eyes to the inspector and now there was an open challenge in them.

'I didn't hear Gerry go into his room. I thought I might, but I was tired. I fell sleep. Matthew woke me early this morning. He said, There's been an accident in the basement. Something terrible has happened. He ordered me to stay in my room. Of course I asked what accident and pointed out that he had no authority to order me to do anything. But I did stay, like a good boy, until you turned up.'

'So you don't know if Hardy came up to his room at all?'

'I thought I made that clear.'

'When you saw him talking to Sarah by the basement entrance, what was he wearing?'

Nevis seemed surprised by the question. 'The clothes he had on for his appointment with the psychic. He changed after we got here. I mean, changed out of the clothes he'd been wearing for the drive down. Why? Is it important?'

'Are you sure you didn't hear him during the night, either coming in or going out?'

'Of course I'm sure. It's not something I'd be likely to forget.'

Chris suspected that Nevis had left his room that morning, after Matthew had told him to stay put.

The only other thing that had happened the previous evening, while Nevis enjoyed his half hour by the fire, was the phone ringing at reception. Manoli had left the bar to answer it.

'So, Blackie,' Masterson said, after Nevis had agreed to remain in Queenscliff, 'Do you believe it's possible to make contact with departed spirits?'

Chris drew in a deep breath, trying to work out how best to reply. He settled on, 'I shouldn't think it matters what I believe.'

'The point being that Mr Hardy did?'

'It seems that way, Sir.'

'What do you make of that little tête-a-tête by the basement door?'

'They could have been arranging to meet later.'

'It's the obvious inference, isn't it? Kent had opportunity and means.'

Chris thought that Nevis had timed his revelation about Sarah in order to turn attention away from himself. He was trying to work out how to put his thoughts into words, when Masterson spat out, 'What blasphemy!'

The inspector's face was red and angry, all the more so for having held himself in check. 'I want you with me when I question that psychic and I want a search done on her background and credentials.'

DS Thomas had taken Anthea with him to interview Bridget McGuire. After that, they'd 'have another go' at

Sarah, who, Masterson told Chris with a note of satisfaction in his voice, had said nothing about talking to Hardy by the basement door when he and Thomas had questioned her the first time. They were expecting two DCs, who couldn't be released from their current duties till tomorrow.

'Maybe the fortune-teller travels around fairs and markets. If she does, I want to know about that too. Where she came from, what the locals think of her, whether Kent's a customer of hers. Ring and let her know I'm coming. Let's say in an hour?'

'Yes. But – '

'What?'

'Didn't you ask Sarah Kent about that?'

'She said no. But she would, wouldn't she? Your job is to get the information from another source. Did Matthew tell you why the girl went down to the basement first thing this morning?'

'To check the wine.'

'Do you believe that?'

'I don't know.' Chris didn't add that he would have to question all three of them, Sarah, Manoli and Matthew, before making up his mind.

When he asked Masterson if he was sure they were dealing with a murder, the inspector smiled as though something he'd been wondering about had been proved right.

'While you were down there, Blackie, you may have noticed those good strong oak beams holding up the ceiling. Plenty of spots for a man to hang himself if he's that way inclined. Hardy may have managed death by strangling without loosening his grip, but those hands clinch it as far as I'm concerned.'

Chris waited for Masterson to reprimand him for having explored the basement on his own. The inspector went on smiling, but said nothing further. Chris recalled the broken blood vessels under the skin of the dead man's face. The whites of his eyes had been bloodshot, indicating retinal haemorrhaging, which would occur whether or not he'd tightened the dressing-gown cord himself.

Autoerotic asphyxiation: the idea made his stomach churn. What if Hardy's death was the result of an experiment that had gone badly wrong? Someone could have found him in the basement and fixed the hands in place; but surely Masterson would have thought of that.

Chris called the medium, who introduced herself as Mrs Evelyn Marr, and they agreed on an interview time. She sounded as though she was looking forward to it.

Gerard Hardy had believed the spirits of the dead could communicate with living human beings, and, if Charles Nevis were telling the truth, had been about to put this belief to the test. If he'd been successful, he would have turned literary scholarship on its head. Or would he? Perhaps Hardy's 'discoveries' would have been ridiculed and dismissed.

Chris knew quite a bit about Ethel, alias Henry Handel Richardson. He'd read her books and letters, and the volumes of letters her parents had written to each other during times of separation, copies of which were kept at the historical museum. He recalled the small and probably irrelevant fact that Ethel had loved detective stories, and that Agatha Christie had been a favourite.

FIVE

Inspector Masterson didn't speak much on the short drive to Bridge Street, but he implied that Chris ought to have known who Mrs Marr was and what she did for a living. He said nothing about his and Thomas's interview with Sarah. Chris reminded himself that the inspector didn't need to share his thoughts with a constable at the bottom of the pecking order.

He'd established that there were no other psychic mediums operating in Queenscliff, and that Mrs Marr had moved from Torquay several months ago. He'd had no time to go through the lists of market stall-holders, though he'd requested them from each of the weekend markets operating on the Surf Coast as well as the Bellarine Peninsula.

The inspector introduced them both, and Mrs Marr nodded without offering to shake hands.

'Come in', she said simply, before leading the way down a central corridor that ran the whole length of the house, to a back room with curtains partly drawn against the afternoon sun. They were heavy curtains and looked warm as well. Chris imagined wrapping himself in them, going to sleep and waking up to find the murder in the basement of the *Royal* had been a bad dream.

The medium's brown eyes were deeply shadowed, the expression in them hard to read, though Chris did not think she looked defensive or ill-at-ease. She was dressed in a plain grey suit that would not have been out of place in an office. Her very dark hair seemed to create shadows both around and across her face.

The wall next to the windows was hung with Indian cotton, glittering with tiny mirrors, tasselled round the edges. Wicker chairs were piled with cushions covered in the same bright, thin material. Low sitar music was playing, though Chris could not see any speakers in the room. He glanced up at the ceiling. The light fitting was covered in a paper shade. Two chairs were free of cushions, on either side of a small table holding an unlit lamp, a small clock and several packs of cards.

The inspector took one chair. Chris hesitated; Mrs Marr swept cushions from a third.

Chris sat down and took out his notebook. He wondered if she'd put on a CD before opening the door, or if she habitually left it playing in the background. The air smelt sweet as well as warm, not with incense, but a different smell, one he thought he ought to recognise.

Masterson said, 'Switch the music off, please.'

The silence that followed seemed to have a voice of its own. Chris guessed that this was an effect the medium had planned, though why she would bother he had no idea.

Mrs Marr sat with her hands together on the table and glanced in Chris's direction.

'Do you have enough light, Constable Blackie?'

'Yes, thank you.'

The psychic gave the impression of a woman used to being listened to, used to being the centre of attention. Chris supposed that, if you made your living giving tarot readings at fifty bucks a shot, connecting grieving people with their departed loved ones, then you might grow accustomed to believing in your own importance. Policemen, too, could become so accustomed.

He watched Masterson from the relative dimness of his corner. The table was a small one, and the inspector and Mrs Marr were sitting close enough to touch.

Listening to her answering questions in a calm, low-pitched voice, Chris found it hard to believe that Gerard Hardy had sat at the same table less than twenty-four hours ago. Hardy's clasped hands came back to him, accompanied by a strange feeling, almost of dread, that the psychic knew about them. She'd had plenty of time to work out her story; she delivered it smoothly and confidently.

Chris took notes, reminding himself that, for people who believed in spirits, death was not the end. What had Walter Richardson called it? 'That change called death.' He watched Masterson, wondering what impression Mrs Marr was making on him.

The DI asked about correspondence, how the meeting with Hardy was arranged.

'Well, you know, he was a writer! Three paragraphs where a sentence would do.'

'Email?'

'Mr Hardy was old-fashioned. He wrote letters and sent them through the post.'

When asked if she still had them, Mrs Marr nodded.

'Go and get them now, please.'

The two men didn't speak while the psychic was out of the room. Masterson seemed to be lost in his own thoughts, looking through the gap between the curtains. There was nothing of any note out there, as far as Chris could see, just an ordinary back yard. He realised with a start that the inspector was studying his own reflection in the glass.

Chris would not have called Masterson a handsome man. His features were irregular. Even when he smiled, he seemed to Chris both grim and condescending. But because of his impressive build, he was the sort of man you would automatically turn to look at.

Mrs Marr returned and placed two letters on the table. They were still in their envelopes, which had been precisely cut.

She said, 'A medium is exactly that, Inspector. I am no more than a conduit, and I never have been.' Her tone of voice suggested that she considered a conduit to be a special kind of being, far more important than a detective.

'I explained to Mr Hardy that I would open myself to what was coming through, but that nothing might. I warned him to be prepared for disappointment. In his letters, he makes it clear that he wanted to make contact with the spirit of Henry Handel Richardson. That's what he called her. I thought he should have called her Ethel. In the spirit world, she has no need to pretend she is a man.'

'You expected to have trouble with the – spirits?'

'I didn't say that.'

'How does it work then? Explain it to me.' Though the inspector made an effort to keep his voice level, Chris heard the hostile undertone.

Mrs Marr's eyelids fluttered. She's heard it too, Chris thought.

'To contact a relative who's passed over to the other side, that's what most of my clients want. Mr Hardy wanted Ethel to tell him a secret of some kind.'

'What secret?'

'He didn't tell me and I didn't ask.'

'Then how do you know that was Mr Hardy's wish?'

'I said he didn't tell me what the secret was. He made it clear that he believed there was one.'

'What did you think?'

'Of Mr Hardy's chances? As I've explained to you, I keep an open mind.'

Mrs Marr's glance at Chris was brief, but expressive. She's picked me for a sceptic, Chris said to himself. He felt uncomfortable and his uniform began to itch.

The inspector opened the first letter. Mrs Marr reached across and switched on the lamp. Immediately, the rest of the room, outside the yellow circle where Masterson sat holding the letter in his large-knuckled hands, appeared much darker. Again, this seemed to Chris part of a plan thought out in advance. He wondered about fingerprints on the paper and who had held it besides Mrs Marr, Hardy and now the DI.

When Masterson asked if they'd corresponded by phone as well, Mrs Marr said that Hardy had called the week before to confirm the time.

'Called on a landline?'

'Yes.'

'It refers here to a book.'

'That's right. I asked Mr Hardy to bring an object with him, if possible an object that had belonged to the departed spirit. He brought a first edition of a novel. One she – Ethel – had personally signed. He'd bought it at an auction, he told me. I could see that he was proud of it.'

Chris wondered where the book was now: in Hardy's room, in which case the search team would have found it. Or had Hardy taken it with him to the basement?

When Masterson asked what the book was called, Mrs Marr said, 'A funny kind of name. Latin.'

'Can you describe it to me?'

'Haven't you got it, Inspector? Wasn't it with Mr Hardy's things?'

'I was wondering if Mr Hardy gave it to you to look at.'

'He showed it to me, yes.'

'Is there anything particular that you recall?'

Mrs Marr shrugged. 'It was just a book. An old one, with a red cloth cover.'

'In good condition?'

'For its age, I guess so.'

Masterson read the second letter without comment. He placed them both back in their envelopes, then said, 'I'll keep these for now. So Mr Hardy arrived with high expectations. Then what happened?'

Mrs Marr's answer was to reach for a pack of cards.

Hardy had chosen his own birth sign as the significator. It was also Ethel Richardson's, she informed them, laying out cards face downwards in front of the inspector as she spoke. They formed a pattern rather like a wine glass.

The psychic explained the meaning of significator, turning the cards over slowly as she did so, one by one. Chris stared at the significator card, wondering if Hardy had really believed himself represented by it, and what this might mean.

Mrs Marr said, 'A channelling chalice reading is designed to open a channel between the querent and the spirit world, allowing access to loved ones who have crossed over. Cards six to nine indicate a personal message from the spirit to the querent, in this case Mr Hardy.'

'These are the same cards?' The inspector's voice was sharp.

Mrs Marr allowed herself to sound offended. 'Mr Hardy shuffled the cards and I set out the spread, exactly as you see it here.'

All very well, thought Chris, but who was there to challenge or deny this? There'd only been two people present and one of them was dead.

Masterson asked Chris to photograph the spread. Chris moved the lamp a little and took shots from different angles, while Mrs Marr leant back in her chair and half closed her eyes.

He checked to make sure each card was identifiable, then took his place again.

When Masterson asked, 'Did Hardy have his own pack? Had he done this for himself?' Mrs Marr opened her eyes wide and, for the first time since their arrival, seemed disconcerted. She recovered quickly, saying, 'If he had, then he didn't tell me. The answer to the question, or questions, which the querent seeks, are found further down, in cards ten to fourteen. I'll come back to them in a moment. You'll see that cards six to nine include three swords, and swords designate objects, amongst them books.'

Mrs Marr looked at the inspector, to see if he was with her so far. 'The Seven of Swords means crime, jealousy or theft. The Nine of Swords is the death card.'

'It's a warning,' Chris said, unable to stop himself.

Masterson frowned. 'Did you warn Mr Hardy, Mrs Marr?'

'I hardly needed to, Inspector.'

'Yet from what we've been told, Mr Hardy was happy and excited when he left here.'

Mrs Marr said, 'That's because his question was answered in the affirmative. The spirit whom he wished to contact indicated that she was open to receiving him.'

'So they did make contact.'

'Not yesterday. Mr Hardy understood that the spirits can't be rushed. He was pleased because, in spite of the warning, he had every reason to hope for success next time.'

'You mean here. Today.'

'That's right.'

'You both saw danger in the cards. You must have spoken of it.'

'Why?' she asked.

Because to do so would be normal and natural, Chris thought, while not to do so –

'Were you worried?'

'Inspector Masterson, I've been in touch with the spirit world in one way or another all my life. The spirits know what they are doing and I have no power to influence them. Mr Hardy understood that, and he also understood that no journey can be taken without risk.'

'Is that what he told you?'

'Perhaps not in those words. But he understood.'

Masterson sat large and solid in his chair, physically dominant, though not in any other way. Chris realised that, under the guise of answering questions, the psychic had subtly turned the tables. She was interrogating him.

Chris loosened his shirt collar and resisted the urge to scratch his neck.

The lamplight shining directly on the cards emphasised

their bright, clear colours. The figures looked both natural and stylised. They were wearing medieval costumes, but were designed by a modern artist, he was sure.

Murder was not, for Mrs Marr, the shock, the inconsolable bereavement that it was for ordinary, non-believing folk. Death, including violent, untimely death, marked a threshold, not the end. What about the Christians who went to church on Sundays, praying that their loved ones would go to heaven? Chris felt instinctively that the psychic was as different from them as she was from him.

Masterson's next question was one Chris had been waiting for. 'Where were you last night?'

'At home, right here. I cooked dinner then watched TV for a while, then I went to bed.'

'Did anybody phone, or call in?'

'No.'

Masterson returned to the spread of cards in front of him. He asked if it was usual to have so many swords.

'Neither usual nor unusual.'

'This one?' Masterson pointed to a red heart pierced by three blue swords.

'Removal, absence, rupture. You'll notice, Inspector, that it's raining.'

Chris looked up involuntarily towards the window.

Mrs Marr allowed herself a small, private smile and at that moment the room was filled with a piercing scream.

SIX

'Quite a performance,' Masterson said, as Chris unlocked the car and the inspector got into the passenger seat.

Chris felt the hairs rise again on his forearms and the back of his neck.

They hadn't found a recording device, though surely there had to be one in the psychic's room, perhaps behind a wall, or in the ceiling. They'd searched thoroughly enough to be sure there was no living person hidden in the house, outside the windows, on the roof. Mrs Marr had followed them into her bedroom, smiling, perfectly at ease.

'The spirits,' she had murmured, while Masterson grew more agitated, demanding answers, angry and embarrassed. Now it seemed to Chris that he was trying, if not exactly to make light of the psychic's game, at least to reduce it to manageable proportions.

Chris took his place in the driver's seat. Masterson stared out the passenger side window, saying, 'Most hotel guests lock their rooms behind them. Wouldn't you say, Constable, that that's the general rule?'

Chris heard the sarcasm and knew that he should answer straight away. He assumed Masterson was referring to Gerard Hardy, in which case it was a question that required some thought.

He understood the reason for the change of subject. Masterson might instruct the scene-of-crime people to search Mrs Marr's house, but Chris doubted he would do this. Mrs Marr could demand a warrant, which meant the inspector would have to convince a magistrate that a warrant was necessary, by which time the recording device would be at the bottom of the bay.

Finally Chris said, 'It may not have been Hardy's – the

deceased's – decision.'

'So you think his killer called for him and led him by the hand?'

Chris knew it would be unwise to speculate. In his present mood, Masterson was likely to squash his most tentative suggestion, and was looking for someone to blame for the psychic's joke.

He said carefully, 'It may have been pre-arranged.'

'By the Kent girl, during that charming little confab by the basement stairs?'

'Or by someone else.'

'Eyes on the road, Constable. Did you ask the fortune-teller if Kent was a customer?'

'Mrs Marr said her client list was confidential.'

Chris thought the inspector should have asked her himself.

He felt relieved when they arrived at the station. He wanted nothing more than to be allowed go home and have a long hot shower.

Masterson went into the front office and firmly shut the door. Chris heard his voice rising and falling, then an exclamation of annoyance.

The hotel was practically empty. Three-quarters of the rooms were closed for renovation, but even so, why had all four guests been put next to each other? Chris wondered how much sound penetrated from one room to the next, and wished he'd thought to do a test. The walls were thick, but raised voices would almost certainly be heard. He pictured the staff and guests rattling around like too few seeds in a dry pod, the honeymooners leaving their king-sized bed for the dining-room, Hardy and Nevis walking away from Mrs Marr's through deserted streets.

His thoughts returned to the basement of the *Royal*. Why would Hardy want to commune with Ethel Richardson's spirit in that airless and foul-smelling place? The obvious answer was because she'd asked him to. Some time between his appointment with Mrs Marr and the middle of the night, Hardy might have heard Ethel's voice telling him he didn't need to wait until the next day. She was ready to talk to him now. All he needed to do was fetch the basement key from under the reception counter.

Of course Mrs Marr could be lying. She could have told Hardy that Ethel Richardson would meet him in the hotel basement. It was suitably histrionic and the scream showed that Mrs Marr had a taste for histrionics.

The interrupted burial stuck in his throat, literally. Every time he recalled it, he felt like retching.

Hardy wouldn't have stood docilely while his murderer removed his dressing-gown cord and throttled him with it; he would have struggled, fought. There was another possibility, that the killer had removed the cord in advance, that Hardy hadn't been wearing it when he'd descended those steps. But did this mean that he'd been forced down to the basement against his will, that he'd known it was his death walk he was setting out on? Why hadn't he yelled out? If he'd made a noise upstairs, someone would have heard him.

Wasn't there some period of time immediately after death when a person's spirit hung around? Had that been Hardy screaming back at Mrs Marr's? Was that what they'd been meant to think? But surely she would have said so, or hinted at it, not just repeated the word 'spirits'. It had sounded like a woman's voice to Chris, but now he wasn't sure. How easy it would be if they could just call up the deceased and ask who'd pulled that cord around his neck. You'd do away with a police force if answers could be obtained as easily as that.

Chris prepared some grilled cheese and tomato sandwiches, unconsciously making enough for two, thinking of Anthea and wondering how she was getting on. He put the jug on for tea while the cheese was bubbling under the griller, remembering how, before Anthea started working for him, he'd kept the teapot warm with a knitted cosy and how she'd laughed him out of doing this. He'd been offended by her laughter at the time, but the memory made him smile.

Replaying the scene at Mrs Marr's for Anthea, Chris said, 'I think it came from somewhere above our heads.'

When Anthea asked if they'd gone up on the roof to look, Chris said, 'I got a ladder, but I didn't climb right out. I went far enough to see that there wasn't anywhere to hide.'

'You mean for a person?'

Chris nodded. 'Of course there could have been a recording device. But it makes more sense to hide it behind a wall or in the ceiling. The scream was so – so piercing.'

'A woman's scream?'

'I think so, but I can't be sure.'

'What about Inspector Masterson?'

'If it was meant to upset him, then it worked. It's a long time since I've seen anyone so rattled.'

'Maybe Mrs Marr is a ventriloquist.'

Chris smiled. 'I wouldn't put it past her. You should have been there.'

'I wish.'

'And there's another thing,' Chris said. 'I don't reckon that book's turned up, the one Hardy took with him.' He repeated what the medium had said. 'And there's Hardy's laptop too.'

Divisions had been blurred; it was funny to think of a scream doing that. It had made them equal for a short time, detective inspector and uniformed constable. For a few moments, they'd been equally baffled.

Chris looked at his assistant, wondering if he should say what was on his mind. If Anthea was going to tell the DI she was pregnant, or depute him to pass on the news, then she should not let more time pass before doing so. Masterson would be angry if he found out some other way.

It wasn't as though Anthea wasn't capable of working all this out; she obviously had her reasons for keeping quiet.

She told him she'd spent the time, after returning from St Leonards where Bridget McGuire lived, taking notes while DS Thomas interviewed the honeymoon couple and Manoli. Once their statements had been signed, the couple were to be allowed to go home.

They hadn't stirred from their bed all night. Why would they? They'd been married for five months and were in Queenscliff for a belated honeymoon, postponed owing to the sudden death of the groom's older brother.

'An odd choice, the *Royal*.'

Anthea said, 'Maybe they got it cheap.'

Chris looked thoughtful. 'I'd like to interview Mrs Marr's neighbours.'

'You might get a chance when we start the door-to-door.'

Chris thought it more likely that Masterson would delegate that task to his sergeant, or the DCs when they arrived. He wondered where the detectives would stay. Not the *Royal*, presumably. But why not? He pictured the inspector skulking round at midnight.

Matthew had phoned Bridget with the news and she'd had time to prepare a response. Anthea was sure, from Bridget's expression, that she'd rehearsed it carefully. She'd spent yesterday on household chores and caring for her mother, who had multiple sclerosis. She hadn't gone out at all except to shop for food.

'She could have gone out in the evening without her mother knowing. She's really got no alibi,' Anthea said.

Neither had Nevis, Chris pointed out. Or Mrs Marr.

They returned to what Nevis had said about Sarah talking to Hardy at the entrance to the basement stairs.

'I don't think Masterson's got anything more out of Sarah. Not with her solicitor there.'

Anthea raised an inquiring eyebrow. 'Do you think Sarah arranged for Matthew to go home early so she could meet Hardy? What if they went down then?'

'Hardy would have had to go up to his room and change into his dressing-gown. Nevis would have heard him because he'd only just gone up himself. And Hardy's supposed to have died around midnight.'

Sarah and Matthew alibied each other, but what if Matthew was lying to protect Sarah? What if they'd returned to the hotel to throttle one of their guests?

Anthea began typing up Bridget's statement, which was comprehensive and included when she'd begun working at the *Royal*, her interview with Matthew prior to starting, her duties and how these overlapped with Sarah's, her opinions of her employer and the rest of the staff.

She looked up from her keyboard to say, 'Manoli left shortly after Sarah last night and went out the back way. He lives alone in a one-bedroom apartment. Claims he went straight home.'

Chris nodded, remembering how frightened Manoli had looked, but his thoughts were still on Charles Nevis.

'People give themselves away by their expressions,' he said, 'even when their words are well rehearsed.'

Chris uploaded the photos he'd taken at the psychic's and printed out two sets, one of which he took to the front office. The second he folded into his jacket pocket.

'Let's see if we can go to my place and grab a bite to eat.'

'Good idea. I missed lunch.'

Chris bit the inside of his cheek to stop himself from mentioning the toasted sandwiches, and that he'd eaten his assistant's share as well as his.

He straightened his uniform and knocked on the door of the front office. Masterson and Thomas were eating Chinese take-away sitting at their desks. Thomas looked as though he was trying to suppress a smile. Chris wondered how much the inspector had told his sergeant about what had happened at Mrs Marr's.

'All right, Blackie.' Masterson wiped his mouth with a blue paper serviette. 'But be back here in three quarters of an hour.'

SEVEN

As Chris opened tins and stirred, he recalled Mrs Marr's back room, fitted out like Aladdin's Cave. He held his head over simmering pasta sauce, breathing in garlic and fresh herbs, and thought of a hotel basement filled with a century and a half of death.

Anthea had said there was something she wanted to do and that it would only take five minutes.

She walked in holding a pack of tarot cards.

Chris smiled at her evident excitement. 'Where did you get those?'

'That funny little shop,' said Anthea, ripping off the cellophane wrapping. 'The one that calls itself an emporium. The owner was about to close. I had to hunt for them. I bet nobody's been through the stock in that place for years.'

She took off her jacket and sat down with a puff of satisfaction, while Chris set out bowls and glasses.

'What are you going to do with them?'

'Learn how to tell fortunes and predict the future.' Anthea returned Chris's smile, but there was tension round her eyes.

The packet's cover design included the Page of Swords, a beautifully dressed youth in golden boots and embroidered cotte, holding a white rose in one hand. He looked like a hopeful young man setting out to seek his fortune, though he stood at the edge of a precipitous cliff.

Anthea raised her water glass. Chris was drinking wine. 'To prudence,' she said, nodding at the different liquids, 'and the powers of divination.'

Chris wasn't sure he was prepared to go along with that, but he lifted his own glass and took a sip.

'Mmn,' Anthea said after a few moments. 'This is good.'

Their tastes were similar, the need for comfort food understood. Fresh pasta with a tomato and herb sauce was one of the scratch meals they'd cooked for each other in the past, in the middle of a case, wanting to stay out of the way of detectives who'd taken over their station.

The fisherman's cottage where he lived alone was too small to include a dining room, so Chris and the few guests he invited for a meal ate in the kitchen. He had cleaned and restored the old hearth and brick chimney and had picked up some iron pots and a kettle of the type his grandparents had thrown away. He cooked on a modern stove, with the best stainless steel kitchenware; but the hearth, with its working fireplace and an easy chair on either side, was the centre of the room.

There were two small bedrooms. For a while, Chris had used what had been his parents' then his mother's room as a study, then he'd decided that he preferred reading in one of the easy chairs and writing at the kitchen table.

There was an instruction leaflet with the cards. Anthea read while she ate, looking up to say, 'When arranging a channelling reading the querent is advised to bring an object belonging to the spirit when he or she was alive.'

'The book,' Chris said. '*Ultima Thule*. Third and last volume of *The Fortunes of Richard Mahony*. It was published as a single volume in 1929. You can still buy first editions and they're not all that expensive.'

'But if Hardy's was signed?'

'I agree that makes a difference.'

'You've read it, haven't you?'

'A while ago now.'

'What did you think?'

'Of the trilogy? It's a masterpiece,' Chris said.

Anthea fell silent after listening to Chris's opinion of the novel. She studied the spread of cards he'd photographed, sorting through her own pack as she did so. The new cards smelt of plastic and looked slippery. To Chris, there was something slightly repulsive about them.

Anthea looked up to ask, 'Mrs Marr warned Hardy, you said?'

Chris responded to the question with a sideways movement of his hand. 'She claimed the cards did that, and that Hardy understood the risk.'

'Look at this.' Anthea handed Chris a card. 'The Four of Swords,' she said. It showed a knight lying on his tomb with his hands clasped in prayer position on his chest.

'Just like Hardy.'

The stink of mouldy sand filled Chris's nostrils. He shuddered. He wanted to say something to reassure his young assistant, who was sitting very still.

'It's not in the spread.' Chris was aware that his voice was shaky and his words sounded lame. He was glad Anthea hadn't come down to the *Royal's* basement with him.

'Mrs Marr must be familiar with the card,' she said. 'The DI didn't give anything away, did he, about the way the body was arranged?'

'Not that I'm aware of.'

Anthea's phone rang.

'I'll just take this outside.'

When she came back in, her eyes were red. Chris asked what was wrong.

'I don't want to talk about it.'

'Olly?'

Anthea's only reply was to shake her head.

The briefing Masterson gave them that evening was short and to the point. They were to start door knocking first thing in the morning and concentrate on the streets between Sarah's and Matthew's apartment and the *Royal*. So Masterson does think Sarah came back, Chris said to himself. The couple shared a car, a dark green Corolla, which they parked behind their flat.

The clearest print on the basement key belonged to Matthew. Partials were probably those of Sarah and Manoli.

'The Kent girl's got a history of mental illness.'

The sneer in Masterson's voice was unmistakeable. DS Thomas winced, a slight movement, but Chris caught it. There were questions he would have liked to ask, but he didn't think the inspector was in a mood to answer.

Thomas had written a list of names on the whiteboard. Sarah's headed it, then Matthew's, then the rest of the hotel staff, followed by Mrs Marr, Charles Nevis and Isobel and Tony Travers.

'I've spoken to the deceased's mother,' Masterson said. 'She claims to know nothing about her son's visit to Queenscliff, or his interest in Henry Handel Richardson.' There was no hint of sadness or compassion in the inspector's face.

Chris, who was standing behind Anthea, saw the muscles tighten in her neck.

She'd taken the man's measure from her first sight of him. She was right to keep her pregnancy a secret. He felt a deep sense of unease.

Chris stayed back, hoping for a word with Thomas. Luckily, Masterson left first and Chris was able to catch the sergeant shutting the front door behind him.

He showed Thomas the Four of Swords.

Thomas stared at the card for a long moment, then said, 'Let's go back inside.'

He found the print-out Chris had brought to the front office earlier. He asked to see the Seven and the Nine of Swords. He didn't ask where Chris had got his cards from. Chris was glad, because he didn't want to say that they were Anthea's, in case the mere fact of having bought a pack might get her into trouble.

'What happened at the psychic's?'

Chris was unsure where to begin. He decided on a question of his own. 'Did Inspector Masterson tell you about the scream?'

The sergeant nodded. His expression was grave, but Chris didn't miss the gleam of amusement in his eyes.

'Mrs Marr played a trick on us, and the DI – '

'Doesn't want to admit that.'

'No.'

'It doesn't make her a murderer. Sarah Kent had opportunity and means. And we know Hardy talked to her about access to the basement. Nevis was on the spot as well.'

'Hardy would know about the Four of Swords if he's at all familiar with the tarot.'

Thomas nodded. 'Leave it with me, Blackie. And – thanks for drawing it to my attention.'

A word of thanks from a detective felt like praise indeed. Chris smiled as he said goodnight.

EIGHT

When he finally got to sleep, Chris dreamt of monsters. All of them wore Mrs Marr's dark hair and business suit. Chris was detached enough in the dream to compare his friend Minnie Lancaster to this woman of the monstrous yet respectable shape and puckish, knowing smile. But Minnie's hair was red; Minnie's hair was as like the sun on a gloomy winter's day. Minnie was clean light, compared with the psychic's shadow.

Chris woke up sweating. He reached for the switch of his bed light, almost knocking it over, and checked his phone. It was 2 AM. If the preliminary assessment of the time of death was right, Gerard Hardy had been dead for at least twenty-four hours.

He got up and put on his dressing-gown, adding socks and slippers, pulling his socks up over his pyjama bottoms in order to minimise the draught.

He knew it was a mistake to drink anything with caffeine in it, but the comfort of a pot of hot, strong tea beckoned irresistibly.

Chris put both lights on in the kitchen, the strong overhead one in the middle of the ceiling and the light over the stove. He couldn't understand why people went for low wattage bulbs in kitchens. He waited, standing in front of the sink, for the jug to boil. The images were fading. By dawn, they would probably have faded right away. Chris did not believe they had anything significant to tell him; he'd had a nightmare, that was all. He remembered being awake in the small hours, getting up to attend to his mother, helping her to the toilet, how she always apologised for disturbing him and how this always made it worse.

His mother had known he found it difficult to get back to sleep, although he never said this to her, never breathed a word. How could he when it was a tiny inconvenience compared with what she was going through? That was the worst of mothers and sons who knew each other too well. Chris recalled his days at the station during that time - gritty-eyed, struggling to keep awake. He prayed he wasn't in for another bout of insomnia, then cursed himself for being so foolish as to offer up a prayer when all those old ones – please God, make her better, please God, don't let her die – had spectacularly failed.

Perhaps Gerard Hardy's mother was sitting in a kitchen somewhere, staring at a wall.

Chris fetched the doona from his bed and arranged it round his shoulders. He told himself that if he wasn't going to be able to get back to sleep, he might as well make notes.

This meant fetching his notebook and pen from his jacket pocket, but he was soon back, warming his hands on his mug and biting the end of his pen as an aid to memory.

He was surprised to find that he'd already formed clear opinions, not only of the detectives and Mrs Marr, but of Matthew, Sarah and Charles Nevis. Sarah was frightened; she and Matthew, perhaps at her instigation, perhaps at his, were holding something back. It was a black mark against Sarah that she hadn't mentioned meeting Hardy at the basement stairs the first time she was interviewed. Nevis believed he was far smarter than the police and could afford to amuse himself at their expense. As did Mrs Marr.

As he jotted down this bit of remembered conversation and then that, Chris's mind was busy with the gaps, with what had not been said.

He pictured the medium as a strong, yet amorphous presence, as though she possessed the ability to shape-shift. During the interview, Mrs Marr had been conscious of her double meanings, pleasurably anticipating the surprise she'd planned.

Chris drained his mug – where the sugar had settled

at the bottom the tea was deliciously restorative and sweet – and decided to avoid giving the detectives an excuse to reprimand or ridicule him. He'd share his opinions with Anthea and wait to see what kind of job Masterson made of the next few days. With that last tired thought, Chris put his head down on his folded arms, and, contrary to his expectations, fell asleep.

Three hours spent knocking on doors and asking questions did not turn up a single sighting that could have been Sarah Kent. Unless, Anthea told Chris, when they met on the windy corner of Hobson and Learmonth Streets, she'd disguised herself as an old man.

Chris nodded glumly, recognising Anthea's description. Brian Laidlaw was one of the few townsfolk who walked the streets late at night – an irascible, observant, unfriendly soul who'd proved himself an important witness in the past. Brian had not seen anybody else; he'd taken offence, Anthea said, at having been asked.

Chris had been given the flats as a starting point. The couple who lived below Matthew and Sarah had heard their car pull in a few minutes after ten. Neither had heard it starting up again.

'They're very quiet,' the woman said nervously. 'They're out all day. We've never heard them argue.'

'What time did you go to bed?'

The couple exchanged glances. 'Eleven?' the man said.

'A bit after,' the woman added, frowning.

Chris suspected that the couple weren't long married. He felt sure that they were holding nothing back.

Sarah's and Matthew's flat was in a block of four. The other upstairs flat was occupied by a single mother and her daughter. The woman said she'd heard voices after ten on Thursday night, but by ten-thirty all had been quiet next door.

'They know Lou's a light sleeper,' she said, referring to her daughter, playing with building blocks on the floor between herself and Chris. 'They're nice people.'

When Chris had asked if she'd heard a car starting up in the middle of the night, or footsteps on the stairs, the woman shook her head.

The tenants of flat number four weren't home.

That afternoon, Geelong was playing Carlton at Kardinia Park. Those not going in to watch the match would be glued to their TV sets and most reluctant to be interrupted. Did Masterson know this? Would it be out of place to remind him? Chris was afraid the inspector was sufficiently self-assured to believe the witness he sought would be found before kick-off time.

He finished his allotted streets, then decided to make a couple of phone calls.

When Anthea came in, flushed and windblown, hanging up her jacket and putting on the jug for tea, Chris said, 'Mrs Marr's permit for a stall at the Cowrie market hasn't been renewed.'

'Cowrie? I thought they were pretty New Age.'

'She had a stall there for a few months, but then there was a complaint.'

'What sort of complaint?'

'The market organiser I spoke to wouldn't say.'

When Anthea raised an eyebrow, Chris said, 'Inspector Masterson told me to look into the psychic's background.'

Anthea's response was to get out her tarot cards.

NINE

Chris discovered that not only had Mrs Marr's permit to hold a market stall been withdrawn, but when the lease on her flat came up for renewal, it had been refused. The flat, close to Torquay's main shopping centre, had been where the medium had lived as well as her place of work; she'd held her tarot readings there.

'If Mrs Marr was in breach of any regulations,' Chris said mildly, 'then I'd like to know.'

'It was a private matter.' The young man's voice was low-pitched and wary.

'What kind of private matter?'

'I don't want to discuss it on the phone.'

'Mrs Marr would have queried why her lease wasn't being renewed. She would have asked for an explanation. What did you tell her?'

'She didn't make a fuss.'

'Did she tell you she was planning on moving to Queenscliff?'

'This is to do with that murder, isn't it? That young fellow who was strangled.'

'Just a bit of background. Who knew Mrs Marr when she first arrived in Torquay?'

'I have no idea.'

'Did she get on well with people?'

'I – not everybody holds with tarot readings.'

'Who's opposed to them?'

'I'm sorry, but I have to go now.'

'She was an odd one, no doubt about that,' Councillor Williams said.

Chris thought it 'odd' that the councillor was referring

to Mrs Marr in the past tense, as though it was she who'd died and not Gerard Hardy. Ros Williams was the councillor's name – 'call me Ros,' she'd said, when Chris introduced himself.

While Mrs Marr's former landlord had been wary from the word go, Ros spoke as though she had nothing to hide.

From her voice, Chris guessed her age to be midway between his and Anthea's – young for a councillor? Probably not these days.

She'd been acquainted with Mrs Marr, 'though not well'.

Chris noted the qualification, and the rise of Ros's voice as she made it. He wondered if she was telling him she hadn't been a customer.

'That poor young man,' she said.

'Did you and Mr Hardy ever meet?'

'Why should we?'

'No particular reason. Why wasn't Mrs Marr's market permit renewed?'

'A' – Ros hesitated over her choice of words – 'member of the public complained about her.'

'Why?'

'A confidential matter.'

Chris could have replied that a murder investigation trumped all forms of confidentiality, but he didn't want the councillor querying his right to be asking questions.

'Did you know Mrs Marr's landlord refused to renew the lease on her flat?'

'I heard something to that effect.'

'Do you know why?'

'She wasn't tarred and feathered.'

As soon as the words were out, Chris guessed that Ros regretted having said them.

'Did any of her Torquay clients follow her to Queenscliff?'

'I don't know.'

When Chris asked if there was anybody else the councillor could suggest he talk to, Ros said, after another

short silence, 'You could try Bernard Hepson. But be careful.'
Chris assured her that he would. Ros sounded reluctant that
she'd passed on the name.

Bernard Hepson, whose number Chris found in the phone
book, readily admitted to complaining about Mrs Marr,
calling her an 'interfering charlatan' who 'preyed on people's
grief'.

'She gets them when they're at their most vulnerable,
gives them just enough hope to keep them coming back.'

Hepson didn't seem to care that Chris was calling
in connection with Gerard Hardy's murder; in fact, Chris
thought, he scarcely took that aspect in, so keen was he to
vent his anger with the spirit medium. He didn't ask who had
given Chris his name, but launched off his attack immediately,
strengthening Chris's opinion that, while Mrs Marr had not
been 'tarred and feathered', she'd been strongly encouraged
to leave town.

'It was bad enough that Sheila and I – we argued. It
was horrible. You don't know what the death of a child can
do to a marriage.'

Chris murmured something that he hoped sounded
sympathetic.

'I'm on the Surfcoast Business Council. I've been head
of Rotary. I'm well known here, well respected. It was an
affront to me to have that woman practically in the main
street, with her incense and her baubles and her lies.'

'Mrs Marr lied to you?'

'To Sheila. Pretending she could talk to Jenny!
Pretending Jenny was still *there*. The other side, she called it.
What a load of rot.'

When Chris raised the subject of the lease, Hepson
hinted that Mrs Marr's landlord had been encouraged not to
renew it.

'Did Mrs Marr object?'

'She went quietly,' he said with evident relief.

Chris began ringing around the local estate agents. It didn't take him long to find out the one Mrs Marr was renting through in Queenscliff. She'd taken a year's lease on her house. 'No,' the young woman who answered Chris's call said, there'd been no problems. She always paid on time.

Chris wondered why Mrs Marr had rented a whole house, when she'd apparently been satisfied with a flat in Torquay. Because there weren't that many flats available in Queenscliff? Because her business had expanded and she needed more room? That explanation didn't ring true either.

When Chris reported on the results of his phone calls, all the response he got from Masterson was a nod. The inspector was staring out the front office window.

'I don't want you gossiping about that scream,' he told Chris. 'I know what junior officers are like.'

Chris controlled himself with an effort. You have no idea, he thought.

TEN

Chris and Anthea watched the two detective constables arrive from the park opposite the station. They were sitting on a bench under the black lighthouse, sharing a packet of sandwiches.

The DCs were tall and thin, like two sides of a ladder without the in-between bits.

'Tweedledum and Tweedledee,' said Anthea.

'I wonder if we look the same to them.'

'What?' Anthea lifted her chin and frowned.

'People who work together for a long time? No offence,' Chris said.

It was unlike Anthea to be touchy. Chris concentrated on his sandwiches, then said he supposed they ought to be getting back.

Masterson held another briefing, rapping out instructions. Perhaps, even as a young detective constable, he'd expected others to do the leg work and then taken the credit. This method would have been easier after he was promoted to sergeant, easier still now he'd been made inspector. But Masterson had to make an arrest. That was the problem with being in charge.

The DI picked up a sheet of paper from his desk and read aloud a list of the doctors and psychiatrists Sarah Kent had seen over the past ten years.

Bi-polar, schizophrenia, severe depression, unipolar depression, psychotic episodes – the list went on.

'The doctors disagree with one another,' Thomas pointed out.

Masterson frowned at him. 'The Kent girl was seen talking to the deceased shortly before ten o'clock on

Thursday night. This' – he waved the paper at them – 'proves how mentally unstable she is. We need a witness. Get out there and find one!'

Anthea kept her eyes fixed on the floor in front of her, which, all things considered, was a good tactic, Chris thought. The phone rang in the back office and he excused himself to answer it.

It was an inquiry about dog registration. Chris told the caller to ring the council on Monday. He had long since given up marvelling that people rang him about matters that were nothing to do with the police.

He put the phone down and stood staring for a few seconds at the empty space around it, wondering what the detectives knew about him and Anthea.

Masterson would normally consider uniformed constables too far beneath him to merit his attention, but he might have instructed Thomas to find out a bit about them, in which case the inspector would know that Anthea was married to Olly Parkinson, who less than a year ago had been arrested for the murder of ten-year-old Bobby McGilvrey.

Chris had great respect for his assistant's self-control and common sense, but told himself that these qualities were not infallible. When he'd warned Anthea not to tell the inspector that she'd bought a pack of tarot cards, Anthea's reply had been scornful. 'As if I would,' she'd said.

The house-to-house was extended on the assumption that Sarah Kent might have taken a roundabout route to the hotel.

'Geelong's playing at home, in case you've forgotten,' Chris reminded Ferrier and Sanders.

Sanders smiled. 'I grant you, we've lost anyone with tickets, but those planning to watch the match on telly will be getting comfortable with a beer or two.'

Chris returned the young detective's smile. He didn't add what surely must be obvious, that the townsfolk wouldn't welcome any interruption to the game.

Anthea had nicknamed the DCs Tweedledum and Tweedledee, but to Chris Sanders was a 'Rawbones', all angular limbs and a strength that had yet to be put to the test.

Ferrier had smooth pale skin, eyebrows and hair practically the same colour. His habitual expression seemed to be one of disdain. Sanders at least treated uniformed constables as people, rather than bits of furniture, or beasts to be ordered around.

Masterson and Thomas interviewed Sarah Kent again, this time at the station. Chris watched Sarah's solicitor leaving and noted the woman's expression of grim determination.

The inspector announced that he was holding a press conference at the *Royal* at six. A mistake, Chris thought, unless he had something definite to offer; but he guessed that Masterson wanted to appear on national television, that he was looking forward to it.

Chris found himself fretting about what might be lost or overlooked because of the DI's fixation on Sarah. Queenscliff's inhabitants, the older ones especially, were good at keeping quiet if they decided that silence was to their advantage. As for the detectives, no matter what their rank, the townsfolk would consider their own interests first. It took someone who knew them, who'd grown up with them, to be able to assess when and how to poke; when to be patient and wait for them to come to him. It simply wasn't any good demanding answers. If Masterson was smart, he'd know that and make provision for it.

Not for the first time, Chris reflected that his style of policing, his personality and character, belonged to a vanished century. He wondered what his counterpart of a hundred and fifty years ago would have made of a murder in the basement of the *Royal*. Would he – it would of course have been a he – have taken murder in his stride, or been shocked and bewildered by it?

Chris pictured the fellow standing four-square in his boots in the early decades of the town, when Europeans had trod heavily on an earth not at all accustomed to their feet, an earth already blood-soaked, if those early settlers had bothered to look carefully, which for the most part they had not. That constable would have considered tarot readings blasphemous, if he'd ever heard of them. The tarot would have been against his religion, conversing with the dead a dangerous heresy, usurping God's privilege and power.

Calling by the station, Chris found Anthea on the back veranda, half lying on a cushioned chair. She opened her eyes on hearing his approach. Her skin looked pale green, practically transparent.

'I just threw up a glass of water.'

'You're over doing it,' Chris said. 'Go home and lie down.'

'No.'

'Have you told Olly?'

'What about?'

Chris lifted his hands, palms upwards, trying to suppress his worry. He sat down next to her.

'It'll pass. I'll be better by tomorrow.' Anthea turned her head away. 'Olly didn't want me to come back.'

'That's what I figured. I'm sorry,' Chris said.

'It's not your fault.'

Chris considered that. He might have spoken up, argued with Masterson against bringing his assistant back. But he knew the inspector would have insisted. Before going on leave, Anthea had said she'd make up her mind while she was away, whether to apply for maternity leave, or to resign.

Anthea raised herself to a sitting position and ran her hands through her hair.

'I heard them arguing,' she said. 'Masterson and

Thomas. I popped back because I wasn't feeling well. I don't think either of them knew I was here.'

'What were they arguing about?'

'Masterson was shouting something about tarot cards. I couldn't hear what Thomas was saying.'

The Four of Swords, Chris thought.

When Minnie Lancaster rang to check with him about cancelling their dinner, it took Chris a moment to grasp her meaning.

He'd completely forgotten that they'd planned to eat together that evening.

'Don't worry about it,' Minnie said.

'But – '

'Honestly.'

'I was going to say I'd rather spend the time with you.'

'Me too.'

Chris pictured Minnie considering with her head on one side, tired, but fatigue not touching the core of her because she didn't allow it to; he saw Minnie with the slanting late afternoon light catching the gold in her hair.

Suddenly she seemed infinitely precious to him, a friend who made no demands, but understood the demands on his time and energy of those he could not refuse.

'Everybody's talking about it,' she said.

'I'll bet.'

He wanted to tell her that their conversation could wait, that there would be a right time, but he wasn't sure how to put this. He also wanted to tell her about the dream, which had stayed with him all day.

'Ring me when you can,' Minnie said, and then, after a second's pause, 'I'll go now.'

ELEVEN

The surprise was delivered in an offhand way, as surprises often are. Sanders put his head around the door of the back office. He was frowning.

'There was a dog barking,' he said.

Chris was sitting at his desk, studying his computer screen. He half turned towards Sanders to ask, 'When and where?'

'In Bridge Street. Thursday night.'

That was interesting. 'What about a cuppa?' Chris asked. 'I was about to make one.'

Sanders followed him out to the kitchen.

'Getting blood out of a stone,' he said in an aggrieved tone of voice, staring at the fridge.

'You've never lived in a small town?'

Sanders shook his head, as though Chris had asked him if he'd contemplated space travel.

'You know what the DI said when I told him? 'Barking dogs are two a penny. Get back there and find someone who saw the girl.'

Chris made a sympathetic face, but didn't speak again while he made the tea.

They took their mugs out to the veranda.

Sanders didn't seem to find it odd that Anthea was reclining on a wicker chair. Chris noted that his glance at her was an appreciative one and that he seemed in no hurry to get back to door-knocking.

They spoke about their different upbringings, stretching out the break, but Anthea did not mention that her parents had been killed in a car accident when she was three, and Chris didn't say that his father had drowned jumping overboard to rescue a pilot who'd fallen from the side of a container ship. They kept the details brief and undemanding.

When Anthea asked, 'What made you join the police?' Sanders replied, 'Boredom.'

'What about your friend?'

'You mean Ron? We're not friends. What kind of tea is this?'

'Russian Caravan.'

Sanders made a complicated movement with his eyebrows. 'We had our weekend leave cancelled. That's all we've got in common.'

Chris did not miss the note of bitterness. Tweedledum and Tweedledee he thought.

Anthea looked as though she was about to comment, but then changed her mind. Chris saw that she was willing to meet the young DC half way, wherever that might be, and that she'd reached this decision quickly, for reasons of her own.

He was a handsome man despite his gawkiness. Indeed his gawkiness could be part of his charm.

'Masterson's known for making quick arrests.' Sanders's tone implied that, had Anthea not chosen to bury herself in a coastal backwater, she would have known this.

As for Chris's decision to remain in Queenscliff, it was clear that Sanders wasn't interested.

When Chris, returning to the subject of the barking dog, asked if he'd talked to the owner, the DC shook his head.

'He wasn't home. He's a vet apparently.'

'Who told you about it?'

'Two old ducks.'

'Two sisters living together in Bridge Street? That'd be Kate and Lily Watkins.'

Waning autumn sun, soon to disappear behind the fence, picked out the bronze in Anthea's hair. Chris asked himself what man in his senses would not find her attractive.

He asked Sanders about timing. The dog had begun

to bark sometime after midnight. One of the 'old ducks' had been woken up.

'She told me about the dog, but then she clammed up. Like I said, blood out of a stone.'

'She?'

'The younger one. Lily, is it? The other one looked daggers and hardly said a thing.' Sanders snorted. 'You know these people, Blackie. You know how to break through their reserve.'

Chris could have told him that 'breaking through' was not the way to go.

A search of the hotel and Hardy's flat had turned up nothing of significance, Sanders told them.

'So his laptop's still missing?'

'We'll never find it now.'

'The book?'

'Keeping company with the laptop at the bottom of the bay. I thought there might be a back-up hard drive in Hardy's flat, or printed notes.'

'About?'

'What he was really doing here.'

'What do you think?' asked Anthea.

Sanders looked at her as though grateful that she'd asked, but did not answer directly.

'You know the quote? If a man lies with a male as with a woman, both of them have committed an abomination; they shall surely be put to death; their blood is upon them.'

'You know your Bible,' Chris said.

'Not me. Ron Ferrier. Another thing we don't have in common. Ron's got into trouble for homophobic statements. So has Masterson. He restrains himself, but the prejudice is there just underneath the surface.'

'If Nevis is gay and Nevis and Hardy were a couple, why get separate rooms?' asked Anthea.

'Maybe Hardy had broken it off, but Nevis was still

hoping. That's why he agreed to drive him down here.'

Sanders stood up and took his mug inside. There was steel inside that bean pole of a DC, Chris decided, determination and a will to possess what he desired.

He had a sudden vision of Hardy hovering above them all like a self-regarding and capricious ghost. Did ghosts retain their sexual orientation? What would he make of the investigation so far?

On impulse Chris followed Sanders to the kitchen.

'What about Sergeant Thomas?' he asked.

'He's a non-believer.'

'Like you.'

Sanders shrugged. 'Ron's convinced we're dealing with witchcraft, devil-worship, Satanism.'

'And he's expressed these views openly, I mean to the DS and the DI?'

'Masterson listens to him.' Sanders made a wry face, then looked at Chris in a speculative, not unfriendly way.

'I probably shouldn't be telling you this, but I heard our sergeant complaining on the phone.'

'Who to?'

'I don't know.'

A press photographer parked opposite the station took a few casual-seeming shots as Chris left the building. The media was concentrating on the *Royal*, which was of course to be expected; they were hungry for details of the basement, and would go on pushing till they got them.

The Saturday papers, which Chris had picked up early in the morning, carried old photographs of the hotel. One had dug up a story about the place being haunted by the ghosts of mental patients; another about two small girls who'd fallen down a well. *The Age* had photographs of Henry Handel Richardson overlapping the Mercer Street house. There was a short history of her life, from the time she'd spent in Queenscliff as a child – Chris was surprised to be reminded that it was only a little over a year – to the time she and her sister had lived with their mother in post offices, to PLC, then Leipzig to study music, then the books that had made her famous – *Maurice Guest, The Getting of Wisdom, The Fortunes of Richard Mahony.*

Chris recalled Sarah Kent as he'd first seen her, hunched in the alcove behind the reception desk. Her eyes had been haunted, no lesser word would do.

On his list, there were more crosses showing that nobody was home than ticks indicating he'd found someone to question. He thought of lighting a fire and waiting till it attained the combination of coals and wood burning at a high temperature that was exactly right. He thought of waiting on Minnie, pouring wine and serving her a meal – Minnie who earnt her living waiting on people at another of Queenscliff's old hotels.

The streets were quiet – well, that was predictable. The wind had dropped and the oblique sun shone with a gentle warmth that seemed surprised at itself. Chris loved autumn sunsets; he loved the way the clouds often parted on the horizon, just in time, or place, for the red and gold. He loved the richness of it, the way the darkness made a breach and was suddenly forbidding.

It was a shock to think of Gerard Hardy alive on an afternoon like this one, such a short time ago, and how a murderer's plans had curled inside the elegiac light.

A woman could have done it, and the fact that Inspector Masterson believed a woman had was the reason for Chris standing on a street corner and procrastinating, instead of finishing the houses on his list.

If Sarah had returned to the *Royal* in the middle of the night, she would have taken a direct route. Why not? If Sarah had disturbed a dog in Bridge Street, causing it to bark, she would have had to go well out of her way to do so.

So most likely the dog hadn't barked at Sarah, but at someone else. Mrs Marr lived in Bridge Street. Had the dog barked at Mrs Marr?

They were polite, the townsfolk who answered his ring or knock; they listened to his questions, after looking round his shoulder to make sure he was alone. A few invited him in; others were so certain they hadn't seen or heard anything that they answered straight away.

Those who did invite him in, even those who offered him something to drink, had nothing of importance to say. They'd been asleep on Thursday night. Some accompanied this statement with a rueful lift of the shoulders, making it into an apology.

It was almost dark when Chris turned into Bridge Street. Nobody had told him that he had to finish by a certain time, though of course he was expected to be at the hotel for the press conference.

Lily Watkins opened her front door a crack and kept it on the chain.

'Oh, it's you. We were just talking about you.' She released the chain with shaking fingers, murmuring, 'Come in.'

Chris followed Lily into her warm, comfortable living-room. He looked around appreciatively before taking a seat near the fire.

Lily's sister, Kate, asked him if he'd like a cup of tea and he accepted, looking from one sister to the other, feeling the tension and the warning pass between them.

Kate was older, but only by a year, and they were very much alike to look at. Kate was a widow and Lily had never married; they'd been living together for the past eight years, perfectly contentedly so far as Chris was aware.

They talked about the match while they drank their tea and ate slices of date loaf that Lily brought in on a painted wooden tray. Chris's interest in the team had faded, but he didn't let this show. He knew the final score, of course, and who'd kicked the goals.

Kate took her knitting from a cloth bag sitting open at her feet. She sat with it on her lap for a moment before looking up at Chris, who understood that they hadn't yet made up their minds whether to be frank with him, and were divided over it.

'What time did you go to bed on Thursday night?' he asked.

Lily went red and Kate laughed without humour. To give them more time, Chris swallowed a mouthful of date loaf and pronounced it excellent.

Kate received the compliment with the placid assurance of someone who'd been called a good cook all her adult life.

Lily said abruptly, 'Half past ten.' Chris knew her bedroom was at the front and that Kate's faced the back yard.

'What time did the dog wake you?'

Kate looked stubborn, Lily unhappy and confused.

Kate said, 'It's that fellow Cartwright's.'

'Does he often bark?'

'No, though I think he's left on his own too much.'

Chris said, 'Someone must have disturbed him.'

Kate and Lily exchanged another glance.

Cartwright lived at one end of Bridge Street, Mrs Marr at the other, with Lily and Kate roughly half way between.

Chris asked, 'What does Mrs Marr think of the dog?'

'Mrs Marr – ' Kate began. Lily interrupted with, 'She likes him.'

'How well do you know her?'

'We don't hold with fortune-telling,' Kate said.

'We just say hello to one another in the street,' Lily added.

Chris said, careful to keep his voice and his expression neutral, 'You got up to see what the matter was.'

Kate was angry. 'We're two defenceless women with a murderer on the loose. Do you want him banging on our door?'

'We're not defenceless,' Lily cut in quickly. Kate glared at her. Chris said to Lily quietly, 'Go on.'

'I came in here to the living-room and opened the curtains.'

'There was someone out there. Who?'

'I don't know.'

Both sisters looked up to the curtained window. Kate was gripping the arm of her chair; her knitting lay forgotten in her lap.

'Man or woman?' Chris asked.

Lily hesitated before answering. 'I think it was a woman, but I couldn't swear to it. I saw a figure in dark clothes, that's all.'

'Doing what?'

'Walking along the footpath.'

'In what direction?'

Lily indicated with her hand. The person had been walking away from Cartwright's.

'You think it was a woman. Did you notice anything about her? Was she short? Tall?'

'I only caught a glimpse, but she looked to be of medium height. I think she was wearing a coat – I mean the figure looked bulky – and a hat as well.'

'What kind of hat?'

'Close fitting. Covering her head.'

'What makes you think it was a woman?'

'Just the way she moved. Mr Cartwright's dog had stopped barking by then. I went back to bed.'

Chris glanced from Lily to Kate. 'Your sister didn't wake you to tell you what she'd seen?'

'No.'

He imagined the rest of Lily's night, lying rigid, or

tossing and turning to find a position that would allow her to relax. But perhaps it hadn't been like this; perhaps it had only been when she heard the morning's news that Lily had been scared.

She said, 'It's not a crime, to be out walking at night.'

Chris agreed that it wasn't.

'We don't want to get an innocent person into trouble.'

Chris said he understood this and was careful to thank both of them.

TWELVE

Chris forced his feet in the direction of the *Royal*, knowing how the figure would be interpreted by Inspector Masterson.

He would treat Lily as the witness he'd been looking for. Lily would be pressured into saying she'd seen more than she had. By the time the inspector had finished with her, the figure would be definitely female and probably with blonde hair too. Never mind that Bridge Street was in the opposite direction for someone walking from Sarah's flat to the *Royal*.

Chris believed that Lily was telling the truth. She'd seen a moving figure. She could not be sure if it was a man or a woman, though she was inclined to the latter. The sensible course would be to question everybody in the street next day when most, if not all of them would be at home.

Chris asked himself if he should go back and warn the sisters to keep their doors and windows locked; but they understood the need for this as well as he did.

He could see the hotel lights ahead of him now; even the derelict tower was lit up. Surely Masterson wasn't planning to run a press conference from up there.

On impulse, he walked around the corner. The *Royal's* back gates were locked, as he'd expected them to be. All activity was concentrated at the front.

Anthea would be keen to hear what Lily had to say. Chris knew he could present the facts, as Lily had presented them, and that his assistant would listen, clear-eyed, keeping an open mind.

DI Masterson walked onto the front steps, with the hotel's exterior lights blazing out across the street ahead of him, meeting and reflecting back the lights above the TV cameras. It was theatrical and over done; the inspector looked pleased with himself as he took centre stage.

He told the reporters, gathered in a semi-circle just beyond the steps, that a terrible crime had been committed and that, rest assured, the perpetrator would be brought to justice. The investigation was only in its second day, but already significant progress had been made.

Names were shouted out by the reporters, and shouted back and forth amongst the crowd as well, for a lot of the townsfolk had turned up. It helped, of course, that Geelong had won. They'd cheered themselves hoarse in the last quarter, but still had energy and breath for this extra excitement. Chris heard Sarah's name, along with Matthew's and Manoli's. Outsiders, the three of them; it would suit the locals if an outsider were found guilty. Chris was shocked to realise how quickly a group of familiar people might turn into a mob.

Standing at the back, out of range of the cameras, he pulled his jacket close and hunched his neck. He'd arrived too late to report on his conversation with Lily and Kate, and he wasn't sorry. He didn't trust the DI not to tell these journalists and the hungry crowd far more than they had any right to know.

There was a surge towards the steps when the inspector turned away from the lights and microphones. Chris moved forward and saw Sanders and Ferrier do the same from the opposite side, in case a reminder was needed that the hotel was still out of bounds.

He found himself close to DS Thomas, who looked worried. The crowd was itching to get into the basement, hot to rush down the stairs and along the brick corridor underneath those arches, past the barred windows to the sandpit.

Thomas raised his voice and told them it was time to leave. For a few moments it seemed they might ignore him, then, in ones and twos, they began to wander off. A man called, 'G'night Blackie' and another, 'Up the Cats!' Chris couldn't spot Anthea anywhere and felt uneasy, hoping that she was all right.

Chris had felt sure that Masterson would want to go straight to interview Lily Watkins, but this was not the case. The DI, pleased with the way the press conference had gone, and looking forward to a good dinner, decided it could wait till morning.

'We'll make the little liar talk. Now she knows someone saw her.'

Chris felt as though he'd eaten something foul. He wondered whether Cartwright, the owner of the barking dog, lived on his own. From what Lily and Kate had said, he'd assumed this, but had not asked them directly.

Cartwright sounded like a military name. Chris had known Cartwrights whose father was stationed at the fort when he was at primary school.

He didn't want to find himself in the position of having to second-guess the inspector, having to think ahead in order to out manoeuvre him. He'd had some experience of this way of proceeding; devious and underhand, but necessary, he'd told himself during the investigation into Bobby McGilvrey's death.

He decided to walk, telling himself he needed to clear his head. It wasn't much past seven, but already the night had settled in to be a cold one, the kind of cold more suited to an inland town than the toe of a peninsula, forever subject to contrary winds and the moderating influence of the sea.

Masterson was in too much of a hurry, too much in love with the image of himself announcing success to listen to anyone advising caution. Chris thought he could go back to Lily's and question her again; but Kate would be there, and returning so soon might put both of them against him. He could warn the sisters that Inspector Masterson would be along first thing in the morning, but they would be expecting this anyway. He preferred to gain the townsfolk's trust and move on from there, but felt in his bones that it was already too late.

He walked along Bridge Street, noting that there were no lights on in the medium's house, at least not at the front. He hadn't seen Mrs Marr at the press conference. There was a back lane, which he considered checking, and told himself he might later on. All of these old streets had back lanes for the night carts. It made for ease of access over a fence, or through a gate insecurely locked, and was worth keeping in mind.

THIRTEEN

The man who opened the door to Chris's knock had no military air about him. He was short, with receding fair hair. His unlined face was fresh and open looking, his skin as fine as though no razor had touched it. Chris noted that he also looked tired.

Troy Cartwright – the young man offered his name, along with a firm, cool handshake – said he was just about to sit down to his dinner, so, if whatever it was could wait, or if Constable Blackie didn't mind –

Chris said he didn't mind at all. His questions would only take a few minutes and he could ask them while Mr Cartwright ate.

The vet looked as though he would have preferred Chris to take the hint and say he'd come back another time. He led the way to a combined living and dining room. His dog, whom he introduced as Jasper, was lying on a rug in front of a well-stocked combustion stove.

Jasper lay with his paws straight out in front of him, head raised and alert. Cartwright sat down at the table, placed at the opposite end of the room to the stove, picked up his knife and fork and took a mouthful from the plate of rice and vegetables in front of him.

The room, clean and uncluttered, felt pleasantly warm to Chris, who was suffering an attack of cold feet. He hadn't been forbidden to continue door-knocking, but he was well aware that Masterson could be angry when he got to hear of it.

When he asked where Troy Cartwright worked, the young man held his hand up to indicate that he'd answer in a moment. The meal looked appetising. Cartwright hadn't offered Chris anything to eat or drink, and Chris knew that this was because he wanted him to leave as soon as possible.

Jasper's brown fur shone in the fire and lamplight. He looked as though he had a bit of German Shepherd in him, and bits of several other breeds as well.

'He's a rescue dog,' the vet said, noting Chris's interest. 'I got him from the pound.'

Chris thought of Max, Bobby McGilvrey's dog, whom Olly had taken in, and who'd died only a few months ago. He asked if Cartwright worked a lot at night.

'Not usually. Why?'

'What about on Thursday?'

'Why?' Cartwright repeated. 'Why do you want to know?'

Chris told him about Jasper barking, watching Cartwright closely as he did so.

Cartwright's eyebrows went up at the mention of Lily Watkins. He said,' I can't help it if Jasper barks from time to time when I'm not here. He's a good, obedient dog considering the miserable start he's had.'

'Nobody's complaining about Jasper. I'm interested in who was out and about that evening. If Jasper barked at someone going by, then I'd like to find out who.'

Cartwright's eyebrows moved again, only fractionally this time, but Chris caught the movement and wondered what it meant.

'What time did you get home on Thursday night?' he asked.

'Late. There was a complication with one of the operations I did.'

'Oh,' Chris said, 'Did the – '

'Cat,' said Cartwright. 'No, she died.'

'I'm sorry to hear that.'

Cartwright shrugged. 'And I'm sorry I can't help you. I've no idea who Jasper was barking at.'

'Did you see anybody in the street when you pulled up?'

'I wasn't looking. I was very tired.'

'Did you notice anything at all that was different, untoward?'

'No.'

'Do you have much to do with your neighbours?'

'We say hello to one another. We're not unfriendly, if that's what you mean.'

'What about Mrs Marr?'

Cartwright smiled and his face became at once more agreeable.

'She likes Jasper,' he said. 'She walks him sometimes, and feeds him if I'm late.'

'Did Mrs Marr feed Jasper on Thursday?'

Cartwright shook his head, still smiling. 'She's a character, that one.'

'How well do you know her?'

'Not – I know what she does for a living.'

'You've never had a tarot reading?'

'No.'

The vet put down his knife and fork. 'Look,' he said. 'If someone was sussing out my place to burgle, then Jasper warned him off. That's good enough for me. Will that be all for now? I've had a long day.'

Chris knew he would get nothing more out of the young man just then, and perhaps there was nothing more to get.

A few years back, he thought, thanking Cartwright for his time and saying goodnight, I would have met this man, or at least known who he was, within a few weeks of his arrival. What this investigation was demonstrating, and Chris told himself he shouldn't be surprised, was how much his town was changing, how many new people were arriving whom he couldn't hope to know.

He stood still for a few moments, noting the position of the street lights, which houses had no tall front fences to obscure the view, and thought again, with pleasure this time, of his own house, of making himself a quick supper and turning the gas heater on; it was too late to light a fire. He wondered how different his life would be if he had a dog of his own, but he couldn't leave a dog alone all day.

That had been his thinking, but maybe he was wrong. What about two dogs, to keep each other company, two dogs who would otherwise be killed? The waste of life, the senselessness of killing an animal somebody had bought as a pet, then no longer wanted, made him feel sick at heart.

He pulled his jacket tight around his chest and turned for home. Half way there, he changed his mind.

Lily looked relieved to see him, as though her conscience had been weighing on her for the past few hours.

She was in her dressing-gown and opened the door with a finger on her lips.

When Chris apologised for coming back, Lily shook her head and whispered, 'Katy's gone to bed.'

Chris had knocked as softly as he could, but the sound could have woken Kate, if in fact she'd been asleep. He steeled himself for Kate's appearance and wondered where he and Lily could go to talk. It was too cold to expect her to stand on the porch.

Lily beckoned him into the living-room and quietly shut the door, offering him a conspiratorial smile that made her seem much younger.

Chris was aware of the risk of coming between the sisters, how easily not only Kate but Lily might turn against him, how quickly her welcome could evaporate.

How would he explain to Masterson if Kate chose to complain? And what would Lily's punishment be for talking to him behind her sister's back?

'Katy doesn't want to get involved,' Lily said in a voice just above a whisper.

Chris nodded to show he understood.

'She says it was just someone walking home, nothing to do with the murder.'

'You're a long way from the *Royal*.'

'I couldn't sleep,' said Lily. 'Kate says I work myself up into states and it's no wonder. She says I just need to relax.'

'You got up because you didn't want to go on lying there.'

Lily nodded, one insomniac to another.

Was it true that she'd got as far as opening the curtains and no further? What if she'd let herself out of her front door, and the person walking had heard and turned to look? If she'd done that, then she really could be in danger.

'You shouldn't have opened the door to me just now,' Chris said. 'Promise me you won't open it unless you know who's there.'

'Kate says we should get one of those eye-hole things.'

'It's not a bad idea.'

Lily said, 'I don't know who it was. Honestly.'

Chris nodded and wished her goodnight.

He went home, made himself a light meal and got ready for bed.

He couldn't sleep; he hadn't really expected to be able to. When he'd entered his cottage, it had been like opening the door to a freezer; not only that, but the air had felt so still and undisturbed, it had seemed as though no one had set foot inside the place for weeks.

The feeling of cold stillness reminded Chris of the basement of the *Royal*. In some part of himself he'd known that it was going to, that the smell would be waiting for him when he went to bed.

Unconsciously – was it unconsciously? – he stretched out on his back and folded his arms across his chest. With a shudder, he flung his right arm out and rolled over on his side.

He'd been reluctant to leave Lily, afraid that something bad was going to happen to her. Yet he hadn't achieved anything by going back there. He would have checked the windows except that he knew Lily was scared Kate would hear him.

Chris squashed his face into the pillow. He wanted Minnie.

Desire lay underneath, or over him, like a mattress or a doona; his tired brain could not decide on which. It was a desire, not so much, just then, for sex; though Chris knew that if he had not desired Minnie in that way, to join his body with hers, to feel her moving and follow her rhythm, then he would not miss her company in other ways.

He knew that Minnie liked him and liked spending time with him. It wasn't a delusion. Minnie was too wise, and – God help them both – too old to waste her time pretending. The notion of Minnie pretending an attraction that she did not feel was laughable.

Chris rolled over on his other side and punched his pillow irritably, admitting what he had so far not allowed himself to admit; Minnie was more comfortable with solitude than he was, as a way of being, rather than a state she'd happened into by default.

He could no more knock on her door, or ring her up and startle her awake, than he could see into the mind of Gerard Hardy's killer. He knew that, were he to give way to his need, Minnie would be calm and friendly. But something would change between them that could not be changed back. A rift would open up, without it being marked, or put into words, and words would be powerless to bridge it. Some breach, not only of courtesy and consideration, would result from his acting out of haste and need.

FOURTEEN

On his way to the station next morning, Chris called by the *Royal*. He knew he might get into trouble for talking to Manoli on his own, but he decided to take the risk. Manoli had been terrified on Friday and there had to be a reason for that.

The cook was in the kitchen. He raised pale brown eyes to Chris when Chris knocked and pushed open the door.

The kitchen's the only place that he feels safe, Chris thought, accepting coffee and a croissant. Manoli sat down opposite him, with a black coffee so thick that it looked solid.

He was a big man, who would run to fat by the time he was forty. But for now, his olive skin was sleek; the muscles in arms looked strong under his white shirt.

Chris asked when he'd arrived for work on Friday.

Though the cook had surely answered this question at least once, he stumbled as though he couldn't get his tongue around the numbers.

'Six – Six forty-five.'

'Did you go straight to the kitchen?'

Manoli nodded. He'd checked that the breakfast menu was in order. All four guests had said yes to breakfast.

'Was the back door locked?'

'Yes. Your sergeant asked me that.'

'Did you notice anything different about the door or the back yard?'

'No – no, there was nothing different.'

The bread and croissants were delivered every day from a bakery at Torquay. 'The best on the coast,' Manoli said, speaking as though Chris hadn't lived in Queenscliff for most of his life and didn't know Torquay from Timbuctoo.

When Chris asked about Sarah, Manoli looked

nervously over his shoulder, as though she was about to appear.

She'd arrived shortly after seven; none of the guests had rung yet, or appeared. Isobel and Tony had asked to have breakfast in their room. The other two, Gerard Hardy and his friend, were expected to come down to the courtyard café.

The owner could put the *Royal* on the market tomorrow, having decided to cut his losses. The hotel might be pulled down and replaced by a block of units. Was Manoli worried about his job? Was that the explanation? Or did his fear have another source?

Hardy's body had been carefully arranged for someone to find. Had the killer known it would be Sarah, assuming the killer was not Sarah herself? How did he or she know that Sarah would be the first to go down to the basement?

Chris recalled the churned-up sand and how it would have been difficult if not impossible to hide signs that Hardy had fought back. He hoped he would be shown the results of the post mortem. It occurred to him that Masterson would expect him to earn this favour in some way.

When Chris asked, 'Do you believe in ghosts?' Manoli looked relieved, as though this was not the question he'd been worrying about.

He said, 'I know there's heaps of stories about this place. But they don't bother me.'

'Which stories?'

'Girls moving chairs and knocking glasses round the bar. When I first heard that, I thought it was kind of fun.'

'What about the girl jumping from the tower?'

'Don't let Sarah hear you talking about that.'

'Why not?'

'Because Sarah's seen her. Sarah believes in ghosts. She's seen that woman in the tower. She won't go up there. She wants Matthew to brick it up. But it's not Matthew's decision.'

'Matthew does his best to look after Sarah,' Chris said in a neutral voice.

Manoli looked as though he was about to comment on this. Instead he asked if Chris would like more coffee.

'Thank you. It's excellent.'

Manoli chanced a smile. 'I'm getting the hang of the machine.'

Chris found he could recall the cook's written statement word for word; where he was living, what hours he worked, when he'd started, as well as a detailed account of his movements last Thursday afternoon and evening.

'Do you go through many bottles of wine?' he asked, recalling the racks in the basement and Sarah's apparent reason for going down there early on Friday morning.

He had no idea why this question should cause Manoli such distress. The cook went white and clutched the edge of the table with both hands.

'Who ordered the expensive wine?'

Manoli hesitated and cleared his throat before saying, 'The owner.'

'You thought it was unwise?'

'No!'

'What then?'

'Just that – with all the renovations – I think he should have waited.'

'Do you have a list, an inventory?'

'Matthew does.'

'Did you have a problem with going down to the basement?'

'No.'

'Will you have a problem now?'

'No,' Manoli said again, too quickly. 'I'd best be getting on with things.'

Chris shook his hand and wished him good-day.

The station's back office felt cramped and claustrophobic. Chris heard voices and then laughter coming from the front. Had the inspector already interviewed Lily Watkins, and had she referred to the fact that he'd returned to talk to her last night?

Chris knew he should volunteer the information; it would be worse if it looked as though he was keeping it to himself. He should also say that he'd stopped by the *Royal* and spoken to Manoli. Both actions could be regarded as stepping out of line, and it wouldn't take much for Masterson to interpret them that way. Chris couldn't really explain the anxiety he felt at the way the investigation had begun, the way the inspector was handling it. It wasn't the first time a superior officer had disappointed him. But he'd woken from a light sleep towards dawn feeling restless, agitated, hungry but not wanting to eat. When he put on his uniform, it felt itchy and too tight.

When Chris knocked on the door, the laughter stopped abruptly. To his surprise it was Sanders in there with Sergeant Thomas; he wondered where the inspector was.

Thomas watched Chris in a speculative way while he explained Manoli's reaction to his question about the wine and said he thought it would be a good idea to check the basement store against the inventory.

'Go ahead, then,' Thomas said. He added that the morning's instructions were to continue with the house-to-house. 'When Constable Merritt turns up, tell her that I want to see her. She wasn't at the press conference last night.'

Sanders was looking out the window. His shoulders tightened at the mention of Anthea's name, but he didn't turn around.

Chris sat down at his desk and pressed in Anthea's number. Suddenly he felt, not just physically tired, but mentally collapsing round the edges, as though there were no boundaries any more to his mental landscape. Those he'd fought to keep in place – created for himself when the natural one, the horizon that was a meeting of sea and sky, had seemed immense and far away and terrifying – these cherished fixtures of his mind he could no longer get a purchase on. He saw again the pit at the bottom of the *Royal*, the rectangle of dun-coloured sand. He pictured Sarah peering into it, Sarah who, according to Manoli, was afraid of ghosts.

Anthea didn't seem disconcerted by his call.

'I was there,' she said. 'I stayed at the back. I didn't want to be – '

'Jostled?'

'We knew we had to turn up to his media circus, but we had no orders about where to stand.'

Chris looked over statements, aware of every noise and movement from the front office, where Anthea had gone as soon as she arrived.

The image of Sarah looking down into the sandpit wouldn't leave him, though he shook his head, stood up and sat down again.

Anthea came in, smiling and saying, 'All good.'

A few minutes later, Sanders propped in the doorway of the back office, holding several sheets of paper.

'Where's Inspector Masterson this morning?' Chris asked.

'At church,' Sanders said. 'He's a Methodist. But they don't call themselves Methodists any more. The Uniting Church.' Sanders seemed about to add something. Instead he waved the sheets of paper. 'I brought you the post mortem.' He smiled at Anthea, who blushed, then began moving around the small room as though he could not keep still.

'Let's say the Kent girl wanted to kill Hardy, I don't think she'd have chosen the basement of the *Royal*.'

'Because of Matthew?' Chris asked.

'If you were the new owner, would you keep either of them on after this?'

'So the killer's someone who hates Matthew or wants to get even with him?'

The sound of raised voices from the front office cut into his question.

Sanders cocked his head. 'The DI's back. Watch out. Fur and feathers are about to fly.'

After Sanders had left, Anthea moved so that she was sitting next to Chris.

The front door banged shut. A car started up.

It wasn't so much a question of flying under the radar, Chris realised, as accepting a peculiar kind of limbo. With the DC's 'gift' of the post mortem, Sanders was testing the limits of what was, for him, a novel situation. It didn't bother him that Masterson and Thomas were in disagreement. He was quite willing to use that disagreement to his own advantage.

The fact that Anthea was married apparently did not deter him. It occurred to Chris that Sanders possessed a quality which was something like a newly-made children's toy. It could be muddied and dented, maybe very quickly, but it still had a lot of bounce.

Anthea and Chris read the report together.

All the signs of death by strangulation had been present; red, bulging eyes, marks on Hardy's neck, bruising round the jaw. Apart from a slight hardening of the arteries, he'd been a healthy man of twenty-nine. He'd had his appendix removed, and had broken his right wrist in his teens. He'd been dead for about six hours when Sarah found him, which confirmed the previously estimated time of death.

There was no evidence that he'd tried to fight off his assailant.

Chris made notes. One thing was curious – a small thing but still it gave him pause for thought – the dressing-gown cord was cleaner than you'd expect it to be if it had been used to strangle someone. There were no tiny flakes of skin embedded in it, though the skin of Hardy's neck had been red and raw-looking. Chris had thought there might be a torch in one of Hardy's dressing-gown pockets, but there wasn't. It had been half filled with sand.

FIFTEEN

No resident of Stevens, Blythe or Bridge Streets, apart from Lily, had seen anyone out walking late on Thursday night, or in the early hours of Friday morning. Some of the householders Chris spoke to were indignant at being asked again. Others shook their heads with regret at not being able to help.

Chris muttered under his breath, recalling false witnesses and false confessions in the past – the local handyman and painter who'd confessed to the murder of a female tourist, and how affronted he'd been when Chris had been unable to see the joke. Time-wasting prankster, Chris said crossly to himself.

He discovered, when he returned to the station, that Lily was holding firm to her original story.

If you didn't want to be noticed, why walk? Why not drive?

Because the sound of a car, at that time of night, was more likely to attract attention than a person on foot. You didn't have to get out of bed and go to a window in order to hear a car.

Lily had been unable to identify Sarah from a photograph or line-up. Masterson's bullying had backfired, with Lily falling back on a native stubbornness. The inspector ranted about 'half-witted old biddies' when Chris reported on the once more disappointing results of his and Anthea's door-knocking.

Nobody in Sarah and Matthew's block of units, or the houses either side, had heard a car pulling out of the carpark after 10 PM. As far as Lily's mystery figure was concerned, Chris decided he would put his money on a teenager sneaking home after curfew. Maybe he or she – Chris thought it was probably a boy – had climbed out his girlfriend's window, and neither set of parents knew. The girl would keep quiet for the boy's sake. The fact that those few hours were now part of a murder investigation would have convinced the young pair to hold their tongues. Given time, Chris thought, he could probably unearth them; but if his assumption was right there wasn't any need.

He reflected that one of the disadvantages of living in a small town, over and above the fact that he could expect the townsfolk to know his personal history, was that the precise limits of his authority were also well known.

As a uniformed constable in a big city station, he would have far less room to manoeuvre. Having room to manoeuvre was a blessing and a curse at the same time.

Matthew and Sarah allowed their flat to be searched again. Sanders reported to Chris and Anthea that Sarah seemed calmer and that she and Matthew were sticking to their story.

Anthea looked up from *The Fortunes of Richard Mahony* and blew on her tea to cool it.

They were accustomed to eating their lunch on the station's back veranda, weather permitting, and though the presence of the detectives made them self-conscious, Chris didn't see why they should shut themselves up inside on a fine day.

Anthea had marked ten or so pages with yellow post-its.

'I found it at the second hand bookshop,' she said in answer to Chris's inquiring look. 'I stayed up reading last night.'

Chris wondered if Anthea had been waiting for Olly to ring. Perhaps that was why she hadn't wanted to get caught up at the press conference, why she'd stayed at the back and slipped away.

'How are you finding it?'

'Good. I started at the beginning and then I thought I might skim through looking for references to spiritualism. Do you remember this one? It's from Mary's point of view.'

Anthea put down her tea and held the paperback in both hands, as though it was a precious first edition. She opened it at one of the marked pages.

'He – Richard she means – had let himself go as never before: he had forgotten to change his under-clothing or have his hair cut; had neglected his meals, neglected the children – lost interest even in his beloved garden. And for all this they had to thank that horrid spiritualism! During the last few months it had come to be a perfect obsession with him; and from a tolerably clear-headed person he had turned into a bundle of credulous superstition.'

Chris smiled. 'Yes, I do remember. They argued over Richard's beliefs, sometimes bitterly. Mary was so practical and down-to-earth. It's interesting how the fictional Mary differs from Ethel's mother, Mary Richardson. And of course having the same name's confusing.'

But Anthea had a different comparison in mind. 'Do you think Hardy might have been the same?' she asked.

'In what way?'

'His obsession. No one's described Hardy as having let himself go physically. But his obsession could have become overpowering. There's a bit further on where Mary describes Richard sitting for an hour with a pencil in his hand waiting for it to write by itself.'

Chris couldn't remember that passage, but others came vividly to mind – Richard swimming in the sea at Queenscliff, the Ballarat goldfields, women dying in childbirth. What an extraordinary novel it was! He should have got out his own copy and looked for references to spiritualist beliefs, should have thought of that himself. No matter though, since Anthea had done it.

'By overpowering, you mean his trip to the basement.'

'If he heard Ethel's voice telling him that she was waiting for him down there.'

Chris nodded, recalling his own thoughts about that. 'He may have seen death – his own death – as a way of getting close to her, meeting her at last. I have wondered about that. And I've read a bit about auto-asphyxiation. The inspector doesn't believe it, but it is just possible.'

'Doesn't believe because of the hands?'

'Yes. Though I've been thinking that could have been done afterwards.'

'As a prank, you mean?'

'A particularly nasty one.'

'Who by?'

'Charles Nevis. If they were, or had been lovers. If Hardy had ended it. If Hardy cared more about the spirits of the dead than living human beings - '

'You think Nevis killed him then?'

'Somehow I don't see Nevis as a killer. Of course I could be wrong. In that taped interview – the one where I was present – he acted like it was a game to him. A game the police couldn't possibly hope to understand.'

'It'd be worth listening to the interview again.'

Chris made a face. 'I doubt if Inspector Masterson – '

'Maybe wait until he's out. Ask Thomas.'

'It comes down to a failure to show proper leadership,' Chris said. 'If Masterson wasn't such a strutting peacock, if he didn't insult people, and wasn't bent on bullying Sarah into a confession – '

'I didn't realise you disliked him so much.'

Chris hadn't realised it either. He tested the feeling; yes, he actively disliked the man.

Anthea sighed and closed the novel. 'I've ordered all three volumes of Ethel's letters through inter-library loans. I wish I could go to the National Library and read the originals. There are scrap books of reviews as well.' She looked at

Chris and smiled. 'Did you know she kept getting called Mr Richardson? I wonder if that gave her a laugh.'

Chris remembered reading that the novelist had wanted reviewers to think she was a man. He wondered if the original owner of Hardy's signed copy had done so.

'A lot of the letters are at the historical museum,' he said, aware of sounding defensive, but unable to help himself. 'Photocopies of course.'

Anthea made a face, as if to say she couldn't be bothered going through folders of photocopies when there was a better alternative available.

Chris imagined Hardy discovering that a signed first edition of *Ultima Thule* was coming up for auction, bidding for it, treating it as the most important purchase and possession of his life. He thought with pleasure of the hours he'd spent at the historical museum. There was one volunteer who'd liked him, and whom he'd liked in return. He'd got to know her at a time when nursing his mother occupied almost all his out-of-work hours. While his mother slept, on Saturday and Sunday afternoons, when the winter sky was heavy and grey and the townsfolk were at the football, or watching it on television, Chris had taken himself down there for an hour or two. His mother had a buzzer she could press and it would ring his phone; but she knew his need to get away.

It was then, on those dark winter afternoons, that Chris had read Mary and Walter Richardson's letters to each other. He recalled his disappointment that, of their time in Queenscliff, only Walter's had survived. What had Walter done with Mary's? Had he lost, or burnt them? The loss had seemed almost criminal to Chris.

He'd never thought it was possible to understand the feelings of people who'd lived a hundred and fifty years ago. You could read their letters and attempt to understand them, but you couldn't avoid doing so in the light of what they simply couldn't know. He'd read enough history and biography to realise that modern day biographers and historians had ways of accommodating this.

Many of Walter Richardson's letters either expressed false optimism, or complained when his hopes and predictions turned out to be groundless. Chris had no time for this kind of person, but he'd gone on reading for hours in a state of suspended disbelief, looking for a glimmer of honest self-reflection, knowing the end of the story, knowing what the letter-writer could not possibly have known.

Mary's letters, by comparison, were straightforward and sensible. They made few demands on the recipient, certainly not for indulgence or forgiveness.

Chris wondered where the volunteer was and what she was doing now; she'd left a few months after his mother died.

They'd spoken of the Richardsons, while rain kept other visitors away, remarking – it had seemed strange to both of them – that though the family had lived in that house in Mercer Street for only a short time, a strong sense of their presence remained. You could feel it walking past. They'd laughed, agreeing on this, catching each other's eyes then looking away.

Walter had taken his keen interest in spiritualism back to England with him, and had sought out spiritualist circles wherever he happened to be. A sentence leapt up from Chris's memory. 'The light shineth into darkness whether the darkness comprehendeth it or not.' It was from an essay published in the first Australian spiritualist magazine, *The Harbinger of Light.*

Chris mentally reviewed the letters he had read. Most of Walter's were to Mary, but some were to his professional colleagues. He'd met a clairvoyant in Leicester – nothing remarkable about that – but this one was reputed to help the police in their investigations and to be a dab hand at finding lost objects.

Chris allowed himself a wry smile, thinking they could use her now. He wondered how she'd assisted the police. Had spirits spoken to her and told her where to look for clues? Had they told her who was guilty? How dangerous, Chris thought, dangerous and wicked. No better than denouncing witches. Anyone the medium disliked or had a grudge against could find him or herself in trouble.

To give Mrs Marr her due, she hadn't gone down that path, at least not yet. Mrs Marr was too clever to reveal her true intentions, and Chris felt suddenly sure that the inspector did not have what it took to persuade or trick her into doing so.

Anthea made a face, self-deprecatory and determined at the same time.

'I did a finding reading last night. More than one, in fact.'

Chris looked up at the sound of footsteps, but the back door remained shut. 'Show me,' he said.

Anthea found the photos on her phone. 'I did a hidden meaning one as well. I think I know where that book might be. Or I know where I want to look.'

Chris peered at images of cards and tried to look as though they meant something to him.

'Is the book in the hotel?' was my first question,' Anthea explained. 'Three nos in a row. I shuffled the cards and asked the same question again. Four nos. Can you see? I can zoom in a bit if you like.'

Chris looked up from the small screen to his assistant's face. 'But we know that already,' he said.

Anthea gave him a look that said, I'm getting there. Don't rush me.

'Is the book in Sarah's flat?' was my next question. Four nos again.'

'The Six of Cups – see the picture – children in an old garden – it's a card of memories and of the past, in particular past things that have vanished. The Ten of Pentacles reversed means fatality, loss, robbery. Three wands in a row, all pointing downwards, means the bottom of a building, in the *Royal's* case the basement. But it also means the cellar of a house. And what house do we know old enough to have a cellar, that Gerard Hardy would have loved to get inside?'

'Ethel Richardson's house. But why would anybody hide the book there? How would they get in for a start?'

'I don't know,' said Anthea. 'I don't believe in the spirits sending messages any more than you do. But I don't see that we've got anything to lose by trying to find out.'

From the sadness in Anthea's eyes, the way her face fell when she wasn't speaking, Chris guessed that Olly hadn't rung last night. His assistant was distracting herself with research into Henry Handel Richardson and tarot readings. He told himself he must be careful not to hurt her feelings.

SIXTEEN

The two constables walked quickly. If challenged, they would say that Sarah might have taken a detour round the harbour. If Masterson could believe she'd gone as far out of her way as Bridge Street, then it wasn't so far-fetched.

'We'll say we're using our initiative,' Chris said, and they laughed.

Anthea said, 'What I didn't understand before is the significance of the Swords taken as a group. Number four, the Knight, is obvious. Whoever arranged Hardy's hands wanted to draw our attention to that. But all of the Swords taken together tell another story, one you'd have to be familiar with the tarot to grasp.'

'As Mrs Marr is.'

Anthea nodded. 'Surely they would have discussed it on that Thursday afternoon.'

Instead of replying, Chris looked up the hill.

Anthea followed his line of sight. 'The owners haven't been questioned yet,' she said. 'I checked with DS Thomas. There was no one home on Friday, or yesterday when he went back.'

'That's an oversight.'

'It is.'

Anthea's tone of voice indicated that she was as aware as he was of the blinkered way the investigation was proceeding. 'One more thing - of the last five cards in Hardy's spread, number ten is the Hermit which, when it shows up in the context of a lost object, indicates that the querent should look in a dark place.'

Chris nodded. 'We can ask if they saw or heard a car, or saw someone walking past. That's what we're supposed to be doing, after all.'

'And if no one's home?'

'Then we'll come back later.'

The *Royal* was only a short walk away from the house where the two small Richardson girls had been trapped with their father, while their mother spent her days at the post office learning Morse code and bookkeeping so that she'd have the means to feed them after he was dead.

Walter Richardson had been laughed at in the street. He'd been incontinent, struggling to stand without support, or else had wandered off and lost himself. Medical knowledge had progressed amazingly, but people still went mad. He was said to have been suffering from tertiary syphilis – a disputed claim, but one Chris thought had a good deal of evidence to support it.

Chris had had to put up with raised eyebrows at the idea of a police constable taking an interest in their local author – if such a claim could be made for someone who'd spent her adult life in Europe. Yet Ethel's time in Queenscliff had been portentous, shaping the small girl into the woman she became: Chris had always believed the Mercer Street house to have been a heart of darkness.

The woman who opened the door to them was black-haired, wild-eyed, as though she'd ridden in from who knew what private nightmares.

Another one, Chris thought, careful not to catch Anthea's eye.

Her name was Delia Robbins. She held her hands behind her back, and Chris knew better than to offer his.

But Delia answered their questions politely enough. She'd been away for a few days. She was afraid she couldn't help them. She'd read about the murder, of course. A dreadful thing.

When Anthea asked where she'd been staying, Delia looked as though she was about to point out that this wasn't any of their business. Then she said, 'With my sister. She owns a property out past Inverleigh.'

Chris had already taken in the fact that the family was well-to-do. Delia's accent was private school; she was fashionably and expensively dressed. And the heritage-listed house would have cost a million and a half at least.

Delia said her children were due home from boarding school. She didn't sound as though the prospect pleased her. Chris noted that there was no mention, or evidence of, a husband.

When Anthea asked if the house had a cellar, Delia stared at her. Anticipating trouble, Anthea quickly asked if she'd mind them having a look round. It seemed that Delia was going to object, but once again she appeared to change her mind and led them through a hallway towards the back of the house.

When Anthea remarked that she was reading *The Fortunes of Richard Mahony* Delia looked bored, as though she was sick of people drawing attention to the fact that a celebrated novelist had once lived in her house. Now was the moment to mention the connection between Richardson and Gerard Hardy, but neither of them did.

The front rooms, which they looked into in passing, had been freshly painted and wall-papered, but the basic room design appeared to Chris much the same as it would originally have been.

The kitchen, by contrast, had been completely re-modelled, and not all that long ago.

Delia pointed to an area of wall beside the stove. 'That's where the entrance to the cellar was. The previous owners had it bricked up. Or maybe the ones before them. I don't know.'

Delia ran her hands through her hair. Her eyes were bloodshot and her skin, in the clear, bright light of the kitchen, had an unhealthy pallor.

Chris thanked her for showing them. To his question about whether the house's original plans had been passed down to successive owners, she shook her head impatiently.

'We'll just have a quick look round the back yard, if you don't mind.'

Delia waved a hand as though to say, make it quick.

Anthea walked ahead. She got down on her hands and knees and felt about in the long grass around a water tank, and between the tank and the back fence. She stretched her arm out underneath the tank, but it was built too close to the ground for her to be able to do more than that.

Chris watched his assistant, then turned at the sound of shouting from inside the house, a rising wail of anger and frustration.

It stopped as abruptly as it started and Delia was suddenly at the back door.

'What the *hell* are you looking for?'

Anthea stood up. Her hands were wet and grubby and she held them away from her uniform.

Delia marched forward, almost spitting the words out. 'You've no right to come nosing around without a search warrant. I want you to leave.'

'We're sorry to have disturbed you, Mrs Robbins,' Chris said mildly. 'I think we'll go out the back way.'

The gate was latched, but there was no padlock. Chris stood aside for Anthea to walk ahead of him, but instead of moving forward she turned to ask, 'Did Mr Hardy write to you, Mrs Robbins? Did he write and tell you he was coming down to Queenscliff? Did he tell you why?'

Delia's answer was to shake her head. 'Just go.'

It occurred to Chris that the house's present occupant was the kind of person who would always see herself as the injured party and who was more inclined to lie than tell the truth. Even if photographs could be produced showing her with Hardy, Delia would deny it, say that they were fakes.

He wondered if it was her scream he'd heard coming from the psychic's roof, then counselled himself against letting his imagination run away with him.

'Here,' Anthea was saying. 'There's a lane.'

They walked along it without speaking and turned left at the end.

The sun was unexpectedly warm and Chris felt the tension easing in his shoulder and back muscles.

Anthea said, 'What did you make of that?'

'Delia phoned someone and they told her to get rid of us.'

'Did you see her face when she came out and saw where I was?'

Chris nodded. 'Do you think the book's there, under the tank?'

'I don't know. I couldn't get my hand in far enough. If it was she'll move it.'

Chris wondered what to tell Masterson.

Anthea said, 'You know, I thought it was silly really. The cards. All those wands pointing downwards. I thought it was nice of you to humour me.'

'And now?'

'What do you think?'

'She's hiding something.'

'Yes.'

Chris glanced across at Anthea. Their strides were evenly matched. Delia Robbins would vent her anger and frustration on whoever came within reach. A woman like that would never make an exception for the police; indeed their uniforms were so many red rags to a bull.

They separated and continued with their door-knocking. But Chris's mind was only a quarter on the job. Three-quarters of it was back there, wondering what Delia was doing now. Was she burning Gerard Hardy's letter? Had she already done so? Or were they mistaken in thinking he had written to her?

Chris called in at the historical museum, where a volunteer he'd never met before helped him find photographs of the Mercer Street house taken in the 1870s and 80s. None showed plans of the house's construction. Perhaps, somewhere in the volumes of Richardson letters, were references to a basement or a cellar; but Chris did not remember, nor did he have the hours it would take to check.

There was a copy of *The Fortunes of Richard Mahony* at the museum, not a valuable first edition, but the trilogy published as a single volume.

Chris half recalled a reference, very near the end, to Cuffy's secret hiding place, where no one, not even his sister followed him, at the bottom of the yard, between the tank and the WC. That was at Koroit, where Mary had taken up her first position as postmistress and Richard had come home to die.

It was typical that Ethel's counterpart in the novel was a boy, not a girl. Was it wrong to think of Cuffy as a 'counterpart'? Chris knew that literary scholars argued over it. Cuffy had twin sisters, one of whom died. Richard believed her spirit had come back, or perhaps never left. The surviving twin, after her father had been committed to an insane asylum, became terrified that she'd lose her one remaining parent.

Ethel's sister Lil, in real life, had been frightened of that. It was a muddle, history and literary creation, but thankfully not one he needed to untangle.

When it came to Delia Robbins lying – yes, he wanted to discover the truth behind that.

Ethel Richardson had loved swimming. Should he call her Ettie, Chris wondered, when thinking of her as a child? The girl he imagined was a kind of working backwards from the woman, yet with no way of foretelling the future, no knowledge of the adult life that was going to be hers. Chris thought of her as a child more or less like other children, until traumatised by her father's illness. He pictured her backwards from the woman, almost as though it was the woman who'd come first, the childless woman who'd given birth to herself as a child. This was fanciful, yet not completely so. It was what novelists and other kinds of artists did; they re-created themselves as children from their knowing adult selves, and, if they were clever enough, if they became famous enough, they took their readers with them.

Suddenly, without warning, Chris saw Minnie's bright head bent over a pack of tarot cards, Minnie listening to a reading with her head on one side. Minnie was nobody's fool, but faced with this novel form of prophecy and divination – he was sure Minnie had had nothing to do with the tarot up till now – she would be open-minded, possibly amused, keeping a distance between herself and any new experience till she found out its shape and substance. This distance was not compounded of anxiety and prejudice, such as Chris was aware of in himself, but a sweetness like the air over grasslands a long way from the sea.

SEVENTEEN

Instead of returning directly to the station, Chris decided on another detour past the black lighthouse and the fort.

Normally it was a walk he avoided – you could hardly take it without looking out across the bay. He ambled along what he thought of as the top way, though the rise was minimal. When he was a boy, he'd believed the crumbling cliffs enormous, full of caves and hidden places. For years after his father drowned he'd hated and avoided them.

He skirted the fort, which had been built in case the Russians decided to invade overland, thinking of how the post office had once been housed inside the enclave – right in the castle keep, for safety – the post and telegraph office had to be kept safe from the Russians. Chris smiled at the idea. He pictured Mary Richardson learning Morse; according to the accounts he'd read she'd found it very difficult, though arithmetic and bookkeeping had come more easily to her.

You could get your head around the history of Queenscliff – the European history – the town was small enough for that. Chris wished he wasn't so ignorant of pre-European history; he'd tried, from time to time, to make dents in his ignorance, without much success. But since the arrival of Europeans – he could make pictures of that in his mind.

Until recently, he'd felt that his relationship with the departed townspeople was a manageable one. Even Walter, raving and wandering and getting himself lost, having to be searched for and brought home by his small daughter – Walter Richardson incontinent and mad – had not alarmed him.

And there, almost as though he had conjured her in response to his musings, was Sarah Kent.

She was sitting with her back against the red bricks of

the fort's outer wall, eyes half closed against the sun.

Chris stopped while he was still some half dozen steps away.

Sarah opened her eyes and looked straight at him. She did not seem surprised. She lifted her right hand slowly to make a cushion for her cheek.

Chris, standing with the sun behind him, wondered if Sarah saw him as a solid shape with a strong outline, his uniform a kind of armour. Could she read his expression, and what did she make of it, if so?

He walked forward, then sat down next to her.

'When I was a boy, I used to think those stories about the Russians invading might actually come true.'

Sarah was silent for a moment before asking, 'What stories?'

While Chris recounted one she smiled, at first a tiny smile and then a real one.

'I like it here, with my back against the wall.'

The sadness in her voice was for having begun to make a new life, as a thirsty person, deprived of water, might begin to drink.

'Do you ever get the feeling that the ground might be water, might turn into water?'

'No.' Chris shook his head.

'I often feel that I could fall through it, the ground I mean. But not right now.' Sarah smiled again. She shook her hair away from her face and twined her arms around her knees. 'They picked a good place to build their fort.'

Chris thought that he should walk away and leave the girl to her few minutes' peace, but instead he said, 'Tell me exactly what happened the morning you found Gerard Hardy. No – start with the day before and don't leave out a thing.'

Sarah sighed as if to say that she'd already told the story, oh so many times. What good could come from telling it again?

But then she rallied, responding to what was, perhaps, a natural wish to please. She said that she'd driven home to their flat on Thursday night, arriving shortly after ten. She and Matthew had both been tired and they'd gone to bed pretty much straight away. She'd had a better night's sleep than she'd had for some time and had woken feeling refreshed.

She'd had a shower and a bowl of cereal and set off for the *Royal*, leaving Matthew 'to have a bit of a lie-in.'

'Wasn't Matthew feeling well?'

'Just tired,' Sarah said. 'He's been working long hours for weeks. And he was worried about the renovations. Sometimes the owner – Mr Ling – well, he's not all that easy to communicate with.'

'In what way?'

'Just long distance I guess. The time difference and – cultural differences as well.'

'Mr Ling's Chinese?'

'Yes. He lives in Hong Kong.'

'Is he going to put the *Royal* on the market?'

'He hasn't told us yet.'

By the time Sarah got to the hotel, Manoli had brought in the bread and made coffee on the new machine.

'What were you thinking when you went down to the basement?'

'I was thinking about Manoli and the coffee. I hope - ' Sarah's voice became a whisper – 'they'll brick it up. I hope no one will ever have to go down there again.'

'Why did you go down there on Friday morning?'

'It was – I was – facing my fear.'

'Of what?'

'Of the spirits.'

'How long have you been frightened of them?'

Sarah's blonde hair shone in the sunlight, and the sun made golden highlights on her cheekbones. But she'd lost weight and, close up, her eyes looked bruised and deeply troubled.

She leant forward, tightening her grip on her knees. 'Sometimes they speak, but more often they're silent. It began when I was a child. Other kids laughed at me and I learnt to keep it to myself.'

Chris settled himself into a more comfortable position. He forgot about leaving Sarah on her own.

'What about Gerard Hardy? Have you see his ghost?'

'It's not that personal, if you know what I mean. It's hard to explain. It's just that, beyond the material world, I see shapes, figures, lights and images. Sometimes I hear voices.'

'More so since finding Hardy's body?'

'What I'm really frightened of is that I'll be locked up as a murderess. That will be the end of me.'

There was nothing Chris could say to this. He had no way of reassuring her. A suspicion came into his mind that Sarah had been waiting for him; but how could she have known he'd come this way?

'What does Matthew think?'

'Matt's wonderful. He was – he's a saint.'

When Chris asked about medication, Sarah said, 'I've tried all kinds. I've been diagnosed as schizophrenic and bipolar. Not shock treatment though. I never had that, though it was recommended to my mother. That I should, I mean.'

'Where's your mother now?'

'She's dead. She died of breast cancer. I can see what you're thinking.'

'I doubt that,' Chris replied. 'Did Mrs Marr help?'

Sarah stared at her knees, then asked in a small voice, 'How did you know I went to her?'

Chris said he hadn't; she'd confirmed his guess.

'Matthew disapproves, doesn't he?'

'You're right. He didn't like me going. He was cross, so I

told him I'd stopped.'

'And you persuaded Matthew to say nothing to Inspector Masterson.'

'I didn't have to. He knew it would make me look bad, I mean worse. And Matt hates the inspector. He says he's cruel and unjust.'

'You told him you'd stopped, but you hadn't. How do you pay Mrs Marr without Matthew finding out?'

'I – I found a way.'

Chris waited, but Sarah said nothing more about payment. He thought he knew the answer.

The road was free of traffic. There was only the sound of the wind in the casuarinas, and behind them the waves that, as usual, Chris tried not to hear. It seemed to him that Sarah was staring at shadows at the edges of her vision, something only she could see.

'Mrs Marr was trying to help me understand. She said the trouble with doctors and medical treatment were that they assumed my visions were abnormal. They all tried to cure me. But she said plenty of people had visions - intelligent, sane people. They were nothing to be ashamed of. She said she could help me understand myself better, help me to accept. I didn't need to go through life believing that I was a freak.'

Chris nodded. Sarah made it all sound reasonable. He asked, 'What did you and Gerard Hardy talk about on that Thursday afternoon?'

'He told me he had an appointment with her, with Mrs Marr.'

'Did he tell you what he hoped to do?'

'He showed me his book.'

'And asked about the basement key.'

Sarah looked at Chris from under lowered eyelids. There was something calculating in her expression. 'I've got into so much trouble over that.'

'When you met at the basement entrance on Thursday evening, whose idea was that?'

'It was his. Gerard Hardy's.'

'Did he want you to take him down there?'

'No, oh no.' Sarah was suddenly emphatic. 'He – I got the idea he was toying with something, exploring a plan in his mind. But the plan didn't involve me directly. I was useful because I could show him where things were.'

'Is that what you told Inspector Masterson?'

'I tried to.'

'Did you get the feeling Hardy was planning to go down there alone?'

'I don't know. The inspector asked me that as well. Mr Hardy talked about the tarot reading, how Henry Handel Richardson was going to contact him. It's such a mouthful of a name.' Sarah raised her chin, then lowered it again onto her knees.

'Ethel,' Chris said. 'Or Ettie. Have you ever seen her?'

'No. I – I don't think so.'

'Where had Mr Hardy been?'

Sarah looked confused.

'Hardy and Nevis had dinner together, then walked back to the *Royal*. Nevis decided to have a drink at the bar. He says Hardy went up to his room. Then, as I understand it, you were getting ready to lock up when Hardy approached you and asked you to show him the basement door. Did he say where he'd been before that?'

'In his room, I guess.'

'Did he look as though he'd been out again?'

'It's dark there in the corridor. I didn't – I'm not sure.'

'What was he wearing?'

'It wasn't the same clothes he had on in the afternoon. He was dressed quite formally. In slacks. A shirt and tie.'

'Tie?'

'Yes. A blue and white one.'

The question of Hardy's clothes, apart from the dressing-gown, hadn't come up in any of the briefings. Chris assumed the forensic team had packed them up and sent them to the lab.

'What did you and Mr Hardy talk about?' he asked.

'The tarot. The reading he'd had done – well, naturally – it was fresh in his mind. We talked about the reverse meanings of the cards. Three cards of the spread Mrs Marr did for Mr Hardy, with a possible two more, point to a basement or a cellar.'

'Did he talk to you about the Swords?'

Sarah frowned. Her eyes held a hint of derision or contempt. 'Specifically? No.'

Chris waited for a flicker of movement, a slight change in her expression that meant the Four of Swords meant something special to her.

'Did Mr Hardy say anything more about the basement key?'

'He knew where it was. I'd already told him, in the afternoon.'

'When you went down there on Friday morning, how did you know he was dead?'

'I saw the marks around his neck. I – I touched him. It was so frightening, so horrible!'

Chris back-tracked to Thursday afternoon.

Matthew had signed Hardy and Nevis in and given them their room keys. Neither had spoken to him about the reason for their visit; Hardy had told Sarah later, when he'd come downstairs on his own. They'd both left their room keys at reception when they'd gone out.

'Did you go into Mr Hardy's room?'

'No.'

'Did Matthew?'

'Why would he?'

I don't know, Chris felt like saying. You tell me.

Surely Matthew would know if Sarah had left their flat in the middle of the night. Matthew might be lying, but Chris didn't think he had the kind of personality to sustain a lie in the face of persistent, hostile questioning. He hadn't hired a lawyer for himself, only for Sarah.

'When you were leaving the hotel on Thursday night, after you'd locked up, did you see anybody in the street, or a car driving by?'

'I don't want to get an innocent person into trouble.'

'So you did see someone.'

'I thought I saw Bridget's car.'

'Parked or stationery?'

'Going up the hill.'

'Away from the *Royal*?'

'Yes.'

Chris went on probing, but all Sarah could, or was willing to say, was that she thought she'd seen Bridget's car.

He said goodbye and began to walk away, then stopped and looked back over his shoulder. Sarah was hunched into herself, crouched against the wall. Perhaps that place where the stones of the fort met the ground was reminding her that she still had a back that could be scraped, muscles that could stop her from sinking through the earth.

Chris drove on automatic from Queenscliff to St Leonards, not so much thinking as replaying images of Sarah at the fort – the sun on her fair hair, the way her hand cradled her cheek, her backbone pressed into the wall.

Bridget McGuire reacted with anger to his request for a few minutes of her time.

'I'm washing my mother's hair.'

Never, to Chris's ears, had a mildly useful activity sounded so much like an accusation.

For some reason, he expected Bridget's mother to be sitting in full view, towel around her shoulders, hair full of shampoo, closed eyes echoing her daughter's impatience. Following her to the back of the house, he noticed that Bridget had a stumpy walk, perhaps developed for heaving cleaning equipment up and down old-fashioned stairs.

She was stout, plump-cheeked, with the expression of a disgruntled marsupial. Chris reminded himself how easily appearances could deceive.

At the very least, he expected Bridget's mother to call out, for a querulous voice to echo along the corridor. But no one called out. The house seemed preternaturally quiet, and the room where Bridget took him almost bare of furniture.

She sat down and motioned Chris to take a seat opposite her.

'What were you doing outside the *Royal* last Thursday night?'

'I wasn't – ' Bridget began aggressively, then her shoulders slumped and her head bent as though her neck could no longer hold it up.

'Did Manoli tell you?'

'No,' Chris said. 'You drove up Mercer Street. What did you do then?'

'I waited.'

'For Manoli?'

'We needed to talk.'

'Why that night?'

'I had to get Mum to bed, didn't I? And it had been my day off. I'd been with her all day. I try, you see, and get no bloody thanks for it. Oh, what's the use!'

'Where did you go?' Chris asked.

'We drove to the pier and walked. I told him he needed to make up his mind. He promised me, you see. He promised he'd get a divorce. He and his wife have been separated for two years. He should never have said it if he didn't mean it.'

'When you parked in Mercer Street, did you get out of your car?'

'As a matter of fact I did. Manoli was late. I couldn't bear just sitting there. I got out and started walking.'

'Did you see anybody in the street?'

Bridget looked as though she wasn't going to answer, then she said, 'I heard running footsteps. Two people, I think. Someone called out, Don't be a fool!'

The voice had been a woman's, but not one she recognised.

'Why didn't you say anything earlier? You must have known it was important.'

'I'd have to admit to being there then, wouldn't I? Are you sure Manoli didn't tell you?'

'Yes. Does Manoli always use the hotel's back entrance?'

Bridget hesitated before nodding her head.

'What did you do then?'

'I went back to the car. I texted Manoli and he texted back to say he was sorry he was a bit behind and he'd be finished in ten minutes.'

'Did you see or hear the people in the street again?'

'No.'

'And your talk, your conversation?'

'What do you think? It was a disaster. His wife won't give him a divorce and he won't pressure her into it.'

'Does marriage matter all that much to you?' Chris asked gently.

'He *promised* me. I've got to go and finish washing Mum's hair.'

For an odd moment, Chris wondered if Bridget's mother existed. Instead, he allowed Bridget to show him to the door.

There was something dogged about her, he thought, dogged and determined. Chris put it down partly to her size. He'd be flattering himself to say their eyes were on a level. Bridget had lowered her chin, not raised it, in order to look him in the eye.

Big-boned and muscular, she'd have had no trouble strangling Gerard Hardy.

'I've just made some cinnamon buns,' Manoli told Chris. 'Would you like one?'

Chris sat down and thanked the cook, who looked nervous and did not meet his eyes. He indicated that Manoli should take a seat at the table opposite him and decided not to beat around the bush.

'Why didn't you tell Inspector Masterson about meeting Bridget after you finished work on Thursday night?'

Manoli's nervousness increased. 'We didn't do anything wrong. She – we had to talk, that's all.'

'Which way did you leave the hotel?'

'By the back gate.'

'Did you see or hear anybody in the street?'

'No.'

'Think carefully. Are you sure?'

'I'm sure.'

If the running figures had reached the front of the hotel before Manoli left, it was possible he hadn't noticed them. He claimed that Bridget had said nothing about them and that, too, was understandable.

Manoli might have walked back to the *Royal* after Bridget had dropped him at his flat, and Bridget, for her part, might not have returned to St Leonards as she claimed. The question was why would either of them want to kill Gerard Hardy?

'Did Sarah say anything to you about the Four of Swords?'

Manoli seemed surprised by the change of subject, but he answered readily enough. 'I don't go in for fortune-telling. Have another bun. I'll make more coffee.'

'Thank you. In a minute.'

They were at a small round table in a corner of the

kitchen. Chris guessed that this was where Manoli liked to sit; perhaps, on fine days, out in the courtyard too: but the courtyard would have to be empty of guests and other staff; he would have to have it to himself.

Chris understood the need for solitude in a building where there were always others with some claim on you. The cook wanted to feed him, and he knew that the way to help Manoli relax was to eat the food he served. But did he want Manoli to relax?

Finally the silence paid off. Manoli cleared his throat and said, 'Sarah told me about the hands. Friday morning before you got here – how he was laid out like a – like he was praying.'

'Did you go down and see for yourself?'

'No! Sarah said the pour souls down there, who'd been held in confinement in the morgue, and later on, the living ones who'd been labelled mad – she said they call to her.'

'What do they say?'

Manoli was about to answer when his phone rang. He walked to the door to answer it.

'Yes,' he said, and then, 'Five minutes.'

'There's a delivery coming,' he told Chris, making it sound like an important event.

Chris got up to go, then said, as though it had only just occurred to him, 'Eight bottles of expensive wine are missing from the basement. Did you know they were missing and do you know who took them?'

'What?'

Chris repeated his questions. Manoli clutched the door handle. The skin over his knuckles was so taut it seemed to Chris that it must break.

'When was the last time you counted the bottles?'

'I didn't' – Manoli gained control over his voice with visible effort – 'I didn't count them. Matthew supervised the delivery. The delivery men stacked them down there and

Matthew was there to supervise.'

'Who do you think took them?'

'It could have been the carpenters or plasterers.'

'How would they get into the basement, and how would they know the wine was there to steal?'

'I don't know.'

'You had access to the basement. You, Sarah, Bridget and Matthew himself. Can you think of anybody else?'

Manoli cried out, 'Why would I steal wine? I'd be the first to be suspected! Why would I do that?'

Chris was silent, waiting for Manoli to answer his own question. When he didn't, Chris asked, 'Do you know if the owner plans to keep the hotel now?'

'No. I mean I don't know.'

'Does Matthew?'

'If he does, he hasn't told us.'

'Us?'

'Me and Bridget. Why would I steal wine?' Manoli repeated in a desperate voice.

Chris went to find Matthew.

'Why didn't you report the missing wine?'

'What?'

'You heard me,' Chris said patiently. 'Between the delivery on February 20th and when I checked your inventory against what's in the basement, eight bottles have gone missing. Why didn't you tell Inspector Masterson?'

Matthew shook his head, then leant his elbows on the reception counter. 'I locked the basement,' he said through gritted teeth.

'But that didn't stop the thief.'

When Matthew didn't reply, Chris said, 'Come down and count them for yourself.'

EIGHTEEN

Inspector Masterson was furious. 'It's fundamental to policing Blackie, not to involve yourself with suspects, surely you're aware of that!'

Chris had given a lot of thought to his report. Until he sat down to write it, it hadn't occurred to him that he should have gone straight from Sarah to the inspector. He was paying for that now.

'Why did you stay there talking to the girl? Why didn't you fetch me or Sergeant Thomas?'

Chris didn't say, because Sarah's frightened of you. She would never have spoken to you the way she did to me.

'You took it upon yourself to interview suspects with no other officer present. What if the Kent girl claimed that you'd assaulted her, what then? She's deranged. She could have said anything.'

'Sir, I – '

'Your problem, Constable, is that you've been a big fish in a puddle for far too long. Well, that's about to change. This cosy little station where you and your girl have done so well for yourself won't be here this time next year.'

Calling Anthea 'his girl' stuck in Chris's throat like a prickly sea urchin.

'A separate station for a tiny borough like this? A waste of resources when the whole area could be much better managed from Ocean Grove. Stay away from Kent! Stay away from all the suspects unless I instruct you to take statements from them. Do what you're told and I might find one positive comment to make in my report to Superintendent Ashworth.'

'Constable Merritt knows nothing about this. She's obeyed instructions.'

Masterson looked unconvinced. 'You've jeopardised

the investigation, Blackie. You deserve the sack.'

Chris tried to console himself with the thought that he'd kept his temper. But what kind of victory was that? He needed to be alone to think. He didn't even want to talk to Anthea.

It was ironic that he'd referred half-jokingly for years to being made redundant. Would closing the station make Anthea's decision easier?

Closure would strengthen Olly's argument that she should resign from police work rather than apply for maternity leave. She could be re-assigned to another station, but would either of them want this? They were settled in Queenscliff with a baby on the way. Having to persuade Olly to move as well as accept her continuing to work would be too much for Anthea. And who was he to judge what was best for his assistant in the end? She might be happy staying at home, then finding some undemanding part-time work further down the track.

An image came to him of Anthea alert and excited, all her senses alive. Could the Anthea he knew really want to give that up?

Neither of them had gone looking to become detectives. They'd fallen into it when a camel had disappeared from a farmer's paddock and a black coat belonging to a missing woman had turned up in the nearby sandhills. They'd persisted because no one else was there, in Queenscliff, asking the right questions, or indeed any questions at all.

Chris had believed his life would settle down to its old routine after the woman's killer had been charged; but then ten-year-old Bobby McGilvrey had been found strangled in the railway yard. Bobby's death had changed him in ways he was still trying to figure out. Though they hadn't spoken about the boy for some time, Chris knew that Anthea had been as deeply affected as he had.

Masterson was a piece of work, but the insult hit home.

He'd concentrated on his own small patch, been blinkered to what was going on within the force in Geelong and Ocean Grove. He had no friends or even acquaintances to whom he could go now for advice. He had no idea how Masterson was thought of, how much weight his word carried. He'd known the future of his station was uncertain; he'd known that much for years. There was that word 'his'. He did think of the station as his; there was no getting round the fact. But there was a world of difference between uncertainty in general, and the letter or phone call which would mean the end of his job.

'Hardy and Nevis had dinner at *The Chandler*,' Chris reminded Anthea when she arrived back at the station, pink-cheeked with the cold. His voice sounded detached, disembodied, even to his own ears.

'Is something wrong? What's happened?'

'I'll tell you on the way.'

They walked to the restaurant briskly, as though they could outwalk the plunging temperature. Chris told Anthea what Masterson had said.

'Promise me you'll say questioning those three was my idea. Nothing to do with you.'

'But – '

'Promise me.'

'You're a stubborn old codger. If it makes you feel better, then okay.'

'I thought – maybe Sarah knew I was coming and was waiting for me. But how could she have known I'd come that way?'

'Listen,' said Anthea, reaching across and taking Chris's hand. 'Sarah's not clairvoyant, and neither's Mrs Marr, in spite of what she'd like us to believe.'

'Do you really think I'm stubborn?'

'Of course. Stubborn and stuck in your ways. That's a compliment. I like you the way you are.'

Chris went red and looked down at his hands. 'Now we've got that out of the way, what two women could have been running down Mercer Street last Thursday night?'

Chris replayed the scene as Bridget had described it. Bridget had been confident she'd heard a woman's voice and Chris felt sure, without knowing why, that both figures had been female.

Delia Robbins lived in Mercer Street. She claimed not to have had any contact with Hardy. But what if she had? What if, on that Thursday night, she'd just found out that he was in Queenscliff?

It was warm inside *The Chandler*. Chris took his jacket off and hung it on the back of his chair, nodding hello to an acquaintance. He seldom took his evening meal at a restaurant. Mostly, he cooked for himself or ate with Minnie, sometimes with Anthea and Olly at the weekend. On summer nights, when tourists overdid their drinking and he was too busy breaking up fights to stop for dinner, he grabbed a salad or a toasted sandwich.

In one small way at least, luck was on their side. One of the waitresses on duty, Danielle, had been working last Thursday. Chris had taken the trouble to check who'd been rostered on, and now was glad he'd done so.

Danielle walked across to them, smiling and saying, 'Evening Mr Blackie. Ms Merritt.'

They spoke about the football. Danielle was one of the few locals who did not support Geelong.

After taking their order, she walked away with a swift, light step, letting the swing doors to the kitchen flap behind her.

Danielle reminded Chris of Minnie in some ways – Minnie as she'd been twenty years ago – light of step and quick to laugh, enjoying taking the mickey out of customers behind their backs.

Chris described Manoli's and Matthew's reactions to

the missing wine.

When Anthea asked, 'Why hasn't Matthew done anything?' Chris said, 'Because he knows who took it.' He told Anthea what he suspected.

Anthea looked thoughtful. 'It would account for Sarah's trip to the basement on Friday morning.'

Chris nodded. 'If Sarah paid Mrs Marr with expensive wine, then what's she done with it?'

They were silent for a moment, imagining the psychic leaning back comfortably on her cushions, calling up the spirits in a mellow frame of mind.

They glanced at one another and smiled.

'Fancy storing Grange Hermitage down there,' Anthea said. 'For that matter, fancy spending umpteen thousand dollars doing up the *Royal*.'

'Mr Ling owns racehorses. Maybe he had a big win. Manoli's frightened,' Chris added.

'It doesn't have to be because of the wine.'

'No. But I think it is.'

Danielle brought bowls of rich vegetable soup and crusty bread.

Anthea filled Chris in on her research while they ate.

'Have you read *Myself When Young*?' she asked.

Chris had found Ethel Richardson's autobiography disappointing, but he waited to hear Anthea's opinion.

'This is great soup, isn't it? Ethel didn't write much about her childhood directly. She wrote about it in her fiction, dramatised and to an extent disguised. But in her autobiography she leaves out what's painful. And a lot of her correspondence, journals possibly as well – a lot of that was burnt.'

'Hardy might have believed that he could persuade her to talk about it.'

'That's pretty arrogant, don't you think?'

'I think Hardy was arrogant. I think he used people.'

'Charles Nevis?'

'If they were, or had been lovers, yes.'

'I wish we could find his laptop.'

'I can't see Hardy taking it to the basement, so whoever stole it has to have gone into his room.'

'Who had the best opportunity? Charles Nevis. Did Sarah even know he'd brought a laptop with him?'

'And to dispose of it, Nevis has to have left the hotel.'

'He wouldn't have gone far, surely. He would've known how important it was to get back to his room.'

'What about his car? When was his car searched?'

'I don't know.'

'The honeymooners didn't hear a thing, not Hardy's door or Nevis's, no footsteps in the corridor or voices.'

When Danielle came to ask if they wanted dessert, Chris invited her to take a seat.

'Those other policemen,' she said, 'I think they're detective constables? They interviewed the boss and our cook.'

Danielle frowned and seemed about to add something. Chris waited to give her time, then decided on a simple question. He asked what Hardy and Nevis had ordered for their meal.

'The one who got himself murdered had chicken parmi. The other one had steak. It wasn't good enough for him. He complained.' Danielle shot Chris a wary glance. 'Do you think they're gay?'

'Possibly,' Chris said.

'I think they are. My first boyfriend turned out to be gay and I learnt to pick 'em.'

'Did either Mr Hardy or Mr Nevis talk to you about what they were doing here?' asked Anthea.

'You mean here?' Danielle's quick glance took in the restaurant.

'In Queenscliff.'

'No.'

'Were they arguing with one another?'

'Not that I saw.'

'Did you get the impression that they had been arguing?'

'I didn't eavesdrop on their conversation, if that's what you're asking me.'

Anthea said she was sorry if she'd given that impression.

'The other one, the dark one – he waved his arms about.'

Danielle lifted both hands high, palms downwards, in an odd gesture that reminded Chris of a heavy bird trying to take flight. Then she flicked her hands over so that her palms faced upwards, and waggled them a few times.

'And then the first guy reached round and took something out of this little backpack and waved it at the dark guy, as if to say, I'll show you.'

'What was it?'

'A book. After he'd waved it in the dark guy's face, he wiped it with a serviette and put it back in his bag.'

When Chris asked if she'd seen what the book was called, Danielle shook her head.

'What did the dark-haired man do then?'

'He laughed.'

'Was there anything about the book that caught your eye?'

'It had a red cover. I don't mean like bright red. Kind of an old red, and the book looked old as well.'

'Do you know where the two men had been before coming here?'

'The detectives asked me that. How could I?'

'Do you know Mrs Marr, the psychic who gives tarot readings?'

Danielle frowned and seemed uncertain whether to say yes or no.

Anthea leant forward. 'Did Mrs Marr do a reading for you?'

'No. I asked her, but it cost too much.'

Danielle went red. Chris thought it strange that the admission made her uncomfortable, while she appeared to be taking murder in her stride. But perhaps she was hiding what she felt about the murder.

'Is there anything more you can tell us, anything that perhaps you didn't think of telling the DCs?'

Danielle shook her head.

Chris thanked her for her time and gave her a tip that made her smile again.

NINETEEN

When they left *The Chandler*, it was windy, cold, the moonlight over the town sullen and metallic.

Walking towards the station, Chris thought of other questions they could have asked Danielle, such as whether she'd made Sarah Kent's acquaintance. Danielle was a friendly girl, even if the impression Chris had formed about Sarah and Matthew keeping to themselves was right. They could have asked if she'd seen Charles Nevis again, and where. Chris didn't imagine Nevis would have chosen to return to the restaurant, but Queenscliff was still a small town.

Then it occurred to him, and the thought made him feel sick, that they might get into trouble for questioning Danielle. Anthea had been with him so he couldn't pretend she hadn't been involved. He'd been told to stay away from suspects. Was Danielle a suspect? Surely not. Even so, he wondered if he should go back and warn the waitress not to say they'd talked to her about Hardy and Nevis.

It didn't seem as though the difficulty had crossed Anthea's mind. She looked thoughtful and pre-occupied. He guessed that these were the worst hours for her, between dinner and bed-time.

'Do you want to come back to my place for a while?'

'What? Oh, no. Thank you but no.'

They continued in silence for a short while, then Anthea said, 'Revenge would be my bet.'

'A revenge killing?'

Anthea hunched her shoulders into her jacket. Her nod was almost imperceptible.

Chris thought again of Nevis. If they had been lovers and Hardy had ended the relationship, then why take revenge in such a bizarre fashion? Why choose the basement of the *Royal*?

'What about vengeance from the spirit world?' Chris asked, feeling embarrassed by the question, which had just popped out. He was glad it was dark and Anthea couldn't see his face.

'You mean Ethel didn't want him asking awkward questions so she had him killed?

'Mrs Marr would consider that a serious proposition.'

'But no one else, surely.'

Except Hardy himself, Chris thought.

'Sarah reminds me of that woman in *A Streetcar Named Desire*,' Anthea said. She stopped walking, and Chris stopped as well. 'Blanche, who said she'd always relied on the kindness of strange men. I don't recall what she says exactly, that's not a perfect quote, but you know what I mean.'

Chris recalled that Blanche Dubois had been labelled mad and sent to an asylum. 'What strange men?' he asked.

'I think we're all strange to her.'

'Are you sure you won't come back? I can make hot chocolate.'

'I'm only pregnant. I'm not about to throw myself off a cliff.'

'I only – '

'I know you mean well,' Anthea said. 'I'll curl up with Ethel Richardson. I'll be alright.'

They said goodnight on the footpath outside the station.

Chris kept on walking once he'd watched Anthea get into her car. He felt furious with Olly and had half a mind to phone him. But Olly would be angry with him for interfering, and so would Anthea when she got to hear of it.

Later, he was to recognise the moment as stepping over a line, but at the time it just felt like putting one foot in front of the other.

Though Masterson had accused him of disobeying

instructions, he had not done so deliberately. Sarah had been sitting by the fort; it had seemed natural to go up to her, just as it had seemed sensible and natural to drive to St Leonards after she'd told him about Bridget's car.

It was too early for sleep; if he went home, he'd just worry about Anthea.

It was pitch dark between the street lights, the moon hidden behind clouds. What's the bet Nevis is having a drink in front of the hotel's open fire? Chris said to himself. And if he is, I might as well be killed for a sheep as a lamb.

Chris ordered a Jack Daniels and Bridget brought his drink over to the fireside, flashing him an anxious look. Chris smiled to reassure her that he hadn't come to talk to her again, but she did not look reassured.

He wondered where Sarah and Matthew were. It appeared that Bridget had been left in charge.

Before climbing the front steps, he'd checked for lights. The kitchen was in darkness, as were all the upstairs windows.

The *Royal's* one remaining guest smiled a greeting. 'Evening, Constable. Off-duty, I see.'

At a noise behind the bar, Nevis turned his head to look at Bridget. His expression went suddenly and completely blank.

When Chris asked him what he thought had happened to Hardy's book, Nevis took his eyes away from Bridget with what seemed like an unusual effort.

'I expect the murderer took it,' he said quietly. Chris noticed, in the firelight, lines around the younger man's eyes and mouth that he hadn't seen before.

Nevis was drinking red wine. He sipped appreciatively, then looked straight at Chris. Would I be so rash and stupid as to kill my companion in such a melodramatic way? his expression seemed to ask. If I wanted to do away with Gerry, I'd choose another time and place. I'd pay someone to do it for me. Which you might have done, Chris said to himself.

'Why?' he asked.

'Are you asking me to speculate about the mind of a psychopathic killer? I've already told those chaps in suits everything I know.'

If this was a dig at Chris's uniform, he felt like telling Nevis not to bother. 'You don't seem worried,' he said.

'Oh, I really don't think whoever it was is after me, do you?'

Chris did not attempt an answer. He wondered if it was his imagination, or if Bridget's anxiety had increased. He could feel it like a solid weight at his back.

'Do you prefer Australian wines?' he asked with a nod at Nevis's glass.

'Australian and New Zealand. They've actually a good selection here.'

'That surprises you?'

'All things considered, yes.'

'I hear the new owner's something of a connoisseur.'

Nevis stared at the fire. If he knows about the stolen wine, he's not going to admit it, Chris said to himself. It occurred to him that Nevis might be waiting for a signal from someone. That's why he was sitting in the bar.

'Who knew Hardy had a first edition of *Ultima Thule* with him?'

'Apart from me? That psychic lady, obviously. Sarah Kent. Gerry told her. He was proud of it, you see.'

Chris said, 'Mr Hardy might have told the other hotel staff as well.'

'I don't know. I only know about the Kent girl because Gerry told me he'd spoken to her. She'd read Henry Handel Richardson. He was surprised by that. Why not? Hotel staff can be educated.'

Nevis smiled. He knows I'm fishing out of bounds, Chris thought, and so long as it amuses him, he doesn't mind.

'When you saw Sarah and Hardy talking by the basement door, are you sure you didn't hear anything they said?'

'I'm sure. I just paused for a moment on my way upstairs.'

No you didn't, Chris said to himself. You were jealous of Sarah spending time with Hardy when you'd hoped to be spending time with him yourself.

'What was Hardy wearing?'

Nevis gave Chris a sharp look. 'Your inspector asked if he was in his dressing-gown.'

'Was he?'

'No.'

'You didn't go straight to sleep,' Chris said. 'You lay awake listening for Hardy to come up to his room.'

'For a while I did, but then I – I gave up.'

'Did you hear voices outside the hotel?'

'I fell asleep.'

'Before that.'

'My deceased friend heard voices, or he wanted to.'

'I'm not asking about spirits,' Chris said patiently. 'I'm asking about human voices, in Mercer Street, under your window.'

'No.'

'Why did Mr Hardy shake his book at you?'

Nevis's eyes widened, then he laughed without humour. 'Who've you been talking to? It must have been that waitress.'

Chris cursed himself for giving Danielle away.

'Gerry was making a, well, a rather dramatic point.'

'And your response upset him?'

'I didn't say he was upset. That's your interpretation. Gerry wasn't upset.'

'I think you argued. I think you wanted Hardy to spend the night with you, and that's what your argument was about. Why else drive him all the way to Queenscliff?'

'Why else?' Nevis repeated bitterly, his face suddenly that of an old man.

'Gerry shook his book at me, but I was the one who was upset. I'll tell you something, Constable. Gerry was beautiful. He made no effort to be. He just was. I used to love looking at him, and he let me do that. He laughed and let me look.'

'Beautiful to women, too.'

'Of course. Women made fools of themselves over him. As I did.'

And perhaps got your own back with interest, Chris said to himself.

'What do you think of Mrs Marr?' he asked.

'I never spoke to the woman, except to say good evening.'

'Mrs Marr came to the door to show Hardy out. You were waiting. You exchanged a greeting. What was your impression?'

'It was dark. The porch light – 'Nevis seemed to change his mind. 'I thought she looked formidable,' he said.

'Not a woman to be crossed?'

'Definitely not.'

'And you're quite sure you never sought a session with her?'

'It's hardly likely to be something I'd forget.'

'Did Hardy suggest it?'

'No.'

'Do you believe that the spirits of the departed can return?'

'Of course not. I'm interested in my heritage,' Nevis continued after turning his now near empty wine glass to and fro, 'my forebears who landed here looking for gold, and stayed. But that doesn't mean I think they can talk to me, or I to them.'

'Do you have any brothers or sisters?'

'I had a sister. Unfortunately she died.'

Nevis stared into the fire. Then he turned and looked straight at Chris, as though needing to prove the point. 'I don't believe in ghosts.'

Chris was struck by the man's expression – stripped of defences, vulnerable, as though a private game had become menacing.

Chris used the rest room on his way out and was about to turn on the tap to wash his hands when he heard voices in the corridor, a man's and a woman's.

He recognised Bridget's, but the man's was pitched too low. He heard the word 'wine', then something else he couldn't quite make out, followed by an angry 'tell them!' before the couple moved away, towards the back of the hotel. Chris waited for a few more moments, then left by the front door. He wondered again at Matthew leaving Bridget in charge. Was he deliberately staying away? And had his absence last Thursday evening been deliberate as well? Sarah had said that, with so few guests, it wasn't necessary for both of them to be there in the evenings, and Matthew had been busy in the daytime supervising the renovations and liaising with the tradesmen.

The different suspects twirled around Chris's head like a scene from a bad movie.

Mrs Marr circled Queenscliff on a broomstick. Hardy, that odd fish, swam in seductive circles, Charles Nevis swimming behind him in a vain attempt to capture his attention.

Sarah Kent had a gift – it had been apparent at the fort – of drawing men towards her, making men want to shield and protect her. Matthew was evidence of this, and Anthea, who'd had little to do with Sarah directly, had noticed it and made a reference to Blanche DuBois. When Sarah twirled, it was with a pretty flight of golden hair, a smile that was at once sad, vulnerable and sly.

Sarah had claimed that the spirits sometimes spoke to her. She saw them, was aware of them. 'Visions', she called it, an ability or curse for which she'd been punished since she was a child.

Suddenly it seemed inconceivable to Chris that she would not have mentioned this to Gerard Hardy, given his own interest in spiritualism, his own passionate and personal interest.

They would have recognised a bond. Sarah would have been charmed, and charming in her turn. Was it too much of a leap to picture the two of them going down to the basement together last Thursday night, to take part in an experiment which had gone horribly wrong?

The picture of those two descending the basement stairs, ethereal, waif-like and insistent, kept pace with Chris along the street as he walked slowly home.

If Sarah had been lying all along, then Masterson was right. He might be right for the wrong reasons. The inspector had fixed on Sarah as mentally unstable, which meant that he did not need to find a motive for murder. Whereas in Chris's scenario, no murder had been intended or committed, but Hardy had ended up dead just the same.

Chris fell into bed exhausted and slept much better than he'd thought he would.

TWENTY

Next morning, Chris decided to check on Charles Nevis's relation.

He walked to the house in Bay Street and knocked on the door.

There'd once been many more streets of fishermen's cottages, but the few that were left had become an important part of Queenscliff's history. The one Nevis's great-uncle lived in was painted bright blue. Chris knew the old man to say hello to. Other old men living near the harbour were better known to him – Brian Laidlaw for one.

'Charles phoned on Friday morning. Dreadful business.'

Chris agreed that it was.

'That sergeant's already been to see me.'

The old man's eyes and tone of voice said, what more do you want?

'Has your great-nephew visited before?'

'His parents brought him down here when he was a little chap.'

'Not since then?'

'Why does it matter? What difference does it make?'

Chris could understand his nervousness and his wish to distance himself from a murder inquiry.

'Have you and Mr Nevis made another arrangement to meet?'

'He said he'll phone. He's at your beck and call, he says.'

'Mine?'

'The police.'

Chris wondered why Nevis had given the impression that his time was not his own. Because the visit to his great-uncle had only ever been an excuse? But why had Nevis needed one? He could have driven Hardy to Queenscliff as a favour, whether a relative of his lived there or not.

Chris wrote a report on his conversation with Nevis at the *Royal*. This time, he waited until Masterson was away from the station before handing it to Sergeant Thomas.

Thomas looked up from the printed pages, his expression grim. Chris expected the sergeant to reprimand him for talking to Nevis on his own and taking it upon himself to visit the man's great-uncle. Thomas must know about the inspector's threats. Given what Chris knew of Masterson's character, he'd probably boasted to his sergeant about it.

There was a stale smell in the front office that reminded Chris of the *Royal's* basement. He tried to breathe evenly.

'What do you think of Charles Nevis?' Thomas asked.

Chris took a moment to organise his thoughts. 'I think he's been lying to us from the start. I believe Hardy threw him over – '

'How did he know to arrange Hardy's hands in prayer position after he had killed him?'

'It wouldn't be that hard. Nevis claims he isn't interested in spiritualism or tarot readings, but all he needed was access to a pack of cards.'

Thomas indicated the report, his expression thoughtful. 'Leave this with me, Blackie. Nevis is going back to Melbourne. He's been kind enough to let us know.'

Chris turned towards the door, but doubled back to say he'd like to listen to the first taped interview.

'Shouldn't be a problem.'

Chris thanked the sergeant, recalling the argument Anthea had overheard. Maybe Thomas was still smarting from the inspector's insults. Maybe he had had enough.

Chris rewound the tape. He and Anthea listened to it carefully.

'Had the deceased met the present owner?'

Chris repeated Inspector Masterson's question aloud, and Nevis's answer.

'I don't know. He didn't tell me if he had.'

Anthea said, 'Nevis sounds like he's laughing at you, daring you to prove him wrong.'

'He often sounds like that.'

'Yes, but's it's more obvious just there, don't you think?'

'Masterson doesn't really react to Nevis, I mean suspiciously, until it dawns on him Nevis might be gay.'

'And then?'

'Then it's as though a switch is flicked inside him. He has to work to keep a lid on his revulsion.'

Anthea nodded. 'When Nevis talks about meeting Sarah at the door to the basement, it's as though he's taunting the police with that too.'

'But they did meet. Sarah admitted it.'

'And got into trouble for not having said anything when Masterson first interviewed her.'

'She should have known it would make him more suspicious if she held things back.'

Chris said, 'If Masterson hadn't annoyed Nevis with that question about being gay, he might have kept the bit about Hardy meeting Sarah to himself.'

'In order to protect her?'

Chris thought before replying. 'He might have kept it in reserve.'

'The DI made us do all that door-knocking, but if Sarah and Hardy went down to the basement together, then she didn't need to come back to the hotel at all.'

'What about the dressing-gown?'

'I agree that it's a complication. It doesn't make sense for Hardy to go upstairs and change into his night things while Sarah waited for him. Unless there was a special reason for it.'

'What would that be?'

'I don't know.'

There was the timing. Sarah's car had been heard

pulling into the carpark behind her flat shortly after ten. The post mortem put the time of death at close to midnight.

Anthea raised her head at the sound of footsteps in the corridor.

Ferrier leant with one shoulder in the doorway. His pale skin was drawn tight over his cheekbones and his hands were clenched.

Chris switched off the tape and turned to face the DC.

'That girl Bridget tried to force the Greek boy to get a divorce.' It sounded as though Ferrier was opposed to divorce on principle.

'I understand that Manoli's been separated from his wife for years,' Chris said.

'It was a mixed faith marriage. His wife's a Catholic. The cook's family is Orthodox.'

Ferrier's eyes flickered towards Anthea's shoulder bag, then back to Chris.

'What about the figures Bridget saw, the voice she heard?' he asked.

'Two people walking along the street, that's all. Mad people don't need a motive for murder.'

Anthea asked in her most reasonable voice, 'Do you really believe Sarah Kent is mad?'

'All that nonsense about ghosts. It was a Satanic rite.' Ferrier looked pleased with his choice of words. 'Ghosts and witches. The Black Mass. Kent believes the spirits of the dead can talk to us. One of them told her to kill the sodomite and that's what she did.'

'As punishment?'

'Sodom and Gomorrah. Homosexuality's a deadly sin.'

'Good Lord,' Chris said, when Ferrier had left them. 'I wonder what brought that on.'

'Good Lord is right,' said Anthea.

They smiled at one another, then they laughed.

'Oh dear,' Anthea said, wiping her eyes. 'That did me good.'

'What a pair,' Chris said.

'Ferrier and Masterson?'

'Be careful, won't you.'

'You too.'

Where did Ferrier's spite come from? Did it have its roots in the DC's childhood? Why so much spite directed against one suspect? A pair indeed, Chris thought.

There'd been that period, at the end of the nineteenth, going into the twentieth century, when spiritualism had almost become respectable. Chris thought that Ferrier would have held out against it even then, spitting out the words 'blasphemy' and 'heresy'. A few centuries before, men like Ferrier would have lifted their hands in prayer as they watched heretics being burnt at the stake.

The image on the Four of Swords came back to Chris, this time with a familiarity he hadn't experienced before. He felt connected to the young man on the stone sarcophagus, connected to the golden light. On the tarot card, three swords were hanging on the wall, the fourth imprinted on the yellow stone beneath the body of the knight.

Gold was in the stained glass windows too, and in the light shining through them; clearly this man had been blessed in life, and his death also was a form of blessing.

A short paragraph described the card's divinatory meaning as 'vigilance, retreat, solitude and exile'. Curiously enough, no mention was made of violence, yet the knight – he looked to Chris to be no more than twenty-one or two – was surely dead by violent means.

The Swords as a suit signified danger and destruction, yet this one did not, or not directly, so far as Chris could tell. Even its reversed meanings prophesied less harm than the other Swords.

Chris felt sorry for Ron Ferrier, who seemed lonely and

lost, as well as angry. He thought it might be a good idea to talk to the DC on his own.

He got his chance later that afternoon, on the corner by the Catholic church.

The sun had already lost its warmth; it would be another cold night.

When Chris said hello, Ferrier looked nervously up and down the street.

'Which church is yours?' Chris asked.

'What?'

'Which congregation do you belong to?' Chris lifted his head towards the spire, as though their proximity to it had prompted the question.

'I – ' Ferrier began, then bit his bottom lip.

'Is the problem that Inspector Masterson disapproves?'

'You could say that.'

Ferrier blushed the way very fair-skinned people do, red on white so stark that it looked painful.

He began to walk away, then turned back to face Chris, saying bitterly, 'I believe in Jesus Christ, the son of God, our Saviour. You'd think that – being Christians – sharing that belief – would mean something, surrounded as we are by atheists and devil worshippers.'

Chris re-phrased his question. 'Is the inspector critical of your church?'

'I'm a Baptist. That's what I was brought up and that's the way I've always been. The DI goes to the Uniting Church. I know what your disagreement was about,' Ferrier said, suddenly changing tack. 'I know why you got into trouble.'

Did Ferrier mean talking to Sarah and the other suspects on his own? Chris wasn't about to explain, much less make excuses.

'It's in the Bible. It's God's warning. I try to forgive sinners, to hate the sin and not the sinner.'

'But?'

'When the sinner persists and shows no remorse – then let them be damned!'

Chris imagined the routines of the young man's life – church on Sundays and possibly during the week as well – Ferrier at police academy, abstemious and careful, teased from day one, lacking any sense of humour. He knew what it was like to be solitary, looked down on. Was that how Ferrier had always felt?

They parted, Chris saying goodbye and that he'd see him later, Ferrier barely acknowledging this with a nod.

Chris told Anthea about the meeting by the church over a cup of tea on the station's back veranda.

'Do you think that's enough?' she asked. 'I mean the whole of it?'

'His religion? For Ferrier it's a personal crusade. Saving souls is what matters most. And if the soul refuses to be saved, hellfire and brimstone. Damnation, as he said.'

'Do you think that's why he joined the police?'

'I don't know.'

'And Masterson? Sanders says he's got into trouble for homophobic statements.' Anthea blushed slightly as she said the DC's name.

'You'd think by the time he got to be inspector he'd have learnt self-control.' Chris recalled the scream at Mrs Marr's, then his thoughts returned to Ferrier, who'd hoped for a personal understanding from his boss, perhaps even friendship, and was now angry and disappointed.

'What about us?' asked Anthea.

Chris was startled. 'We're not like that.'

'Why not?'

'Because we're not religious is the obvious answer.'

'And?'

'Our personalities and characters.'

Anthea leant back in her wicker chair and sighed.

Chris thought about safety. For men, women and children to be able to walk the streets of a small coastal town without fear of being set upon and robbed, or worse: hadn't that aim, which he'd thought of as modest and achievable, been destroyed when Bobby McGilvrey was killed? How could he possibly claim to ensure anybody's safety after that?

If you chose the police force as a career; if you chose a church which demanded adherence to a set of rules with no exceptions, no room for back-sliding, then those two combined might exert a powerful compulsion.

Masterson had taken Sanders to interview Hardy's department head at the university and his PhD supervisor. If it had been up to me, Chris thought, I would have done that well before today.

Hardy's teaching salary had been small, but it seemed that he'd been a frugal young man. His bank account showed that his scholarship, plus a bit of extra money, had covered his rent and food, and of course he hadn't had the expense of a car. His flat was close enough to the university for a single bus ride or a longish walk.

Sanders filled Anthea and Chris in on the details soon after he returned to Queenscliff.

Hardy didn't seem to have made much of an impression on anybody at his place of work. 'Quiet and studious' had been the adjectives most often used to describe him. His area of interest – spiritualism in the work of Henry Handel Richardson – seemed to have no more than mildly amused the staff and students. None claimed friendship, or even close acquaintanceship with the deceased.

TWENTY-ONE

The missing book turned up in Charles Nevis's flat in Melbourne. Masterson was cock-a-hoop about it, Sanders told Chris and Anthea, though he shouldn't be. It was Thomas who'd applied for the warrant and organised the search.

Sanders was leaning in the back office doorway, trying to look relaxed, but watching Anthea closely. Chris wondered if he'd spoken to her in private. He wondered how Anthea, still upset and angry with Olly, had responded.

Chris said, 'I wonder where he hid it those days he was here.'

'In a locker at the swimming pool.'

Sanders laughed and suddenly the two constables were laughing with him, though the joke was surely on themselves.

'Where did Thomas find it in his flat?'

'On a bookshelf. Under R for Richardson.'

'So he took the book before Hardy was killed?'

Sanders shifted from foot to foot. 'That's what he says, but we've only got his word for it.'

'What's Inspector Masterson going to do now?'

'Interview him again. But he's not taking Thomas. He's taking Ferrier. And Nevis's got a solicitor. Well, you would, wouldn't you?'

Chris nodded, aware that Sanders wasn't interested in his reaction and that Anthea was tense. It was interesting that Masterson was taking Ferrier. Would they get through the interview without the subject of homosexuality arising? Surely not. Would Ferrier give vent to his feelings and his prejudices? How would Nevis and his solicitor react?

Ferrier came to the door. 'The boss is asking for you,' he told Sanders, ignoring Chris and Anthea.

Sanders turned to go, but looked back at Anthea over his shoulder. She rewarded him with a brief smile.

'So I was wrong about the water tank,' Anthea said when the two constables were alone together. 'All those wands pointing downwards, leading us to Mercer Street.'

Chris reflected on the clarity of hindsight, with what a pure light it could shine; he thought about the bounce in his assistant's step as they'd made their way to Ethel Richardson's house, following the tarot, how Anthea had understood that he was humouring her, then how he'd ceased to do this, but instead had followed her in his imagination.

He compared this with how the detectives interacted with each other, but maybe the comparison was unfair. The detectives had been thrown together; they'd not had time to learn each other's ways. What expression had Sanders used? Fur and feathers flying.

The theft accorded with what Chris thought of as Nevis's malicious temperament, as did the elaborate details of the murder.

The *Royal* looked closed up and deserted. Chris wondered if the renovations would ever be finished, or if the hotel would be sold with half its face lifted, to someone willing to take a gamble on notoriety.

The press vans were gone. There'd been a gang murder in Melbourne and the attention of the crime reporters had shifted to that.

They'd talked about it, Anthea wondering if the inspector would be pleased that the journalists had more gruesome killings on their minds. Recalling Masterson preening in front of the cameras, Chris had asked himself what could be more gruesome than to be strangled with the cord of your own dressing-gown?

Somebody had washed the hotel steps. It seemed an

oddly futile gesture, and at the same time understandable. There'd been no blood in the basement. The contamination and misery Hardy's death had caused could not be washed away, yet trying to do so was a very human act.

Chris was conscious of fatigue dragging at his muscles, a dragging and bearing down sensation, but was glad that he could walk home alone in the pearly dusk.

The building was too big, he decided, turning the corner from Mercer into Stokes Street. The *Brewhouse* was too big as well, and the *Vue Grand* – those nineteenth century palaces with their echoing, high-ceilinged rooms.

Matthew was walking towards him.

'Can I talk to you?' he asked.

'I shouldn't – ' Chris began.

'Please.'

Chris nodded. 'Alright.'

Matthew switched lights on. They sat in the lounge in front of an empty fireplace.

'I've told Manoli and Bridget to take the rest of the week off. There's nothing for them to do.'

'Is Mr Ling going ahead with the renovations?'

'He can't make up his mind.'

'Is Manoli an alcoholic?'

Matthew stared at Chris, an unnatural glitter in his eyes. 'How did you know?'

'I didn't, but he was frightened that you'd accuse him of stealing the wine.'

'Manoli was dismissed from his last job because of his drinking. His boss found him surrounded by empty bottles.'

'You knew that when you took him on?'

'He was learning to trust his will-power. Sarah was helping him. They helped one another. Manoli's an excellent cook, imaginative and conscientious. I wanted to give him a chance.'

Chris thought how the explanation fitted. Manoli was

in Matthew's debt and would do whatever Matthew told him to.

'When did you first learn about the missing wine?'

Matthew raised his hands, then let them fall back on the table. 'Some – several weeks ago.'

'When did you realise that it was Sarah?'

Instead of answering, Matthew said, 'I wrote to Mr Ling and suggested that he hold off sending any more deliveries until the ground floor renovations were completed. He agreed.'

'So you never told him about the theft. What did you think he'd do when he found out?'

'I don't know.'

'You were buying time,' Chris said. 'Did you think of replacing the missing bottles? They were worth a lot of money.'

'At first I thought Sarah might have been protecting Manoli. It's the sort of thing she'd do.'

'And the thefts stopped?'

'Yes.'

'You would have talked to Charles Nevis,' Chris said. 'You talked to him about Sarah meeting Hardy at the basement stairs on Thursday evening.'

'He said he had to tell the inspector what he saw. Hardy came downstairs and asked her to show him the door. He was curious. He'd already asked about the keys.'

'Did they go down there?'

'No! They just stood talking for a few minutes, that's all. Sarah didn't think anything of it till the next day, when, when he – '

'When you found out he was dead. How did Sarah seem when she got home?'

'I was already in bed. I was very tired. We didn't talk. She kissed me goodnight and we went to sleep.'

'Didn't talk at all?'

'She said something about getting in early in the morning, to help Manoli with the breakfasts. But we'd already agreed on that.'

On the surface it all sounded reasonable, and Matthew had been over his story many times. But someone in this whole tangle – perhaps more than one person – had been lying from the start.

'What did you want to talk to me about?' Chris asked.

'Sarah did not kill Gerard Hardy. She can't kill an insect. It's preposterous.'

'Where's Sarah now?'

'Home. She's scared to go out. I – it's – I feel as though I'm being suffocated.'

Chris thought that an interesting choice of words.

'How did you and Sarah meet?' he asked.

Of course the detectives would have asked this question, but Matthew, giving Chris a swift, sidelong look, didn't seem surprised to be asked again.

'At a concert. The John Butler Trio. It was the first time Sas had heard them live.'

And it was the first time Chris had heard Matthew call his girlfriend by a nickname.

'I knew she – well – she saw things,' Matthew said as though anticipating Chris's next question. 'She said that if she didn't tell me straight away, it would look bad when she had to.'

'Is that why Sarah consulted Mrs Marr?'

'That woman got her hooks into her. She preys on vulnerable people.'

'Why did Sarah go all the way to the end of the brick passage on the Friday morning?'

'She said she smelt something.'

'Did you go back with her?'

'Yes.'

'Did you touch the body?'

'No.'

'Did Manoli?'

'No.'

'But Manoli went with you. The three of you went back there.'

'He followed us down the stairs. I didn't even know he was there until he said - he cried out, I don't remember what – '

So Manoli had lied about that. Chris wasn't surprised. 'You took Manoli and Sarah back upstairs. You left them together while you called the police. You made sure you'd locked the basement door. Didn't it occur to you that the killer might have his or her own key?'

'Of course. But why would he go back there? What was there left to do?'

Chris pictured Sarah with her back against the fort's bluestone wall. One can be hounded for one's gifts, then lose them, he thought, and then spend the rest of one's life trying to convince oneself that they weren't gifts at all.

He suspected that Matthew had wanted to tell him something different and then changed his mind. He reminded himself that he shouldn't have been talking to the hotel manager at all.

TWENTY-TWO

Masterson held a short briefing after his return from Melbourne. He acted as though he discovered the book, not Sergeant Thomas.

'The tosser had men's magazines.'

The inspector smiled as he spoke, then glanced at his reflection in the window. Ferrier was standing in the shadow by the door. Sanders was looking amused. Chris wondered where Thomas was.

Nevis's hotel room had been next to Hardy's. By his own admission he'd gone in there and taken the book. So much for claiming that he'd fallen asleep and not stirred till Friday morning.

What other lies had Nevis told? But if he'd killed his lover, why had he been so stupid as to display the stolen book? Hidden in plain sight – had that been his reasoning? Had his scorn for the investigation been such that he felt confident his flat would not be searched?

Masterson raised his large, powerful right hand.

'Before he left here, our dear Charles boasted to Bridget McGuire about the book. He didn't tell her where it was. That'd be too much to expect. But he hinted that he knew and the bitch kept it to herself.'

After the briefing was over, Chris and Anthea sat on the back veranda. Chris didn't know what they'd be asked to do next. Ferrier had gone to St Leonards to bring Bridget to the station.

'And don't listen to any tripe about not leaving her mother,' Chris had overheard the inspector saying.

He wanted to go home; suddenly he thought, why shouldn't I? He was tired and Anthea looked ill.

'Come on, I'll drop you at your flat.'

Anthea hesitated, but did not object.

Manoli's car was parked outside his cottage. The cook got out as Chris was unlocking his door. Chris, trying to hide his surprise, invited him in.

Manoli looked haggard, more frightened than when Chris had seen him last. He wouldn't sit down, but stood staring out the kitchen window while Chris put on the jug for tea.

'You've got to help us.'

Chris turned to face Manoli, saying, 'I'm not even meant to be talking to you.'

'But you must!'

'When you withhold information, then – '

'What? We should have told you our life stories the moment we were introduced?'

'You know I don't mean that. Did Charles Nevis talk to you about Hardy's book?'

Manoli gathered himself together with an effort. 'No,' he said.

'So he talked to Bridget, but not you. Why was that?'

'He – Mr Nevis came down to the kitchen. I tried to make him welcome but – '

Chris pictured the scene – Manoli doing what he did best, making coffee on the new machine and serving fresh, delicious food.

He guessed that Nevis had flirted with the cook. Perhaps he'd touched Manoli on the arm or shoulder, a friendly touch at the same time offering something more than friendliness.

'Did you tell Bridget?'

'I didn't have to.'

'You talked about it. What was Bridget's opinion?'

'She said to stay out of his way.'

'So it was Bridget's idea not to say anything about the book?'

'She said the less we had to do with the police the better.'

'You knew Sarah was taking the wine,' Chris said. 'Did she tell you why?'

Manoli hesitated before answering. 'She didn't say exactly, but I gathered that it was to pay a debt.'

'You must have known you would be suspected. Why did you go along with it?'

'I felt sorry for her. And – '

'Yes?'

'It was daft of the owner to order all that expensive wine while the place was a building site. I said so at the time.'

'Did Matthew accuse you of taking the wine?'

'He asked me. I said no.'

'Do you think he believed you?'

'He didn't want it to be Sarah.'

'I can see how that would have been hard for him,' Chris said.

Manoli stared down at his hands which were clasped firmly together.

'You were going to tell me something more about Bridget. Something else that Bridget saw or heard?'

'No. No, not that.'

'What then?'

'She's planning to get her mother into a nursing home in Melbourne. Then she'll look for a job and move. She says she's had it with this place and with me as well.'

After Manoli had left, Chris closed his front door behind him and walked around the block to clear his head. He badly wanted to continue on to Minnie's cottage, to be welcomed there, to see Minnie's dear and earth-bound face, to kiss her cool lips and look into her calm, accepting eyes.

Chris completed a circuit of his block. When he returned to it, his cottage felt as though it had been empty for a long time. He looked up a phone number and checked the time difference between Australia and Hong Kong.

The voice on the other end carried the trace of a Chinese accent, but was predominantly English and, Chris guessed, English learnt at a public school. Perhaps the *Royal* was no more than one of Mr Ling's minor investments. He could afford to hang onto the hotel in the hope that notoriety might gain, rather than lose him custom in the long run.

Though Mr Ling said he'd faxed a signed statement and had nothing more to add, Chris continued with his questions, hoping the hotel owner was too polite to hang up on him. Yes, Matthew had hired his own staff. Matthew had wanted to return to Australia and when the *Royal* had come on the market it had seemed a perfect match. As for the Greek boy, he'd come second in his year at hospitality school, reputed to be one of Australia's best. If a young man like that wanted to work in a small seaside town, then that was his choice.

When Chris said casually, 'Just to confirm, Matthew was working in Hong Kong for you at the time you bought the *Royal*?' Mr Ling replied impatiently, 'Of course.'

TWENTY-THREE

Next morning, Sanders came out to the back office to announce, 'Our sergeant's leaving.'

Anthea and Chris looked up, startled, while Sanders moved restlessly around the room.

'He didn't want to come here in the first place.'

'But surely – ' Anthea began.

'Oh, he couldn't have asked for a transfer just because he wanted one, but he got under the DI's skin sufficiently, so - '

'Who's replacing him?' Chris asked.

'I don't think there's going to be a replacement. The four of us are stuck with each other.'

'Four constables and an inspector,' Chris said. 'An interesting mix.'

Anthea looked at Sanders with her head on one side as if to say: what next?

Chris and Anthea took mugs of tea out to the back veranda. Chris hoped they'd be left alone for a while.

A wind came up, blowing Anthea's hair about her face. She grimaced. Her skin had a green tinge.

'Are you okay?' he asked.

'Not really.'

'Olly?'

'It's just – he doesn't see – the tarot cards were – ' Anthea began, then pressed her lips together.

'The last straw?'

'Kind of. Yes.'

'Why did you tell him?'

'I don't know. It just slipped out.' After a pause, Anthea said, 'I hate talking on the phone.'

Chris didn't say what was obvious, that Olly should have come back days ago.

'Come on. Let's go to my place and have a decent meal.'

'I don't think – I don't know if – '

'Something light and nutritious,' Chris said.

They walked with their heads down against the southerly blowing off the Strait. Anthea pulled the collar of her jacket tight around her throat, holding it with one hand, while with the other she stopped her bag from slipping. Her expression was severe; her white, exposed hand looked small and fragile. Chris wondered if they should have driven.

He understood that part of his dizziness, a strange vertiginous sensation that he'd gone to bed with, and woken up with that morning, was to do with Anthea and his feelings of protectiveness towards her.

She seemed all the more vulnerable to him because of her insistence that she did not need his help.

Over a herb and tomato omelette, Anthea browsed tarot sites, every now and again pausing to consult her pack of cards.

She looked up to say, 'You know, there's a water tank in one of Richardson's short stories. And a description of children hiding treasures from the grown-ups.'

Chris nodded as he stood up to clear away the plates. He felt impatient and tried not to let it show.

He said, to introduce a different subject, 'No one's mentioned visitors to the *Royal* on Thursday afternoon or evening. I mean customers who dropped in for a drink.'

Anthea took her time before replying. 'That could be because there were none. Or because someone saw them and is keeping quiet.'

She turned her attention back to the cards. 'They point to Ethel's old house, but you can't expect them to cross all the 't's and dot all the 'i's. Did you notice that the space between the water tank and fence is just big enough for a kid to hide?'

'But Charles Nevis had the book.'

'We agreed that Delia was lying about something.'

'She won't let us back there.'

Anthea said firmly, 'I think it's worth a try.'

Delia Robbins looked at Chris's outstretched hand without taking it. Her glance at Anthea was one of condescension bordering on contempt.

'School holidays. The pits,' she said by way of greeting. 'What do you want now?'

Two children came up quietly and stood behind their mother in the hallway. They were expensively dressed, their hair stylishly cut, their expressions anxious.

Anthea smiled and said, 'Hello. My name's Constable Merritt. What are your names?'

The children stared at her without speaking. Their mother said, 'David and Sonya. Not that it's any of your business.'

When Chris asked if they could come inside for a few minutes, Delia said, 'No, you can't. I've nothing more to add and it's inconvenient. I was on my way out.'

'You say you weren't here last Thursday. Do you mean in this house, or in Queenscliff?'

'Here!' Delia shouted. 'Don't you understand plain English!'

The children started backwards. The girl tried to hide behind the boy, who reached out his hand.

Chris said, 'Gerard Hardy wrote to you about Henry Handel Richardson. He wanted to see over your house.'

'Whoever told you that's a liar.'

Delia slammed the door. Chris and Anthea walked a short way along the street and waited. Nobody came out.

'Did you notice Sonya's face?' said Anthea. 'Two bruises,

here and here.' She touched her own face lightly.

'She was told to stay out of sight. I hope she isn't punished for it.'

Anthea looked bleak. 'I bet she will be. Do you think Delia was one of the women Bridget heard?'

'It crossed my mind.'

'Who was the second one?'

'It could have been her sister.'

Chris wondered how often the boy and girl escaped to their father's and if it was any kind of an escape. He'd found out since their last visit that Delia and Justin Robbins were divorced. It would be easy to seek there for the cause of Delia's bad temper.

TWENTY-FOUR

Chris had to wait to see Masterson. He told the inspector that he and Anthea had called in on Delia Robbins and what they suspected with regard to her daughter.

'I'm going to put in a report to the child protection unit.'

The phone rang on Masterson's desk and he reached towards it greedily.

He waved Chris away with a nod which Chris took to mean go ahead.

Chris wrote his report and submitted it. The child protection unit was a relatively new police initiative, specially trained to deal with family violence. Chris had no doubt Delia would respond angrily to a visit from one of their officers. She would have prepared an explanation for why Sonya had bruises on her cheek and chin. Still, Chris didn't see that he had any alternative but to follow the proper steps. In the meantime, he would make his own inquiries.

He told Anthea he was sure a woman like Delia Robbins would have a cleaning lady. It shouldn't be too hard to find her.

Anthea said she'd have a go, then swivelled in her chair to say, 'Masterson believes Delia Robbins's alibi. That's why he's not interested in her or her children.'

Delia's house cleaner's name was Edwina Miles. When Chris and Anthea knocked on her door, she invited them inside. She didn't ask why they'd come to question her; indeed, she opened the door as though she'd been expecting the police.

'You know, I never clean that back room of hers,' she said, inviting them to take a seat in a pleasant sun-room. 'It's out of bounds. Not that I mind, but. One less room to bother with is how I look at it.'

'Would you mind telling us about it?'

Chris kept the surprise out of his voice. It seemed Edwina thought they'd come to question her about Mrs Marr. It was another black mark against Inspector Masterson that, so far as Chris knew, he hadn't even found out that the psychic had a cleaning lady.

Edwina didn't mind at all. She described Mrs Marr's living room and bedrooms. 'Not but that she only uses one.'

'Does Mrs Marr ever have visitors to stay?'

'She could do. No one's been there on my cleaning day. That's all I can tell you.'

Edwina had begun cleaning for the psychic soon after she arrived in Queenscliff. Chris wondered about income; employing a cleaner in Mrs Marr's circumstances seemed unnecessary.

Edwina said confidingly, 'I never did like the smell of incense.'

She cleaned for Mrs Marr once a week, usually for two hours on a Wednesday morning. When Anthea asked who'd chosen the day of the week, Edwina said that Mrs Marr had. Chris wondered if it was significant, if the medium had a regular Wednesday afternoon or evening visitor, for whom it was important that the house should look its best.

Sometimes Mrs Marr stayed in while Edwina worked, sometimes she went out. Edwina made it clear, without actually admitting to snooping, that she'd had a good look round when she'd had the chance. She described the wall hangings, the lampshade and cushions, the table with the cards, seemingly unaware that she'd just told the two constables she wasn't allowed in the back room.

'Does anyone ever come while Mrs Marr is out?'

Edwina could not recall this happening.

When Chris asked how the psychic paid, Edwina said,

'In cash.'

'Would that be your choice?'

Edwina reddened. 'I pay tax on what I earn.'

'So cash was Mrs Marr's idea?'

'She suggested it at the beginning and I said, That's fine with me.'

Anthea took up the questioning. 'What about the clients, how do they pay?'

'Oh, I wouldn't know that.'

'But you'd know if Mrs Marr had a machine for people to pay by card?'

'I've never seen one.'

'From your Wednesday mornings, and from talking to Mrs Marr,' Chris asked, 'would you say most of her clients are women?'

'Yes, I would.'

'And how would you say they look, I mean any that you've seen.'

'What do you mean?'

'Do they look excited? Worried?'

'It depends on the individual, doesn't it?'

'Have you ever had a tarot reading Mrs Miles?'

'Me?' Edwina looked as though Anthea had asked her if she'd flown to the moon. 'What would I be doing that for?'

'Curiosity?'

'I've got better things to do with my money, thank you very much.'

'Did Mrs Marr suggest it?'

'Well, yes she did. It was more of a hint than an outright offer. I said I'd clean her house for her and earn my wages, but I drew the line at fortune-telling.'

'Did Mrs Marr object?'

'To what?'

'Your use of the term fortune-telling.'

'She knew I wouldn't change my mind.'

When Chris asked where Edwina had been on the night of the murder, she said, 'Right here. In front of the telly.'

Chris thought, as he had before, how often television sets were wheeled out as alibis.

'Do you know any of the hotel staff – Sarah and Matthew, Bridget and Manoli?'

'I say hello to Bridget if I see her in the street and ask after her Mum. Those others, they're incomers, aren't they?' Edwina hesitated and seemed about to add something.

'Yes?' Anthea prompted.

'I saw that Sarah once. She turned up just as I was leaving.'

'For an appointment?'

'I couldn't say. All I know is that she came to the door.'

Edwina's expression was both relieved and satisfied. She'd clearly been waiting to get this off her chest, but waiting too, Chris reminded himself, for the police to come to her.

'What happened then?'

'I let her in and she went down the back.' Edwina hesitated, then continued, 'They were arguing. I could hear them from the front.'

'What about?'

'I don't know. I got on with my cleaning.'

'Did Sarah bring anything with her?'

'What do you mean?'

'A parcel of some sort? Was she carrying a bag?'

'She had a shoulder bag. A brown one, I think.'

'A largish bag, was it?'

'Just normal sized.'

Chris and Anthea exchanged a glance.

'Is there anything else you recall about the visit?' Chris asked.

'Not really. The girl let herself out. Mrs Marr didn't come with her to the front door.'

'How did Sarah seem to you?'

'She looked angry and – like she was in a hurry.'

'What can you tell us about Delia Robbins and her daughter?' Anthea asked, after another swift glance at Chris, who nodded.

'Sonya?' Edwina went red and looked guilty. 'She goes to boarding school. She – '

'In the holidays,' Chris said curtly. 'When you clean Mrs Robbins's house then.'

'Sonya?' Edwina repeated, looking from Anthea to Chris and back again.

Chris said, 'You've seen Sonya's cuts and bruises, haven't you? If you suspected Mrs Robbins was mistreating her daughter, why didn't you report it?'

'Who to?'

'Constable Merritt or myself.'

Edwina looked defiant. 'I can't afford for her to sack me.'

'We'll leave that for now,' Chris said, 'but we want you to do something to help us with our investigation.'

'How can I do that?'

'See who comes and goes to Mrs Marr's house. Pay attention to who she phones and who phones her while you're there.'

'But that's eavesdropping!'

'Just see what you can do.'

Edwina looked as though she was about to argue further, then she said, 'Alright.'

Chris and Anthea walked, by common and unspoken consent, around the corner by the fort, skirting old haunts known to Chris from childhood.

They returned to the station slowly and reluctantly. In his mind's eyes, Chris saw the small figure of Mary Richardson hurrying home from the fort along Mercer Street, in the cold and dark. He wondered if Sonya felt the shift in freezing air that was Mary coming home and if, without knowing how or why, it comforted her.

Anthea said, 'Edwina made me angry, standing there and telling us she was afraid Delia would sack her.'

'She didn't want to get involved.' Chris was embarrassed by the cliché. 'Me too,' he added. 'She made me angry too.'

'Why do you think Mrs Marr pays her in cash?'

'Because it's easier. Because her clients pay cash and she's got it sitting there.'

'Some of Mrs Marr's clients may have followed her from Torquay,' Chris said.

'Bernard Hepson's wife?'

'She may be too frightened of her husband finding out. But others.'

'You mean other grieving mothers?'

'It's a possibility.'

As they approached the station, Chris realised that his stomach was clenched tight. He tried to breathe slowly as he hesitated outside the front office, glad the door was shut. He could hear Masterson talking on the phone, in a low voice, then suddenly much louder. 'Now that's a cock-up.' The DI sounded pleased.

Delia Robbins's GP, a man in his sixties whom Chris knew by sight but had never dealt with personally, was reluctant to talk about the family and denied that he'd ever treated Sonya for lacerations or other 'injuries of that kind'.

He told Chris and Anthea, as though they were unaware of this, that the girl spent most of her time at boarding school. He seemed to take their presence in his surgery as a personal affront.

Chris told himself that Delia wouldn't risk taking Sonya to her own doctor. She'd be kept inside until evidence of 'that kind of injury' had disappeared.

He gave vent to his irritation as soon as they left the surgery.

Anthea raised her eyebrows, but said nothing. Chris suspected that Delia had been hitting her daughter for years, so why did he feel such a sense of urgency? Was it guilt at discovering what had been going on under his nose? In a big city, you could make excuses and perhaps end up believing them; not in a small town.

Chris phoned Sonya's school, but was told he'd have to wait till the start of the new term before speaking to her house mistress. The school gave him a phone number for her father, who answered Chris's call in an abrupt voice.

An out-of-the-blue call from the police was enough to put any father on his guard. And if the father was ignorant of what Chris and Anthea had noticed after a single encounter with the girl, then what did that say about the man?

Chris felt his face growing hot and was glad that Justin Robbins couldn't see him. He did have Sonya and her brother David sometimes during the school holidays, he said, and 'for the odd weekend.'

'When was the last time?'

Justin was tied up with work; he was very busy now, as a matter of fact.

When Chris repeated his question, Justin said, 'Over Christmas. Well, around there. In the summer holidays.'

'What about the children's grandparents?'

'What about them?'

'Are they in regular contact?'

'Delia's parents are dead and so is my father. My mother – well, she used to visit before Delia and I separated.'

'Could I have a phone number for her please?'

'Why?'

'Just background,' Chris said mildly.

'Background to what?'

'A murder inquiry. Mr Robbins, I can get the phone number another way, but I'd advise you to co-operate.'

After a short silence, Justin told him and he wrote it down.

'If you have any further questions, I'll expect them in writing.'

Justin Robbins hung up and Chris was left staring at his phone.

Elizabeth Robbins sounded cautious, which was understandable. When she said she visited her grandchildren as often as she could, Chris read into this as often as Delia allowed her to. She refused to comment on the divorce or custody arrangements. Chris let the silence following his question hang for a moment before asking Elizabeth if she had any plans for visiting Queenscliff in the near future. Her answer was no.

Chris reflected that he'd given the children's grandmother an opening, which she'd chosen to ignore. She could be feeling guilty; on the other hand, she mightn't have a clue.

He took a cup of tea out to the back veranda, thinking of Bobby McGilvrey and Bobby's older sister Sharon, and how, to his embarrassment and shame, he'd been avoiding the dead boy's family. He would remedy that, and made a promise to Bobby's ghost, without believing that he had one, that he'd seek out his younger brothers and drop in on Sharon at the bakery.

He leant back, stretched out his legs and closed his eyes, trying to relax. But then he saw Hardy's body on the backs of his eyelids, in that parody of worship.

He felt again his horror and disgust at the smell coming from the sandpit. Neither the inspector nor his sergeant had remarked on the smell, not in his hearing at least.

Chris opened his eyes and stared at the fence in front

of him, schooling himself against theorising in advance of the facts. He mustn't let his antipathy towards Delia cloud his judgment.

TWENTY-FIVE

The sound of raised voices brought Chris hurrying inside.

'What's this? What rubbish have you got here!'

Anthea stood facing the office doorway with her hands grasping the back of a chair. She frowned and shook her head at Chris. Her tarot cards were scattered on the desk. Her face was greenish-grey.

Chris walked forward. 'I don't – ' he began.

Masterson turned on him. 'You don't what, Blackie! Don't use what few brains God gave you?'

Chris moved across to Anthea and put his hand on her arm. 'Sit down,' he said gently.

Anthea looked at him blankly, but she pulled the chair out and let herself fall onto it.

Chris thought of claiming that the cards were his, but Masterson must have made Anthea open her bag. Why had she brought them to the station with her?

Masterson picked up the Lovers card then flung it down again. 'Disgusting!'

Anthea recoiled, biting her bottom lip.

'It's research,' Chris said calmly. He made himself meet the inspector's eyes.

'Research?' Masterson repeated cuttingly. 'Your job isn't research. It's to do what you're told.'

'I think you should go home,' Chris said to Anthea after the inspector had stormed off.

'But – '

'No buts, please. I'll message you.'

'Alright.'

Anthea began picking up her cards. She put them carefully in her bag, then said, 'Here's that phone number you wanted. For the farm at Inverleigh. Cheryl Adamson is Delia's sister's name.'

After Anthea had left, Chris sat down and thought for a few minutes, then went looking for DC Ferrier, hoping to find him alone.

'It was you who told Inspector Masterson that Anthea had bought a pack of tarot cards.'

Ferrier threw him a hostile look, but did not deny it.

'Did Masterson ask you to spy on us?'

'No.'

'So it was your idea. Why do you dislike Constable Merritt?'

'It's not – '

'You dislike both of us. Why?'

'You're too big for your boots.'

'That criticism may be true of me, but not Constable Merritt.'

'I've seen the way you look at one another. You've got your own agenda, anyone can see that.'

'We've worked together for years, managing a station.'

'That's the problem.'

'Is that what the inspector told you?'

'No, I worked it out for myself.'

Chris and Anthea were sitting on Anthea's small balcony. Her skin was still greenish and she looked worn out.

'If they sack me it'll make it easier for Olly.'

'Why doesn't he just come home?' Chris asked.

'He says he – we've – paid for the two weeks. I never thought that he could be so cold.'

Chris tried to think of something that would lift her spirits. He pictured his own future, or the lack of one. He felt like standing on the cliff top and shouting that he wasn't old. Not finished yet!

'Olly knows it's not a nine-to-five job, that things

come up, and when they do you can't say no. But he doesn't understand why I want to involve myself with danger and misery and death.'

'Because of the baby?'

'It's partly that. It's largely that, I guess. But he never could understand it.'

Olly had been wrongly arrested for Bobby McGilvrey's murder and it had looked for a while as though his relationship with Anthea would never recover. Chris didn't think that excused Olly's withdrawal now, but perhaps, from his point of view, it did.

'He wants me to make up my mind before he comes home.'

'Make up your mind to resign?'

'Yes.'

Chris hated seeing Anthea divided and sad. 'If it's any help to you, I'll manage,' he said.

Anthea thanked him. She shook her shoulders, as though to shake off self-pity.

'Do you think police work is something you can leave for a few years and then pick up again?' she asked.

'If it's in your blood.'

Anthea stared at Chris, two hands resting on her belly. His eyes involuntarily went to them. Was she thinking of her own blood that gave blood to another life, or had her hands found that position without conscious thought?

In your blood. The words echoed off the cliff face Chris usually avoided. But after leaving Anthea he'd walked across the road and flashed quick glances at the sea, which today seemed painted on, unreal. He felt a sense of foreboding. Would it be better if he hadn't spoken them aloud?

He'd never really considered an alternative career. Nor had he properly considered, up until that moment, what it was about the job that held him and defined him.

The words echoed. The cliff face was impervious to humans. That had been a comfort to him through the years. He recalled how he'd once suggested half-jokingly that Anthea should train as a detective.

Would the station be re-converted to a residential house? Chris imagined the offices becoming bedrooms, the calls of children back and forth, the old walls relaxing around the smells of dinner cooking. He paused in his reverie and discovered he was smiling. Minnie called out that dinner was ready, Minnie with her red-gold hair and lovely uptilt of the chin and eyes.

Chris realised how important it had been to their relationship that he had a role to play in Queenscliff, work to occupy his days. He had never thought status mattered to him, or to Minnie either. It wasn't losing status that caught in his throat now, but living day to day without a routine. When Minnie spoke of her work at the *Brewhouse* it was often ironically, sometimes derisively, but it mattered to her.

It had seemed to Chris that modesty with regard to employment had been something he and Minnie shared. They'd talked about it, Minnie laughing, saying she was sick of being asked why she stayed on, Chris echoing her laughter, complementing it with his own. He'd used his mother's illness as an excuse for not returning to Melbourne, not seeking employment at an urban station, for refusing suggestions that he should apply for promotion. He realised now that he'd been lucky they were only suggestions, that he'd never been instructed to move.

This symmetry with Minnie would be lost, a common viewpoint they'd taken for granted. What other job was available, or would suit him? Could he work in a supermarket, telling himself that it was temporary, a stop-gap till a 'real' alternative came up? He'd seen middle-aged men at the supermarket check-out, the way they kept their eyes down, their expressions of embarrassment or shame.

No one answered Chris's knock on the front door of the Mercer Street house, but when he went around the back, he saw the two children sitting in a patch of sun. The car wasn't in the driveway; perhaps their mother had gone out. She would have warned them not to answer the door.

Chris climbed so that his head was over the top of the gate and called out hello. Sonya quickly disappeared, but David stood and stared at him.

'What do you want?' he asked.

'Would you mind opening the gate?'

Chris was aware of two pairs of blue eyes watching him intently as the gate swung back, one belonging to the girl, whose outline was visible through the kitchen window.

'My name's Constable Blackie,' Chris said, remembering that they had not been introduced. 'Would you mind if I had a look by your water tank?'

'What are you looking for?'

'I'm not sure.'

In order to give David time to observe and make up his mind about him, Chris knelt down, conscious of the boy stiff and on guard at his back, and the smell of long grass that, once the summer was past, never thoroughly dried out. Delia might employ a cleaner for the house, but she evidently didn't pay a gardener or mow the lawns herself.

He put his hand under the tank and then reached further, thinking ruefully of the green stains on his uniform. He felt something right at the back near the fence.

It was hard and small and cold to the touch. Gently, Chris edged it towards him with his fingers and then pulled it out.

He stood up with a grunt. David watched him carefully, in silence. Chris held the object out on the palm of his hand; it was a small cup, a doll's tea-cup, discoloured and dirty but unbroken. Chris turned it gently by its handle; it wasn't even chipped.

Sonya opened the back door and took a few tentative steps.

'Is this yours?' Chris asked, holding the cup out on his muddy palm.

Sonya regarded him warily. No doubt both children were listening for the sound of their mother's car.

'I found it,' she said.

'Here, underneath the tank?'

The girl nodded. David moved closer to her, with a warning glance.

'I wasn't doing any harm,' said Sonya, in the voice of someone who had often made this claim, only to find it thrown back in her face.

'I'm sure you weren't. I'll put the cup back in a minute. Do you know who it belonged to?'

'A long ago girl.'

'Do you know her name?'

Sonya shook her head. The wind blew her hair back from her face, making the cut near her left ear more visible.

'You're hurt,' he said kindly. 'Do you want to tell me how it happened?'

'It's nothing. I fell down.'

'I can help you. Constable Merritt can help too.'

'Please go now,' David said. 'We'll get in trouble if you're here when Mum comes back.'

Chris handed the boy a card. 'Here's my phone number. Ring me, please, if you need anything.'

Sonya ran towards the house, as though, too late, she'd realised the consequences of disobeying orders. David watched her go with a protective frown.

He took the cup, then shut the back gate behind Chris, sweat appearing along his hairline and his upper lip.

In a house where privacy was impossible for children, a small, strange object might take on magical significance. David would value it on his sister's behalf, even if he didn't fully comprehend the value that it had for her.

It occurred to Chris that the cup might have been regarded as a treasure by its former owner. He pictured Ettie and Lil Richardson playing tea-parties in the long grass by the back fence, safe for a short while from the unreasonable demands of grown-ups.

David and Sonya would find another hiding place. They wouldn't trust Chris not to tell their mother. They would be distressed by his interference and punished if their mother found that he'd been back. He glanced around the lane, hoping no one had been watching through a window. Normally comfortable with the small town habit of one neighbour watching and noting what another did, and more than willing to take advantage of this when it suited him, now Chris felt hampered and restricted by the possibility that other sets of eyes had witnessed that small, sad pantomime.

He didn't normally go around regretting that he'd never had a family. At different times when he'd been younger, when regret had been keen, there seemed to be so much that he lacked. Children had taken their place in a list, and missing them had seemed less real than missing parents, which after all he had had, and had lost.

But now, Chris thought that if he'd had a son, he'd have wanted him to be like David Robbins, with David's on-guard, expressive eyes, his air of anticipating trouble. Chris was surprised he'd taken in so much about the boy from two brief encounters. He pictured Bobby McGilvrey, not dead after all, but by some miracle still paddling his kayak round the bay. He understood that his fears for Sonya and her brother had their roots in the feeling that he'd failed Bobby, a guilt he expected to carry with him for the rest of his life.

Was it the same for Anthea? Chris reminded himself that Anthea was pregnant, her protectiveness towards her unborn child extending to other children; but he thought she would have been determined to help Sonya anyway.

Underneath the surface of his town, whole new layers of experience and meaning were opening up.

Under the *Royal* there was a basement where the dead had lain in times past, and in very recent times as well.

Under the Mercer Street house, there was perhaps a literal cellar or a basement. There was certainly a metaphoric one, made up of childhood fear and dread and longing to escape, stretching all the way from Ettie Richardson to Sonya Robbins, from the 1870s to the present day.

Chris found somewhere to sit, pulled out his mobile and rang the child protection number. An officer had been assigned and a visit would be arranged. A background check had been done and there was no history of child abuse in Delia Robbins's family. No report had been made concerning Sonya or David before.

Sonya's troubles and what to do about them occupied Chris's conscious thinking for the rest of the day, but that night, alone in bed, a picture of Hardy and Sarah Kent in the basement of the *Royal* returned to him.

He got up, fetched his phone and googled erotic asphyxiation.

He reminded himself that Sarah might not have intended to harm Gerard Hardy, but that harm might have resulted from an agreement they had made. All that had been necessary was for Sarah to go along with Hardy in the piece of bizarre theatre he proposed, to be present as accomplice and as witness, to tighten the ligature so that Hardy experienced at the same time the ecstasy of communion with his dead heroine and sexual release.

The Wikipedia article started with a list of names: erotic asphyxiation was also called asphyxiophilia, hypoxyphilia or breath control play. Put simply, it was the intentional restriction of oxygen to the brain for the purposes of sexual arousal. The term autoerotic asphyxiation was used when the act was done by a person to him or herself. A person engaging in the activity was sometimes called a gasper.

Hardy gasping while Sarah looked on and tightened the cord? This was the point where Chris's imagination failed him. Even if Hardy had managed to talk her into going down to the basement, and had given her a general idea of what he had in mind, Sarah would have stopped before he died. But then there were the hands in prayer position, which could be read either as a form of mockery, a cruel last flourish, or, just possibly, as a way of saying sorry.

TWENTY-SIX

Superintendent Ashworth passed three typed pages across his desk, saying, 'I'm disappointed in you, Blackie.'

Chris's eyes blurred and from that blur single words and phrases leapt at him. 'Insubordinate', 'pig-headed', 'dogmatic', 'unable to follow instructions', 'false pride'.

Inspector Masterson's signature was a gigantic flourish at the end.

Chris wondered if Ashworth had already made up his mind and the interview was no more than a formality. He wondered if his letter of resignation was sitting on the superintendent's desk. That would make it easier. All that would be required of him was his name.

'I admit to having gone my own way at times, but Constable Merritt has always followed Inspector Masterson's instructions. I'd like that on record, please.'

Ashworth looked grim. 'What about the tarot cards? Were they your idea?'

Chris took the plunge and began explaining about the reading Mrs Marr had done for Gerard Hardy, the missing laptop, the book that had turned up in Charles Nevis's flat. He spoke of Delia Robbins and the house she lived in, how he believed she was lying about having met the deceased, the voice Bridget had heard, the running figures in the street.

Ashworth listened without interrupting, then he said, 'So you don't think the Kent girl did it?'

'There are too many' – Chris was about to say 'phenomena', then thought better of it – 'too many facts that don't fit. And DC Ferrier – he expresses what I would call fundamentalist religious beliefs.'

'Ferrier has to do what he's told. The same goes for you. DI Masterson's in charge.' Ashworth raised his eyes and there was a different kind of light in them, a gleam that came and went. 'Be careful,' he said.

'Yes, Sir. Yes, of course.'

Chris left the superintendent's office feeling he'd been given a reprieve. He told himself that he must hang on for Anthea's sake, if not his own. Another thought followed quickly from this one. Masterson was incapable of finding out who had killed Gerard Hardy. He lacked the patience and the skill. The fact that Nevis had stolen Hardy's book was important; but instead of working logically through the evidence and what it meant, Masterson had made his jealousy of Thomas apparent and the sergeant had left.

Chris put a match to the combustion stove, sat at his kitchen table, and proceeded to make a list. It felt right to use a pencil; he imagined taking to his list with a rubber fairly soon.

He wouldn't be expected to show up at the station, since it was already after six.

He phoned Anthea to tell her the interview had gone better than expected.

When she asked for details, he said they'd talk about it when he saw her.

'Do you want to come round for a bite to eat?'

'I'm tired. I think I'll have an early night. Did Ashworth ask about the tarot cards?'

'I kind of side-stepped.'

'Side-stepped?'

'I don't know what to make of it, really. I mean Ashworth said the usual things about obeying orders, but there's something else going on. Maybe he's got his own issues with Masterson.'

'Who wouldn't?' Anthea said dryly.

Chris told her to take care and that he'd see her tomorrow.

He folded his list and put it in his pocket, then stared

at the wall, thinking of spirits, who believed in them and who didn't. He'd never felt his mother's presence after she was gone. Memories, yes, but nothing you could call a ghost.

Suddenly he felt beset by doubts, recalling Sarah's expression at the fort, how he'd caught a calculating glimmer in her eye. Just when you thought you'd reached the bottom of an opinion or an idea, you found that there was room for falling lower.

Time was, and not so long ago, when Chris would have argued for the importance of maintaining a clear hierarchy and obeying orders. But that time seemed to belong to a different person, another set of circumstances. He was no longer that person and couldn't behave as though he was. It wasn't just that he mistrusted Masterson as an individual. Those belonging to the lower ranks often despised and mistrusted their bosses; there was nothing new in that.

The police force had seen fit to retain him, when they could have nudged him out. He'd even been praised for his role in bringing Bobby McGilvrey's murderer to justice. The killer had pleaded guilty, so there'd been no trial. But words of praise had been spoken, by the assistant commissioner no less.

Chris put more wood on the fire and decided on a short walk to give himself an appetite. There was some soup he could heat up, or, if he felt like it, he could make a quick fried rice.

He was worried about Anthea, but didn't want to pester her by going round there. He realised that his assistant was irreplaceable. It was strange that the understanding should come to him just then, and in just that way.

The autumn twilight calmed him. He realised how tense he'd been, working himself up to the interview with Ashworth, telling himself he needed to prepare for the worst, but unable to do this in any sensible way.

He pictured what it must have been like to walk the

empty, silent streets of Queenscliff when Ethel Richardson was a small girl and the town was hunkering down to a long evening.

He raised his head and saw – it was much more than an illusion – a small, black-clad figure hurrying towards him on the opposite side of the street.

'Mary.'

Chris was scarcely aware that he'd spoken aloud. He didn't want to startle the woman, who was walking swiftly, with small, regular steps, her face hidden by a bonnet.

He was shivering and his uniform felt too tight.

He knew that the little lady, scurrying home in the cold, was fearful of what she would find there, already seeing, in her mind's eye, the mess Walter had made, the debacle, the ranting and the never-ending childish complaints; while her real children, two small girls, waited for her, watching through the front window.

She'd found a sanctuary for herself in the post and telegraph office, with kind Mr Dodd who helped her and believed in her, protecting her from the telegraph boys who laughed at her behind her back, mocking the efforts of a woman married to a lunatic, a woman with little formal education thinking she could do a man's job.

Mary's children ran to her, wild-eyed and crying. She soothed them, and then Walter, who cried at night like a hungry baby. And when they were all asleep at last, Mary lay exhausted and wakeful, wracked by doubts as to whether she was doing the right thing, leaving Walter with the girls all day while she struggled to learn Morse code.

Chris's heart went out to the figure moving swiftly in the dusk. She had brought the girls through it. The three of them had survived. He wanted to cross the street and put his arm around her, tell her it would be okay. He would explain that he was visitor from the future and he knew what she didn't, what she still had to learn.

Sarah would believe him if he said he'd seen the ghost of Mary Richardson. Would he use the word ghost? It was a dangerous word.

Sarah would smile that sad smile of hers, acknowledging a kinship, making him feel sorry for her, drawing him in.

Who had Gerard Hardy seen? What visions had he entertained?

Chris thought the answer to that was simple enough. He had seen Henry Handel, the famous author, the adult whom the child became.

Murder was paltry and pathetic, tawdry, an admission of failure. That body in the basement with its frozen hands belonged on a B-grade movie set. B-grade was too good for it, Chris thought crossly, turning his back on self-pity, resolving to do better tomorrow.

TWENTY-SEVEN

'Well, all I can say is, I'm glad it wasn't me who found him,' Minnie Lancaster declared.

Minnie was sitting at Chris's scrubbed kitchen table with a glass of Yellow Tail Shiraz in front of her, while Chris chopped vegetables for a stir-fry. When Minnie had rung, he'd said yes without thinking, feeling his heart lift at the thought of her company. Now she was there, he knew she sensed his ambivalence.

'Things are pretty quiet, then, at the *Brewhouse*?'

Minnie took a sip of wine and laughed. 'Trust you to change the subject.'

She stood up and walked across to the bench, where she uncovered the salad which was her contribution to their meal.

Every week or so they'd been in the habit of eating together like this. It wasn't a date, and there were no formalities, or none that these two single, middle-aged people would admit to.

Minnie said she was too sick of the sight and smell of food at the end of a day's work to be bothered preparing dinner for herself. She took home leftovers and made do with them, as she'd done for years, apart from the evenings when she walked the length of two streets and crossed a small park to arrive at Chris's cottage.

Minnie knew how to laugh him out of the doldrums without laughing at him. Minnie never laughed at anybody; that was her great gift.

He wanted to tell Minnie about his interview with Superintendent Ashworth, ask her what she thought. He wanted to talk about Mary Richardson, but his vision was too recent and too personal. Minnie wouldn't laugh, he knew that; but still he couldn't bear even the possibility that she might misunderstand.

Was this how Sarah Kent felt?

Minnie lived in what had been a fisherman's cottage too, close to the harbour and the bridge that led to Swan Island with its golf course and secret training base. But Minnie's house hadn't been 'done up'. Chris thought that 'done down' was a better way to describe the work that had gone into restoring his home, stripping it back to its original form, or as close to this as was consistent with the modern comforts he saw no reason to live without.

They served themselves, speaking about who'd worked at the *Royal* before the change of ownership. There'd been a big staff 'in the old days', dwindling in recent years. Minnie had been acquainted with only one of the waitresses, a girl called Carol Alveretti. She'd heard that Carol had got a job at Harvey Norman in Geelong.

Minnie knew Bridget to say hello to, but she'd never met Matthew, Sarah or Manoli. Chris wondered if this was significant. It generally didn't take Minnie more than a couple of weeks to make the acquaintance of new staff at the town's hotels and restaurants.

Sometimes Chris made dessert; tonight there was only fresh fruit. He had some good chocolate, which he might offer with coffee later; that is, if Minnie stayed for coffee. Sometimes he walked her home after dinner; sometimes they watched a DVD together.

Their shared evening was normally planned to fit in with Minnie's shifts. They'd tried 'going out', to a movie or a concert in Geelong, and still did this from time to time. By mutual consent, and without need for discussion, they adapted to each other's ways. On the whole, they preferred the quiet companionship of sharing a meal to having to get into a car and drive for half an hour, having to cope with noise and other people.

But tonight they weren't easy in one another's company. Chris couldn't tell what Minnie was feeling about him, whether she was regretting having called.

Minnie said, 'That trip you went on, what was that about?'

'To Egypt, you mean?' It seemed to Chris a long time since he'd thought about it.

'You meant to get to Europe.'

'Would you like to travel overseas?'

'I've never really thought about it.'

'What if you did think about it?'

'Now?'

'Well, some time.'

'I wouldn't give up my job.'

'No. Of course not. I'd never ask you to do that.'

'I'd come back here, but what would you be coming back to?'

There it was, the opening he'd been avoiding. 'I don't know,' Chris said.

'You're scared of losing your job, aren't you?'

'I'm too young to retire and there's nothing else I'm fit for.'

Minnie watched him shrewdly, head on one side, the kitchen light catching the red in her hair. Chris was aware of his resolve not to give in to self-pity and aware, too, that it was evaporating fast.

'You haven't worked out where to draw the line,' she said.

'There's Anthea, you see.'

'Who can look after herself, I would've thought.'

'It's complicated.'

Chris opened his mouth to offer some kind of explanation, but Minnie spoke before he could.

'Closing the station – it's been coming for a long time.'

'Tom Maloney and his jokes.'

'Your jokes too,' she reminded him.

'What you said just now Min, about drawing a line. Would you let the wrong person be arrested for a crime?'

'I'm not a policeman. I mean woman.'

'But would you?'

'I don't think so.'

Chris was recalling Olly's arrest for Bobby's murder and wondering whether Minnie was as well. He'd been powerless to stop it happening, or that's what he'd told himself at the time.

If he gave in to the temptation to unburden himself, Minnie would listen without interrupting. She would let him know, by the expression in her eyes, the sudden drop of curls shadowing one cheek, that she respected his judgment, though it might take him to unlikely places.

It was what she'd come for. Minnie knew that his experience with the CIU had been a good deal less than enjoyable. She would listen intelligently if he complained about Masterson; he could count on her for that. But he was afraid that once he started he wouldn't be able to stop.

The woman Chris walked home after they'd washed up together was a guarded friend, a friend who understood that the gap between them had widened, though she'd meant to make it less.

She'd given him opportunities and he'd deflected them. Perhaps she'd needed to satisfy herself about something by seeing him that evening. Some flaw in his character? A confirmation that she hadn't wanted but would now accept? Well, it was too late to do anything about that tonight.

Chris was half way to Geelong next morning before he pulled in to the emergency lane and phoned Anthea to tell her what he was about to do. He recalled Ashworth's warning to be careful. Well, he would be. He would proceed with caution, but he would proceed.

Re-starting the engine, Chris indulged in a brief, sweet picture of Minnie opening up the *Brewhouse* doors, letting out the fug of late-night drinking. He knew she liked the early shift, liked to sit over a coffee and a crossword at reception, though, it being the school holidays, there were families to book in and out.

Carol Alveretti offered Chris her name with a half-fearful glance at his uniform and outstretched hand. It was second nature to Chris to offer his hand to people when introducing himself, but it occurred to him that lately it had been more often rejected than accepted.

Carol told him that her boss was strict and she could only spare ten minutes. They walked to a lane at the back of the arcade where she worked, on one side of them an empty landing bay. Chris sensed that Carol needed privacy, or at least the illusion of it.

It was cold and Carol, who'd left the heated shopping centre without stopping to put on a coat, began to shiver.

When Chris showed her a photograph of Gerard Hardy, she said curtly, raising suspicious eyes, 'Yes, I've seen him.'

Chris took out his notebook and wrote down dates and times.

If Hardy had stayed at the *Royal* before, why hadn't Matthew or Sarah, Bridget or Manoli said something? It was before their time, he reminded himself. The hotel's old records might have been destroyed.

Why hadn't Charles Nevis mentioned it? Had Hardy kept his previous visit a secret from his friend, or had Nevis known about it and chosen to keep the knowledge to himself?

What about Mrs Marr?

Carol had no idea where the former manager or any of

the *Royal's* previous employees had gone; she'd left before the sale, having decided that it was better to find another job as soon as she could, rather than to wait and see. She had no idea what had happened to the old booking and registration records.

She'd not been aware of visitors to Hardy's room, but of course she could not be sure. She'd never said anything more than 'hello' or 'good morning' to him.

When Chris asked why she hadn't contacted the police, Carol looked surprised and said, 'It was over a year ago.'

Chris thought this reply disingenuous.

Carol couldn't recall exactly how long Hardy had stayed at the *Royal*; she thought it was a few days.

When Chris asked if the basement had been kept locked, she nodded. 'It was a junk heap. It wasn't safe down there.'

'Where were the keys kept?'

'At reception. All the keys were, the internal ones that is.'

'Did you ever go down to the basement?'

'No.'

'What room was Mr Hardy in?'

'It was on the first floor. That's all I remember.'

Chris showed Carol photographs of Sarah and Manoli, Matthew and Charles Nevis. When he came to Mrs Marr, Carol said, 'I've seen her.'

'With Gerard Hardy?'

'No. I served her coffee one day, in the courtyard. I remember because someone said that she told fortunes.'

'Who was that?'

Carol screwed up her face, trying to recall.

Had Hardy been a client of Mrs Marr's for over a year? If so, why had he lied about it? Why had she? A year ago, Mrs Marr hadn't been working in Queenscliff. Where had she been before Torquay? Chris felt annoyed with himself for not having found this out.

Could Mrs Marr have booked a room? Had she been staying at the *Royal* as well?

Carol said no, not while she was there. After announcing that she had to go, she disappeared into the shadows at the far end of the loading bay.

Chris watched her departing figure with a feeling of alarm. How much had been going on at the *Royal* that neither he nor any of the detectives had a clue about?

His uniform felt tight again, as though, in a fit of absent-mindedness, he'd shrunk it by washing it in hot water. Carol was young, though anxiety had scored and lined her face. Chris felt a renewal of respect for the way Lily Watkins had stuck to her story, refusing to be pushed into elaborating, or imagining more than she had seen. In some ways, Carol reminded him of Lily, not that they were anything alike to look at.

Chris was keen to get away from the lane, aware that anybody walking past and looking in would wonder what a policeman was doing hanging round the back of the shopping mall.

On the highway, Carol's words returned, in all their clarity, their lack of ambiguity.

Instead of returning to Queenscliff, he turned left and took the road to St Leonards.

'Did you ever see Mr Hardy at the *Royal*?'

'I wasn't working that Thursday,' Bridget said scornfully.

'Gerard Hardy stayed at the hotel last year.'

'Who told you that?'

'Did you see or speak to Mr Hardy during his previous visit to Queenscliff?'

'Of course not!'

It was all very well for Bridget to sneer, but she was clearly worried by the question.

'Why did you take a job at the *Royal*?'

'Because of Mum. You think it's easy to get work down here?'

'What were you and Manoli arguing about the night you were serving at the bar?'

'Stop trying to trap me! Manoli wasn't there!'

Now I know you're lying, and you know I know, Chris thought.

Bridget flashed him a look full of hate, but then some resistance in her crumpled. 'We weren't arguing,' she said in a different voice. 'We were talking. We're all under suspicion. Do you expect us not to talk? And isn't there some regulation about police not listening in secret? You'll be telling me you taped our conversation next.'

Chris said, 'Has it occurred to you that if you were arguing loudly enough for me to hear, then others heard you too?'

'What others? Oh, that weasely little man. Did you order him to spy on me?'

For a moment, Chris thought she meant Ferrier, then he understood.

'You must have wondered why Charles Nevis stayed on at the hotel. Did you ask him that?'

'He said he wanted to observe.'

'Observe? That was his word?'

'Yes.'

'You suspected Nevis of taking Hardy's book and you challenged him about it.'

'Why would I do that?'

'Because you wanted to turn suspicion away from Manoli. You and Manoli argued over Sarah. You wanted him to tell Inspector Masterson that she'd taken the wine.'

'He was always fussing over her, always fetching her from the basement, mollycoddling her.'

'Mollycoddling?'

'Bloody hell! Do I have to spell everything out? Sarah and her ghosts! Sarah and her troubles! Oh, she's so vulnerable, oh, we must look after her!'

Small wonder that Bridget had been jealous of Sarah's prettiness and grace, and of Matthew's obvious devotion to her.

'You sought out Charles Nevis and you asked him about Hardy's book,' Chris repeated.

'Charles sought me out. He wanted to know what I thought of them all.'

'Nevis told Inspector Masterson he hinted to you that he'd taken the book.'

'Why would he do that?'

To make mischief, Chris thought but didn't say.

Bridget was shrewd, he decided, shrewder than he'd given her credit for. He'd been fooled by her marsupial cheeks and expression of boorish discontent. He ought to have known better.

'What did Inspector Masterson accuse you of, you and Manoli?'

'Adultery. Can you believe that? Manoli's been separated from his wife for years. He wants a divorce – he's bloody begged her – and you know what? In the inspector's eyes it's still adultery and I'm to blame for tempting him and leading him to sin.'

'Did you ever see Mrs Marr and Gerard Hardy together?' Chris asked.

'No,' Bridget said. 'I want you to leave now.'

TWENTY-EIGHT

When Chris handed Masterson a report detailing his meeting with Carol Alveretti and what she'd told him, Masterson lifted his eyes from the printed sheets. There was a remote, opaque expression in them.

Chris felt the ground shifting. He had no doubt that the inspector was disappointed Superintendent Ashworth hadn't been harder on him. He was aware of a fraying tightrope underneath his feet. But then he told himself he'd been walking a tightrope for some time. All he had to do was keep putting one foot in front of the other and avoid looking down.

Masterson was watching him, not with respect, certainly not with liking, but with a degree of reluctant acceptance.

'Give me the gist of it, Blackie.'

The gist was, Chris said, that a former employee of the *Royal* remembered Gerard Hardy having stayed there over a year ago. This same employee had seen Mrs Marr as well, not as a hotel guest, but in the courtyard café.

'So the psychic lied about not having met Hardy before last Thursday?'

'It seems that way,' Chris said.

'I'll have to see her again. Ring and let her know.'

Chris was turning to go when Masterson said suddenly, 'You don't have any children do you?'

'No.'

'Never had any?'

As though I might have forgotten, Chris thought.

'Sharper than a serpent's tooth – ' Masterson's voice faltered then recovered. 'We have one child only. A girl. My wife was unable to conceive again. Melanie was such a happy child, happy in her faith, secure in the love of Jesus Christ.'

Chris could guess what was coming. Perfect Melanie had grown into an adolescent and rebelled.

'It's five years since my wife and I have heard from our daughter. Can you imagine what that does to a man?'

Chris couldn't. 'I'm sorry,' he said.

Chris made an appointment with Mrs Marr for that afternoon. He and Anthea began going through the *Royal's* old paper records. Matthew had raised no objection when Chris asked for them.

Only one former employee, apart from Carol, admitted to having recognised Hardy from the media coverage of the murder.

She sounded guilty for not having come forward and insisted she had nothing to tell them, except that Hardy had taken his meals alone in the dining-room and had not attempted to engage her in conversation.

She did not recognise Mrs Marr from Chris's description, and answered his questions with a wariness bordering on fear.

In some ways it was like the DI's first interview with Mrs Marr, in others not at all. Mrs Marr had raised no objection when Chris rang to arrange a time; in fact she'd sounded pleased. Chris had hidden his surprise when Masterson had asked him to be present at the interview, wondering if he should feel flattered that the inspector had chosen him over either Ferrier or Sanders.

Mrs Marr seemed larger than life, opening her front door and asking if they'd like something to drink. She led the way to the room where she gave her tarot readings.

Once there, she removed her jacket and asked them to take a seat. Her pale blue shirt stood out in contrast to the cushions and wall hangings.

The tea she'd made them was a herbal mixture; to Chris, it tasted like decomposing grass.

The curtains were half drawn, the room warm and dim. There was no sitar music playing, and no smell that was similar to incense. Mrs Marr switched on the table lamp.

The inspector leant back in his chair. 'Did you know Mr Hardy stayed in Queenscliff a year ago?' he asked.

Mrs Marr folded her hands in her lap. 'I wasn't here then,' she replied with an edge to her voice.

'A former employee at the *Royal* remembers you calling in there for a coffee.'

'There's no law against it.'

'Why didn't you tell me before?'

'Because you didn't ask me.'

The inspector frowned. Chris noticed that, although Mrs Marr had poured tea for herself, she hadn't drunk any. He cleared his throat and wondered how long it might be before the decomposing grass took effect.

'When did Mr Hardy first get in touch with you?'

'He wrote to me at the end of February. You have the letter.'

'Before that.'

'That was the first time,' Mrs Marr said evenly.

'Did Mr Hardy tell you how he intended spending Thursday evening?'

'No. I think I can help you if only you would keep an open mind.'

There was a long pause before Masterson said, 'Go ahead, then.'

'When Mr Hardy came in here, he was wound up like a spring. He put that book of his down on the table.' The psychic raised her hand. 'Slapped it down like that. He made me look at the signature. You'd think it had belonged to the Dalai Lama himself.'

'What happened then?'

'I held his hand, like this.'

Mrs Marr stretched out her hand and took Inspector Masterson's. He started, but didn't pull his hand away.

'I told Mr Hardy to close his eyes. I closed mine too.'

She did so now. Chris noticed how much softer the psychic looked without those brown calculating points of light.

'I'm climbing under a fence,' she said. 'A low fence, with barbed wire on the top. On the other side there's a kind of tunnel made by bushes. There's light at the end, a green, glowing light. I'm moving through the tunnel and it's guiding me. My spirit guide. I'm seeing a refuge up ahead. I'm making my way towards it.'

Mrs Marr opened her eyes and looked directly into Masterson's.

'What refuge?' he asked.

When the psychic didn't reply he said, 'Could it be the basement of the *Royal*?'

'Hardly a refuge, Inspector.'

'But Mr Hardy may have seen it that way. A refuge or an invitation.'

Mrs Marr's tone of voice was dismissive. 'He was coming back here. He was looking forward to it. Though Mr Hardy received a warning from the cards that there was a risk in attempting to communicate with the spirit world, he was also reassured.'

'That he was in good hands, your hands?'

Masterson looked down. His hand and the spirit medium's were still joined, his own huge, Mrs Marr's tiny by comparison.

He pulled away, frowning and shaking his head. In the lamp light his face was red with confusion and discomfort.

Mrs Marr's smile was satisfied, bordering on triumphant. When Masterson spoke again, he had his voice under control.

'How did you meet Sarah Kent?'

'Most people come to me for counselling of one sort or another. I read the cards for them and help them think their way out of a knotty corner.'

'Is that what you did for Sarah Kent?'

'Sarah is a very special person.'

'In what way?'

'She's been mocked and hounded since she was a child for gifts she should be proud of.'

'But you agree that she's mentally unstable.'

'No more than you or I, Inspector.'

'That scream you put on for us – '

'Put on?'

'It was your recorded voice.'

'Neither you nor Constable Blackie found a recording device.'

Chris wanted to say that if it had been left up to him, he would have gone on looking till he had found it.

Masterson looked as though he wished he hadn't brought up the scream. 'Did you like Gerard Hardy?' he asked.

'It's not up to me to like or dislike a client. I thought I'd made that clear. And even if I happened to take a dislike to someone, I wouldn't respond by strangling them.' Mrs Marr paused, then added, 'Mr Hardy was very single-minded. Any questions that did not relate directly to his wish, he ignored.'

'So you did try and get him to talk about himself.'

'A little. At the start.'

'Did Mr Hardy tell you he was romantically involved with someone?'

'No.'

'No, Mr Hardy didn't mention it, or no, you asked him and he answered in the negative?'

'I didn't ask him and he didn't tell me.'

Chris consoled himself with the thought that, if Mrs Marr wanted to poison the police, she wouldn't choose her own house to do it in.

'After you'd calmed Mr Hardy down with that vision of the green tunnel, what happened then?'

'Then we did the reading.'

'Do it again, please.'

The psychic reached for her cards. Before she began to lay them out, she moved the lamp so that it was shining directly downwards.

Chris knew the original spread by heart. All of the cards were the same this time, except for one important difference.

TWENTY-NINE

'Have we got time to go to your place?' Chris asked Anthea. 'Your cards are there, aren't they?' he added, lowering his voice. 'I want you to show me something.'

Anthea nodded. 'Will we walk?'

'I'd like to. I need to unwind.'

The two constables set off. It was a while before either of them spoke again. Both had their jackets buttoned tightly round their necks. Once they reached the top of the hill, the full force of the south-westerly hit them.

Anthea lowered her head in a practised way. Chris could remember a time when she would have grumbled, making the weather part of her threnody. He knew that, were he to remind her now, she would be embarrassed and offended.

He said as they turned a corner, 'Mrs Marr got the better of Masterson again.'

Anthea raised her head inquiringly.

Chris explained about the addition of the Lovers card. 'Masterson didn't remember. And he didn't ask to see the original spread.'

'And you didn't tell him.'

'I should have. Something held me back.'

'You didn't want to make him angry.'

'He told me that his daughter ran away from home five years ago. They – the DI and his wife – haven't heard from her since.'

Anthea was silent for a long time, then she said, 'That might explain a lot.'

'I think so.'

'I wonder why Sanders didn't tell us.'

'Maybe he thought that we already knew.'

Anthea made ordinary tea. She laughed when Chris described the herbal mixture. 'Cheers,' she said, setting Chris's mug in front of him.

Chris cradled the mug in his hands. He thought he would like to sit there for the rest of the day with something warm to drink.

'What will Masterson do now?'

'I don't know.'

Chris recalled the moment when the inspector had seemed to understand that Mrs Marr was laughing at him, a moment when he might have lost his temper, but held himself in check.

Anthea got out her cards and reproduced the spread.

The extra card stood out like a lighthouse, a warning to passing ships.

'What does it mean?' he asked.

'A complication. Love usually is.'

Chris asked what the position of the Lovers meant. He knew enough about the tarot now to understand that the relationship between the cards was almost as important as the cards themselves.

Anthea did not reply immediately. She sat staring at the colours and the shapes. The couple at the centre of the Lovers card did not look at all erotic to Chris, though a pointed mountain behind them was suggestive.

Directly behind the naked woman was an apple tree with a snake coiled round its trunk; behind the man – Adam, Chris supposed – another kind of tree, taller, with flowers that might also be flames. God looked down on the pair and blessed them – a svelte, New Age kind of God.

'The Three of Swords is the adultery card when it appears in the same spread with the Lovers,' Anthea explained.

'Hardy was having an affair with a married woman?'

'That's what adultery usually means.'

'Delia Robbins? But she and Justin are divorced.'

'What about Bridget and Manoli? His wife won't give him a divorce.'

'So it's technically adultery.' Chris sighed. 'The only thing I'm sure of is that Mrs Marr wants to keep us guessing.'

He wondered what the medium was doing now. Was she sitting in her cave, with her shawl across the chair back, arms stretched out on the table and her cards in front of her? What was she thinking? What questions was she asking?

Perhaps she was doing something more prosaic, talking on the phone, recounting her interview with the law enforcement, sharing a joke about how slow they were. Would whoever was listening offer advice or instructions?

The scenario had its appeal, but somehow Chris couldn't see Mrs Marr confiding in another person, another human being in that way.

He had a headache, and felt cold right through his bones. He recalled the herbal tea and shuddered.

He thought of the saying: take the bull by the horns. Was there a bull in the tarot pack? He rather liked picturing Mrs Marr as a bull. The waving hair around her temples just needed a small extension in order to produce fiery horns.

'Can I have a look?'

Anthea handed Chris the cards and he shuffled through them till he found the one he wanted.

The World had a bull's head in the bottom left hand corner; in the other three corners were a handsome young man, an eagle's and a lion's head. In the centre was a beautiful young woman. The World was an optimistic card, promising success, but also flight and change of place.

'The designs are different on different packs,' Anthea said, pushing her mug away with a deprecating movement of her shoulders to indicate that the point she was making was an obvious one.

'According to what I've read, references to the tarot

date from the fourteenth century. 1377 is the first one I've come across. But I don't think the cards were used to make predictions then. They were hand-drawn or hand-painted naturally, and naturally too, only for the wealthy. Mine are known as the Rider deck.'

Anthea looked up from the World card to Chris.

'They're by a young woman, an American called Pamela Coleman Smith, who was an illustrator and theatrical designer. She worked with W.B. Yeats on stage designs and also brought out her own magazine, *The Green Sheaf*.'

Chris nodded, not wanting to appear impatient with these details, but unable to see their relevance. 'I think it's a fair bet that our killer knows this one – Rider, you said?'

'Rider-Waite. But they ought to be called after Pamela Smith.'

'Maybe she should have used a man's name.'

Anthea's smile was sardonic. 'They're very common. Popular. I've looked up other ones on the net. Some Four of Swords don't have a knight lying on a tomb at all. Smith and Arthur Waite were contemporaries of Ethel Richardson,' she continued. 'Waite was a scholar of the occult who published *The Key to the Tarot* in England in 1910. I wonder if she met them.'

'Gerard Hardy would have known.'

'If you spent enough time looking you could track it down. We know that Ethel Richardson liked being Henry Handel. She liked having a mask to hide behind.'

'And Pamela Smith?'

'I feel the key is there somewhere, in the identities women create for themselves and their pride in those identities.'

Chris reminded himself that Ethel Richardson had been a small, frightened girl when she'd played with her sister in the garden of her home. She'd been ignorant of the identity she was to grow into, the mantle of authorship which went far beyond the adoption of a pseudonym.

'Rider was a publishing company,' Anthea was saying. 'Now they're an imprint of Random House. They published books about the occult in the early twentieth century. They published horror stories such as Bram Stoker's *Dracula* as well.'

She paused and gave Chris a speculative glance. 'I wonder if Ethel met W.B. Yeats? I read somewhere that she admired his poetry. They had at least two interests in common.'

'What's the second one?'

'Literature.'

Anthea began creating a large cross with the cards.

She looked up and smiled. 'I tell you what's ironic. I got into trouble for buying my own tarot pack, and now Mrs Marr's using the tarot to bamboozle the inspector. I'm the only one who's done her homework and knows what the cards mean.'

Chris nodded and was about to say something when his phone rang. It was Edwina Miles telling him that Bridget McGuire had called on Mrs Marr.

When Chris asked if Bridget had come for a tarot session, Edwina said, 'You asked me to keep an eye on who came here. I'm not a mind reader.'

Chris thanked her and asked her to note how long Bridget stayed.

THIRTY

That evening, Chris was called to a house fire in Stevens Street.

The house was old and the kitchen looked as though nothing had been done to modernise it since the 1920s. The stove had caught fire. Mr Dubowski, who was in his 70s and whose sight was poor, hadn't been able to put it out, and it had spread to the curtains before he gathered his cat into his arms and ran outside. His next door neighbour had phoned the fire and police stations.

The kitchen was a write-off, but the rest of the cottage salvageable. Chris hoped the old man was properly insured. There was no reason to suspect foul play.

Once he'd taken statements, he knew that his presence wasn't required at Stevens Street any longer, but he lingered. It was a relief to have something simple and straightforward to deal with.

As soon as he lay down to sleep, Chris saw the Lovers card in front of his eyes, static and yet moving. He opened his eyes wide, then blinked them shut, but was unable to get rid of it. The lovers moved towards one another in the darkness of his bedroom. Chris was both inside the scene and out of it, as is the way with dreams. Yet he was not asleep. The Adam and Eve banality of it annoyed his wakeful mind.

After his mother died – he had not felt he was able to do this while she was alive – he'd had thick, heavy dark blue curtains made, and pulled them tight, on summer nights as well as winter ones.

Finally falling towards sleep, Chris acknowledged that he preferred the cooler months – not just because the summer was hectic, crowded – but because the small, cosy fortress that he'd made of his cottage was appropriate for the closing in of days.

All night long, when Chris woke, which he did frequently, he saw the Lovers and the Devil superimposed on his bedroom ceiling.

'We've come to see Sonya and David,' Chris said when Delia Robbins opened the door.

'They're not here. I know you've been snooping around behind my back.'

Anthea placed her foot firmly in the door. 'Where are the children, Mrs Robbins?'

'Visiting,' said Delia, glaring at her.

'Can we come inside?'

'No you can't! You can't just turn up here without a warrant. I do have some rights!'

'Mrs Marr offered to help you get Justin back,' Chris said.

Delia laughed, a vicious sound that made the hairs stand up on his forearms.

'It was Gerard Hardy's idea, wasn't it?'

'I didn't kill him and I don't know who did.'

When Anthea asked, 'What now?' Chris said, 'Let's try Delia's sister.'

'She might hide the children. Delia might ring to warn her.'

'She can't know that's where we're heading.'

'No, but it's a logical guess.'

The two constables had begun walking towards Chris's car. Anthea glanced over her shoulder towards Mercer Street.

'What if they're in there and their mother's lying?'

'Then we'll come back,' Chris said.

He sat in the driver's seat and phoned the child protection unit. He was put through to the relevant officer, whose visit had gone much as Chris had feared it would. When the officer had spoken to Sonya on her own, the girl said she'd fallen down the back steps.

Chris said he and Anthea were on their way to Delia's sister's farm. He thought she might have sent the children there. He would phone again after they'd had a look around.

He estimated that the drive would take about an hour. Once through Geelong, on the long highway that led all the way to Hamilton and what had once been the great sheep stations of the western district, Anthea leant back and closed her eyes.

She woke up as they pulled in through the driveway.

Chris knocked on the front door, taking in the open space around the farmhouse, realising the impossibility of approaching without being seen.

The children stood together just behind their aunt, David a quarter of a step in front.

Chris introduced himself and Anthea, scrutinising Sonya's face.

Cheryl smiled coldly to let him know that their visit was unwelcome. Her greying hair was pulled back from her forehead and tied at the back of her neck. Her light blue eyes gave nothing away.

Perhaps Delia and Cheryl had agreed that it would be better if her niece and nephew did appear, better if they were seen to be behaving normally.

The living-room was spacious, airy, warmed by north-facing windows all along one wall. The children stood in silence by the door. Sonya kept her eyes down. Chris noted that she stayed out of the direct light. David moved towards her and took hold of her hand.

When asked about employees, Cheryl explained that she grew canola and kept a few sheep.

'I hire help when I need it.'

'You have another job?'

'Oh, no,' Cheryl answered, as though the idea of having to earn her living had never occurred to her. She'd lived alone since her divorce.

'How long ago is that?'

'Five years and two months.'

'And your husband, where is he?'

Cheryl looked as though she was going to object to the question, then she said, 'Ex-husband. In Tasmania.'

They looked into the children's rooms, which were small and neat. The narrow single beds were made. The windows could be dead-locked and there were locks on all the doors.

Brother and sister had remained in the living-room. Chris wanted to ask them how they were, but he knew he couldn't do so in front of their aunt.

'Your sister stayed with you on Thursday the 16th, is that right?'

Cheryl nodded.

'Is that a regular occurrence?'

'What are all these questions in aid of?'

'Background to a murder inquiry,' Anthea said.

When they returned to the front of the house, Chris asked if they could see around the farm. He thought Cheryl was going to refuse, but she hesitated then favoured him with a brief nod.

A warning light in David's eyes told Chris that he and Sonya did not want to go with them and that he shouldn't ask. He suspected that the sheds and paddocks would have nothing to tell him, not with their aunt as his guide. But the itch was back, in his armpits and around his neck, the feeling that his uniform was too tight.

Cheryl led the way. She seemed to have grown physically taller, her grey-brown hair like a cone held up by the wind.

The shed that housed the generator – powered by wind

and solar, Cheryl told them proudly – seemed enormous, like a small aeroplane hangar. Chris wondered if it had other uses.

Anthea said, 'You've got a good supply of tank water.'

Cheryl nodded, flashing Anthea a quick, assessing look.

'Do they ever run dry?'

'The summer I first came here. I only had two then.'

'What's that over there?' Chris asked.

On the far side of an electric fence were two highland cattle, with horns that looked to Chris to be at least a metre across.

Cheryl smiled. 'A birthday present.'

'From your sister?'

'Yes.'

The cattle were of a piece with that aeroplane hangar of a shed, Chris thought. Everything on the farm looked over-sized. He almost expected Cheryl to shoot up like Alice after she'd eaten the mushroom.

Close up, he observed that the cattle were young, and curious.

He said, 'I'm sure your sister told you about the visit from the child protection officer. What I'm less certain of is your opinion of your niece. Do you care about her?'

'Of course I care about her! I have no children of my own. David and Sonya and their mother are all the family I have.'

'But you've chosen to side with Delia,' Anthea said.

'The children are fine! There's no law against them spending a few days on my farm.'

Cheryl turned round swiftly and began walking towards the house.

Anthea caught her up to ask, 'What do you think of Mrs Marr?'

Cheryl kept walking, snapping over her shoulder, 'Who?'

'Mrs Marr has a house in Bridge Street, Queenscliff. She gives tarot readings.'

'Why should I think anything of a woman whom I've never met?'

'Did Mrs Marr suggest that she read the cards for your sister?'

'Why would she do that?'

'Were Gerard Hardy and your sister lovers?'

'Don't be ridiculous! I never met the poor man and neither did Delia.'

Sonya and David stood on the veranda steps, watching them drive off. Chris silently praised their courage. He feared he'd made things worse for them by turning up. He would have to work out a way to question them away from their mother and their aunt, and cursed himself for not making more of his chance when he'd found them alone at the Mercer Street house.

He turned and looked back. The cattle were standing with their heads raised, still as statues.

Delia was impulsive, rash and unpredictable. Now he'd met her, Chris guessed that Cheryl was different altogether. Cheryl would keep her cool and concentrate on outmanoeuvring the police.

Chris phoned the child protection officer and reported that the children were staying at their aunt's farm and that Sonya had no new injuries so far as he could tell. The officer spoke about her workload and said she'd schedule another visit, but it would not be in the next few days.

THIRTY-ONE

Chris was passing the hairdresser's in Hobson Street when he stopped at the sight of a familiar face. He stood sun-dazzled in the street, half blinded by the reflections off two car windscreens behind him and an even stronger reflection from what seemed like a head made entirely of aluminium foil.

Chris blinked, then blinked again. It wasn't Minnie under that extraordinary head-dress, though this had been his first impression. He could see better now; the woman having her hair dyed was older, bigger, an imposing figure.

But Minnie was there, in the chair next to the customer who was magnified under a sparkling weight of silver.

Minnie smiled and waved. Chris waved back, feeling awkward, almost like a peeping Tom, though he told himself not to be stupid. He couldn't possibly have known that she was there.

They sat in a warm corner at the back of *The Chandler*. Chris took off his jacket and hung it on his chair, relieved that the annoying itch had left him.

The café was practically empty. A couple in their seventies, who nodded hello to both Chris and Minnie, were the only other customers.

Minnie reached across the table and laid her hand on his, holding her head on one side and studying him gravely. Her hair, not noticeably shorter, caught the slanting light.

'Did I say something?' Chris said. 'Was I talking to myself?'

Minnie shook her head, still solemn.

The waitress came to take their order, not Danielle this time. She spoke to Minnie about the *Brewhouse*, which was quiet except for bikies at the weekends.

When the waitress left, Minnie turned to Chris.

'I've missed you, you silly old coot. When I saw you through the window, I was that glad.'

Chris felt an immense and corresponding gladness. Minnie's hand was lying next to his; she'd moved it while talking to the waitress. He turned his own hand over and grasped it, in some demonstration of – he scarcely knew what.

They drank their coffee, munched fruit buns.

Chris felt starving. He busied himself with knife and butter, saying, 'I'm not fit company, Min.'

'It's not Bobby all over again, is it?'

'No. Well, yes and no. There's two children mixed up in it, you see.'

When Minnie asked if there was anything she could do to help, Chris thanked her warmly.

She finished her coffee and put her cup down carefully.

'I wasn't going to say anything because it seems like breaching a confidence. And my friends, the other waitresses and hotel staff – Louise, she – well, I've known Louise for years.'

It was unlike Minnie to be tongue-tied. Chris knew Louise had lost her daughter to a heroin overdose, though he had no more than a nodding acquaintance with her. Louise's daughter, Cathy, had come home for a while, then gone back to Melbourne. She'd been dead for about a year.

'Lou told me she just wanted to say she's sorry, tell Cath she loves her.' Minnie looked up at Chris with clear, candid eyes. 'She says she never really said goodbye. We're her friends and we stick by her, but it's not enough. Well, about six months ago, Lou heard about this woman who could call up the spirits of the dead. Channelling, it's called.'

Chris nodded.

'Well, the woman called up Cathy's spirit and Lou

spoke to her.'

'What happened then?'

'That's the thing. Lou's still going to this woman, but I don't believe it's good for her. She won't talk to me about it. She knows how I feel.'

'Is the woman's name Evelyn Marr?'

'I don't know. Lou never told me. It could be – well – it could be that Lou and Cathy do communicate with one another, but Lou's unhappy. She isn't getting better. Anyone can see that.'

If Louise had started seeing Mrs Marr six months ago, it must have been before she moved to Queenscliff.

'Be careful with her,' Minnie said.

'I will,' Chris replied. 'I promise.'

Minnie made an effort to lighten the conversation. 'We could do this again. Meet up for afternoon tea.'

'Two old codgers,' Chris said.

Minnie smiled. Her red hair danced. Chris got up quickly to pay the bill, wanting to take her in his arms.

Inspector Masterson had taken Ferrier to interview Sarah Kent again. Sanders was in the front office alone, but he didn't seem to be doing anything in particular.

'Believes he'll wear her down eventually.' The DC shrugged with reference to the inspector's interview.

'What do you think?'

'Someone should be putting the screws on Charles Nevis.'

Chris said he was worried about David and Sonya Robbins. Sonya was too frightened of her mother to tell the child protection officer the truth.

When Sanders offered to go with him back to the farm at Inverleigh, Chris said thank you. He felt strangely touched. He'd concluded that Sanders was mostly interested in making headway with Anthea, and that his helpfulness –

turning up in the back office with a copy of the post mortem, for example – had been calculated. Now he saw that there was more to the young man than that.

Sanders stood up suddenly, went to the window and flung it open.

'The trouble is that there's no hard evidence,' he said. 'Masterson's still convinced he can browbeat Sarah Kent into a confession, but there's no physical evidence linking either her or Nevis to the body, or the hotel basement late on Thursday night.'

'Sarah was often down there.'

'Which is smart of her, if she did kill him. But she's got no motive.'

'Ferrier believes it was a Satanic rite.'

Sanders laughed without humour. 'I'm amazed he gets away with saying the things he does.'

'It suits the DI to have Ferrier making extreme statements.' Chris recalled Anthea's tarot cards. 'Nevis's motive would be vengeance.'

'In spades,' Sanders said.

When Chris phoned Louise to set up a time to talk to her, he wanted her to think that all of Mrs Marr's clients were being questioned, that there was no reason to single her out.

When he'd told Sanders about Louise, the DC had stared at him as if to say he thought it was a wild goose chase, then shrugged.

Louise had dressed up for the interview and was wearing lipstick and blue eyeshadow. They began by speaking about Gerard Hardy.

'That poor young man. Did someone break into the hotel? A thief?'

Instead of answering, Chris said, 'Mr Hardy had an appointment with Mrs Marr the evening he was killed. I believe you're a client of hers too.'

Louise stared straight at him. Chris found her blue eyeshadow disconcerting, as though she had an extra pair of eyes painted on above her own.

'Yes,' was all she said.

'Would you mind telling me about your sessions with her?'

'Why? You think it's got something to do with – with the murder?'

'I'm just filling in some background.'

Louise frowned, then appeared to accept this. 'Do you know what happened to my daughter?'

'I know she died of an overdose. I'm very sorry.'

'It's over a year ago, but it still feels like yesterday. I know what happened to your father,' Louise said. 'Do you think he drowned himself on purpose?'

Chris hid his surprise. It was a question he'd often asked himself. 'I don't know,' he said.

Louise nodded, as though something she was wondering about had been confirmed. 'What did your mother think?'

'We never talked about it. It was too hard for her.'

Louise said, 'Suffer the little children to come unto me.' She went on staring at Chris and now her eyes were hard. 'Minnie's Larry ran his motor bike off the road and into a tree.'

Chris had never asked Minnie what she'd felt about her husband's death. There were times when he could have, but something – a mixture of his native reticence and his own feelings for her – had stopped him.

He said gently, 'Did you want to ask your daughter if she'd taken an overdose on purpose?'

'I wanted to tell her I was sorry and that she was forgiven.'

'What happened? Were you able to contact her?'

Each time Cathy had been about to speak, Louise told Chris, something had broken the connection. Mrs Marr had explained the chancy nature of the undertaking, but she always offered Louise enough hope to keep her coming back. Fifty dollars a time over six months was a lot of money, but she didn't mind the money. It wasn't the important thing.

Chris recalled Bernard Hepson's anger on behalf of his wife.

Louise was divorced; her marriage had disintegrated as a consequence of Cathy's heroin addiction.

'You would have started seeing Mrs Marr when she lived in Torquay. When she told you she was moving here, did she tell you why?'

'She said she wanted a change.'

'Do you think there are others?'

'Other what?'

'Mothers who seek help from Mrs Marr.'

'There could be. There's' –

'Please go on,' Chris said.

There'd been a girl in Colac. The coroner's finding had been accidental death by drowning, but shortly after the coronial inquiry Mrs Marr had left Colac for Torquay.

'Did she talk to you about the girl?'

'Oh, no. You have to understand, the readings are in confidence. Strictly confidential.'

Chris wasn't sure about that at all.

'I don't want to get anybody into trouble,' Louise said. 'I just, well I did wonder about that girl.'

When Chris told Anthea about Louise, Anthea looked thoughtful, then said, 'It's in *The Fortunes of Richard Mahony*, when Richard and Mary lose one of their twins. Amelia, she's called. Richard believes her spirit's come back, that she's still with them even though she's dead. Mary can't bear it. She writes that it cheapens her grief. This is when she's left Barambogie. She doesn't believe in spiritualism. In fact there's a scene where she exposes a medium, hangs onto her under the table and tells Richard afterwards. It's very powerful, the conflict between them – between Mary's practical common – sense and Richard's, well, Richard's lack of it.'

'I agree,' Chris said. He'd gone back to the trilogy, refreshing his memory. 'It must be one of the most common ways.'

'What do you mean?'

'Reasons why people seek out mediums and psychics. Because a child has died.'

'And parents disagreeing about it,' Anthea said bleakly. 'Marriage breakdowns.'

'Bernard and Sheila Hepson. I wonder if Sheila's still seeing Mrs Marr.'

'Behind her husband's back?'

'She'd have to be lying about the money. Unless she's got a separate bank account.'

'Like Sarah and the wine?'

'Once Mrs Marr knows that clients are visiting her in secret, it gives her an extra hold on them,' Chris said.

'Stop coming and I'll tell your husband? But what's that got to do with Gerard Hardy?'

'I don't know, but my bones tell me it's connected. They're frightened of Mrs Marr and what she represents.'

'Which is?'

'A last hope. They've exhausted all the rest.' Chris thought for a moment, then he added, 'Delia Robbins is frightened, but she's also angry, and she comes from a class of people used to getting their own way.'

Anthea said, 'I think the children know about Hardy contacting their mother. They've known all along.'

THIRTY-TWO

Methodically, they began checking coronial inquiries in the Colac area for the past two years.

Chris's mind kept returning to Ethel Richardson and her spiritualist beliefs.

When she came to dramatise these beliefs through the character of Richard Mahony and set them against Mary's scepticism, it was Mary who came through, time and again, as the stronger character. And then there was the confusion of Mary Richardson and Mary Mahony having the same name, which had to have been deliberate on the part of the author. For all his reading and thinking, Chris realised that he was a long way from understanding Ethel's feelings about her mother.

'Here's something,' Anthea said. 'A drowning in Lake Colac. Deceased's name Emma Sinclair.'

Chris moved across to read the screen.

Twenty-four-year old Emma Sinclair had drowned in Lake Colac. It was assumed that Emma had got into difficulties and there'd been nobody to help. Her body had washed in not far from a popular swimming spot. She'd been wearing a swim suit. A towel and small backpack containing her car keys had been left on the bank, and her car in a nearby carpark.

In his summing up, the coroner included a warning against swimming alone. The weather had been cool that day.

Chris glanced from the screen to Anthea's face, wondering why that detail had been included. Was it to emphasise the fact that it wasn't surprising Emma had been swimming alone? What had made her go to the lake on a day not suitable for swimming? She had died between four and six pm on a weekday. Emma lived at home. She worked in a café and had finished work that day at three.

When her parents were questioned as to their daughter's state of mind, her mother had replied that it was normal. They hadn't known she was planning to go to swimming.

Anthea looked at Chris inquiringly. 'What do you think?'

Chris shook his head. 'Impossible to say from this.'

There'd been no note. Emma had not been pregnant at the time.

Anthea said, 'Why don't we go and see her parents?'

'If they'll talk to us. They might refuse.'

The road to Colac passed through sawmills. Chris and Anthea noticed the smoke before they saw any of the buildings. One of Chris's uncles on his mother's side had worked in a sawmill. It was with some surprise that he recalled his mother's family were country people, small farmers and those who'd sought other work when their farms had failed. His mother hadn't kept in touch with them while he was growing up. No doubt his father knew the reasons why, but she'd never explained them to her son. Chris would have liked to know his cousins. Had it begun then, his mother's withdrawal that became so marked after his father drowned?

'What are you thinking about?' Anthea asked.

'Sawmills and smoke.'

'And?'

'Why people end up where they do. It's the next turn to the left,' Chris said.

Maureen Sinclair was waiting on the front porch. While Anthea was parking, she disappeared inside the house. A man in his fifties answered their knock. His hair was damp and looked as though he'd used his hands to flatten it. He was dressed in a cotton knit shirt and grey flannel trousers.

Jim Sinclair shook hands and introduced himself. He gave Anthea a small, reluctant smile.

Chris had rung the local sergeant to let them know he and Anthea were coming. The sergeant had said, after a slight pause, that that wouldn't be a problem, but they wouldn't get any more out of Emma's parents than was in the coroner's report. Chris had found Mrs Marr's previous address in Colac, with the help of a local estate agent.

Maureen Sinclair's hair was permed; it clung to her scalp in tight, grey-blue curls.

She led the way, not into a formal living room, which Chris, glancing through a half open door, guessed was hardly ever used, but to the kitchen at the back of the house.

They accepted tea. Chris noted that Maureen had everything prepared. He shook his head slightly to indicate that Anthea should leave her notebook in her jacket. He also noted that Maureen and Jim sat with their backs to the window and that their faces were set into lines of endurance.

There was a single photograph of Emma on a sideboard.

'What's all this in aid of?' Jim asked.

Chris had rehearsed his answer to this question in the car, but was suddenly at a loss as to where to begin.

Anthea said, keeping her voice low, 'You'll have seen it on TV – a young man was killed in Queenscliff.'

'What's that got to do with us?'

'His name was Gerard Hardy. The evening before Mr Hardy died, he had an appointment with a spirit medium called Evelyn Marr.'

'So?' Jim said.

Chris noticed that Maureen was sitting very still. He exchanged a glance with Anthea, who said, 'Mrs Marr was living in Colac at the time of your daughter's death. We were wondering if Emma had ever been to see her.'

'A fortune teller?' Jim said scornfully. 'What – '

'Yes,' Maureen said quietly. 'She did.'

Maureen didn't know how many tarot readings her daughter had paid for. Jim scoffed at the idea. Chris wasn't sure if the husband and wife had talked about it, how much the scoffing was for show. If the tarot readings were news to Jim, then Maureen would pay for having confessed to them.

'Did Emma have a boyfriend?' Anthea asked gently.

'No!'

Jim reached out a hand to his wife. She thrust it away and shrank back into herself.

'Emma was a quiet girl. She had her job, her friends.'

'But something was bothering her,' Chris said.

'You can see my wife's upset.' Jim controlled himself with an effort. 'I'm afraid we can't help you with your inquiries into that young man's death.'

The two constables walked slowly to where Anthea had parked the car.

Chris said, 'Maureen knew why we were coming. She knew we were going to ask about Mrs Marr.'

'She could have denied the connection.'

'Do you think she'd talk if we went to see her on her own?'

Anthea glanced at Chris along her shoulder. 'Maybe. I don't think we handled it that well. Do you?'

Chris nodded his agreement. 'Come on,' he said. 'Food.'

He wondered why he felt Mrs Marr's presence so strongly in Colac's main street. There'd been no refusal to renew her lease on a one-bedroom flat. Chris had checked this with the estate agent. No one on the local council had spoken out against her. Her name did not appear in the coroner's report on Emma Sinclair's death. Chris had been keen to speak to the coroner, and disappointed that he was in hospital recovering from an operation to remove a growth from his bowel. He felt sorry for the man, and sorry on his own behalf as well.

Anthea looked up from her focaccia to say, 'It's not a bad place here, but I wouldn't like to live so far from the sea.'

She reddened slightly, remembering, too late, Chris's fear.

Chris recalled his vision of Mary Richardson, that small, energetic woman dressed in black, hurrying home to who knew what domestic crisis, pulling her shawl tight against the wind. But it was a recollection only; she wasn't present to him in the inland town.

Anthea felt a twinge in her abdomen; it was too early, surely, to feel the baby move. The twinge was more likely to be indigestion, but she'd hardly eaten anything. Most food tasted soapy to her; even dry toast and Sao biscuits, which had been her staple for the last few days.

They found an old friend of Emma's, whose name was Sky and who worked in the same café.

Sky told Chris and Anthea, with a sad shake of her head, that Emma had visited Mrs Marr once a week for months.

After she drowned, a man had phoned Sky and asked to meet her. She'd been nervous, even a bit scared.

The man had introduced himself as Gerry and had questioned her about Emma. Had Emma talked to her about Mrs Marr? Had she said why she'd kept going back? How much had Mrs Marr charged, and had the sums increased?

'I didn't know the answers to most of them,' Sky said.

'Why did Emma keep going back?' asked Chris.

'She was talking to someone.'

'A spirit, you mean?'

'You think that's crazy, don't you?'

'No,' Anthea said. 'Who?'

'Em didn't tell me.'

'Could it have been a child?'

'What child?'

'Do you know if Emma had had an abortion?'

'No.'

'No, you don't know, or no she never had.'

'I don't know. In the last few months, she – Em – well, she went really quiet.'

'Did she tell you what was bothering her?'

'I asked her, but she wouldn't say.'

In answer to Chris's next question, Sky said she didn't know how Gerry had found her, or what his purpose had been in seeking her out. She didn't know if he'd driven to Colac, or got there some other way.

'Please don't tell Em's parents that I've spoken to you.'

Chris said he couldn't promise, but he'd bear her wishes in mind.

'If Emma had recently had an abortion, why wasn't it in the coronial report?' asked Anthea, when they were once more on the road.

'I don't know. Maybe the father was – is – '

'A man of influence?'

Chris glanced at Anthea. Her expression was grim.

'Do you think her parents suspect she'd been having an affair?'

'Not Jim. Maureen might.'

'There's no real evidence she was.'

'No,' said Chris, 'but my uniform's itching again.'

Anthea smiled and shook her head. 'There'll be medical records if Emma had an abortion. They may have been suppressed, but they won't have been destroyed.'

THIRTY-THREE

If Emma Sinclair had been pregnant, if she'd sought a termination, then she probably would not have done so through a local doctor. What about the pathology report prepared for the coroner? There hadn't been a full post mortem. Emma's parents hadn't wanted one and the doctor who signed the death certificate had been confident she'd drowned. This much Chris had discovered from talking to the coroner, who was home from his surgery, but short tempered.

When Chris and Anthea decided to drop in on Louise, she made it plain that their visit was unwelcome.

Chris asked without preamble, 'Did Gerard Hardy contact you when he was in Queenscliff last year?'

Louise nodded, her lips pressed firmly together. Chris was reminded of the old superstition that the devil could enter through an open mouth.

'Why didn't you tell me earlier?'

'I had nothing to do with his death. I'm under enough stress as it is. I don't want to get involved.'

'But - ' Chris began.

Anthea shot him a warning look. 'How did Mr Hardy know where to find you?' she asked. 'How did he know you were a client of Mrs Marr's?'

'I don't know. He phoned and said he'd like to talk to me.'

'And you agreed?'

'Not straight away.'

Louise looked indignant, then her expression changed back to its habitual sadness.

Studying her thin, disconsolate shape, her grey skin and hair, Chris felt a sudden, intense anger with Mrs Marr.

'I met Mr Hardy at the wreck bell,' Louise said in a soft voice. 'We walked to the pilot station.'

'Whose choice was that?'

'Mine.'

'You didn't want anyone to see you? It's an isolated spot.'

'I wasn't frightened.'

'What did you talk about?'

'Mr Hardy asked me questions. I didn't want to answer them. I even thought Mrs Marr might have sent him, that it might be a trap.'

'What kind of trap?'

'To trick me into paying more money.'

'But you talked anyway?'

'I – yes.'

'And Mr Hardy reassured you?'

'I felt bad about it afterwards, but it was such a relief to talk to someone who – '

'Was in a similar position to you?'

'He never said that, and I never asked him. But he'd had dealings with her. He knew what she was like.'

'What is she like?'

'She finds out people's weaknesses and uses them to make money.'

'Why didn't you stop going to her?'

'I tried to. I told her I wasn't coming back. She said that was my choice, but she knew how to entice me, she knew all the right words. And I did feel comforted, going there. I went home feeling a bit better.'

'Even though you suspected Mrs Marr was blackmailing you?'

Louise appeared to consider the word carefully. 'In spite of that,' she said.

'What does your husband think about all this?'

'Ex-husband.'

'Well?'

'He thinks I'm mad.' Louise's voice took on a hard, bitter edge. 'Is that the answer you were looking for?'

'I wasn't – '

'Oh, I think you were. I think you agree with him. Well, I'll tell you something. I don't care! Oh, we argued over Cathy. We fought like cats and dogs. Ian always claimed I was too soft on her. You don't cure someone of heroin addiction by shouting at them. Ian said the reason Cath became addicted was my fault.'

'Do you have anything more to tell us about Gerard Hardy, anything that might be relevant to his death?' Chris asked.

'No,' Louise said. 'Please don't come here again.'

Chris and Anthea conferred on the footpath. Anthea said she might go home for a bit.

'Not feeling well?'

'Just tired.'

Chris walked to calm himself, so pre-occupied that he didn't notice he'd reached the edge of Swan Bay till the sudden honking of some swans feeding on the sea-grass made him look up.

That evening, he put a good-sized log on the fire and fiddled with the curtains so that there was no gap between them at all.

Sitting down to draft a report for Inspector Masterson, he heard the scream again and recalled Masterson holding the psychic's hand.

He shook his head to clear it of the vision and the noise. He wrote for a while, then put his draft aside. He was too tired to check over it; he'd read through it again in the morning.

Chris opened his folder on Queenscliff in the 1800s. He'd put it together over the years without any special order or logic in mind. As he began lifting photocopied pages, glancing through them, he decided that he liked the eclectic nature of his bits and pieces.

Here was a description of a man who'd had a treasure map tattooed on his chest, but had never, apparently, found the treasure. The man's name had been Kerosino and he'd been called Kerosene Jack by the English-speaking locals. The treasure was supposed to have been brought ashore and buried by a pirate called Benito Benita. Generations had gone looking for it. Chris supposed that was typical, yet was it? The story seemed to him special and unique; just as the woman who had chosen death by jumping from the *Royal's* tower was special, and Gerard Hardy, who'd met his death in the basement.

Chris put his folder aside and got out the pack of tarot cards he'd borrowed from Anthea.

The log split, giving off a cheerful warmth. Chris stretched his legs towards it, debating whether or not to bother cooking dinner. He thought of Minnie, but no, he wouldn't ring her. She'd suggested meeting in the daytime and he thought it was a wise suggestion. If he phoned now, he'd be tempted to invite her over.

He laid out the channelling chalice exactly as Mrs Marr had the second time, with the addition of the Lovers card. He stared at the figures, which once more seemed to undulate, yet remain frozen. The overall shape was suggestive of a cup – Chris could not stop himself from thinking of all chalices as poisoned in some way – yet suggestive of a woman's figure too.

The firelight played over the naked man and woman. Crude and obvious in daylight, they now seemed to take life from each other, and from the divinatory power of the symbols surrounding them.

Chris shuffled the cards clumsily into their packet, remembering that he'd meant to take his uniform to the dry cleaners. He dropped the Three of Swords, shoving it in with averted eyes, afraid suddenly of seeing a beating, living heart.

He felt amateurish and silly, sitting there toasting his feet, alone with his thoughts.

Anthea had sought for clues as to where the missing book might be, reasoning that the book was a way to Hardy's murderer. The tarot had not led them to the book, but to two vulnerable children and a child's tea-cup. The cup might have belonged to Ethel Richardson or her sister, but equally might have nothing to do with them. Chris was inclined to the latter; but even if it had belonged to one of the Richardson girls, he could not see how that helped.

Nevis had taken the book, and had left it in plain view in his flat. Had he been daring the police to find it? Was Nevis as familiar with the tarot as Hardy had been, his ignorance a pretence? What was he waiting for now?

Chris warmed a tumbler of Jack Daniels between his hands and held it to the fire, its golden colour echoing the gold in the cards. He decided that he especially disliked the Three of Swords, perhaps because there were no people in it, just a heart pierced thrice.

Anthea's pack had a small instruction booklet – tiny in fact, the writing barely legible. Chris remembered Anthea telling him about how the reverse position was usually more sinister than the upright one. It would have made more sense if the lovers had been upside down.

He felt a chill at his back, though the room was warm.

It no longer seemed preposterous to Chris that so many cards predicting disaster were together in the spread.

Another question came to mind, again one that ought to have occurred to him before. What if there'd been a second person present at the reading Mrs Marr had done for Hardy?

Chris's phone rang. It was David Robbins. They'd returned to Mercer Street that afternoon, but then their mother had gone out and still hadn't come home. She had said she'd only be an hour. Now it was dark and they were worried.

THIRTY-FOUR

Chris drove to Mercer Street. One look at Sonya told him she was hanging on by a tiny thread.

He phoned Anthea, who said she'd come at once, then Masterson, who put out an alert for Delia's car.

The children sat side by side on the living-room couch, close but not quite touching. Chris realised he'd never seen the room before. It looked far too neat.

'We'll find your Mum,' he said. 'Don't worry. Did she tell you where she was going?'

Both children shook their heads. 'I hope – ' David began. But to put his hope into words was beyond the boy just then.

Anthea's face was closed and thoughtful as they searched the house. There was no note anywhere obvious, but of course if there had been David and Sonya would have found it.

Chris made more phone calls out of earshot.

When he came back to the living room, David said, 'I think Mum's run away.'

'Did she tell you she was going to?'

'Mum says we're too much of a handful.'

Chris pictured Delia shouting the words. He wished Cheryl would answer her phone. Someone needed to go to the farm. He could go, leaving Anthea with the children, but it would be stupid to head off there alone.

His phone rang. Delia's car had been driven into a fence half way along the highway to Inverleigh. She was unconscious, but alive.

The ambulance was on its way to Geelong hospital. Chris broke the news as gently as he could.

He phoned the after hours number for the child

protection unit and explained what had happened. David and Sonya would need somewhere to stay overnight and possibly for the next few days.

A relative was suggested, or a friend of the family.

Chris was most reluctant to ask Cheryl. 'I'll see what I can do,' he said.

The children's grandmother wasn't answering her phone.

Justin sounded affronted, both by the lateness of the hour, and the notion that he should hop on a plane and fetch his children from the bottom of Victoria; or worse still, stay with them.

'Just the sort of stupid thing she'd – no, it's out of the question.'

Masterson sounded impatient when Chris phoned to tell him of the problem.

'Just organise something, Blackie.'

Anthea knocked on doors until she found a neighbour willing to spend what remained of the night with the children.

When Sonya asked when they could see their mother, Anthea assured them that she and Constable Blackie would be back first thing in the morning and they'd talk about it then.

Anthea made hot chocolate while the neighbour spoke kindly to the children, who looked alarmed and then resigned.

The neighbour, who had the short grey hair and smiling eyes of a woman used to grandmotherly duties, had brought a small overnight bag. She said she didn't want to sleep in Delia's bed and that the sofa would be fine.

Before they left, Chris and Anthea went through the house again. Two shelves in the bathroom cupboard were crowded with prescription medicines. Chris hesitated for no more than a second before pulling on a pair of gloves, fetching a plastic bag from a drawer in the kitchen and sweeping them all into it.

He felt weightless and was aware of fatigue like the passage of something cool across the surface of his skin. He phoned the hospital again. He wasn't going to be allowed to see Delia that night.

Sonya looked at him gratefully. 'Thanks for helping us,' she said.

When Chris and Anthea arrived early the next morning, the children were sitting at the table eating breakfast.

They looked up, huge-eyed, asking for news of their mother.

'She's alright,' Anthea said gently. 'Constable Blackie will visit her today.'

It was a bleak answer, but the best that she could offer.

Chris had spoken again to the child protection unit. The officer who'd visited Mercer Street would talk to Delia in hospital and be down to see the children later that day.

The neighbour said that she'd be off home now, but could come back that night if need be.

Chris thanked her. She hesitated a moment before kissing Sonya lightly on the cheek and taking David's hand.

Sonya blushed. Of course the neighbour would have noticed the girl's bruises, the healing cut by her left ear.

The children sat at the table with their dressing-gowns pulled tightly round their chests. It occurred to Chris that the thick woollen garments were probably worth more than his whole childhood wardrobe had been.

Sonya looked up and caught his expression. 'Mum likes pretty things,' she said.

'You're pretty,' David told his sister.

'No, I'm not!'

'At your age, I thought I looked frightful,' Anthea said. 'Most girls do.'

Sonya's eyes widened, taking in a possibility that had

not occurred to her before.

David reached for the sugar bowl. 'See. What did I tell you?'

'Your mother bought the gowns for you?' Chris asked.

David nodded. Gerard Hardy's dressing-gown was identical, except for size, to theirs.

When questioned further, the children lifted guarded eyes and shook their heads. Their mother had given them the gowns one school holidays. 'Last year,' David said.

Sonya added, 'Our boarding house is freezing!'

Chris said to Anthea, low-voiced in the kitchen, 'If those dressing-gowns cost as much as I think they do, they shouldn't be hard to trace.'

When Anthea walked back to the dining-room, carrying a fresh pot of coffee, Sonya got quickly to her feet.

'Do you need help? What do you want us to do?'

Anthea let Sonya take charge of pouring the coffee and a few minutes later asked to see the label on her gown.

Sonya twisted round.

'Does your mother have one too?'

The girl nodded, meeting her brother's warning eyes.

Chris sat in the back yard near the water tank and googled the name on his phone. The labels were printed with the single word 'Contrapasso' and, underneath that, 'pure wool'. A few minutes gave him the name of a clothes shop in Toorak that stocked the brand.

It didn't take the owner long to check her receipts, once Chris had introduced himself and said his call was in connection with a homicide inquiry. Four gowns, two adults' and two childrens' had been purchased by a Mrs Delia Robbins.

He spoke to Delia's GP, who said he was sorry to hear what had happened, in the tone of voice that suggested he was speaking about some kind of natural disaster outside his patient's control.

When Chris asked about prescription drugs and why there'd been so many in Delia's bathroom cupboard, he replied that he was bound by patient confidentiality.

He rang the children's grandmother, who said she was sorry but she couldn't manage the trip down to Queenscliff, and there was no room in her flat for David and Sonya to stay.

Chris wondered if he should push to have the children sent back to school early, but when he raised this as a possibility, they pleaded to be allowed to stay together.

He found he couldn't argue with that.

'Are you and your sister busy for the next hour or so?'

'Why?' David asked, surprised.

'I had in mind an ice-cream and a walk on the pier.'

David's expression was incredulous, then he laughed.

Anthea took the lead as they headed off towards Swan Bay. Of course she knew that Chris never set foot on the pier if he could help it.

Anthea was looking better than she had for days. She exchanged a glance with Chris in which they silently agreed that there were questions they needed to ask, but they must be careful.

Chris noted that Sonya walked, from what must be long habit, half a step behind her brother, with her face averted. He also noted, as he had before, that David's protectiveness towards his sister was automatic; he didn't need to think about it.

Sonya spoke softly, yet her voice was clear. 'Is Mum very angry?'

'Not with you,' Chris said.

The children stared at him.

'When will she be coming home?' asked David.

'We don't know yet.'

David said, 'Are we nearly there?'

Chris couldn't believe they didn't know the way to the pier, but perhaps it was possible. Perhaps they'd never been allowed to go anywhere in Queenscliff on their own.

The brother and sister's eyes were exactly the same colour, reflecting the bay ahead of them and the ocean at their backs. They sat under the pier's covered end to eat their ice-creams, having chosen carefully and consulted one another.

Sonya finished first and went to lean over the railing.

When Chris asked David about his father, the boy finished his ice-cream with evident enjoyment, licked the stick, then said, 'It's Dad's girlfriends.'

'Girlfriends?'

'We get in their way.'

'What about your gran?' Chris asked.

David shrugged. 'She's old and can't do stuff. But she's okay, I guess.'

Sonya came back from the railing and went to sit beside Anthea, who took her hand. She'd begun to get some colour in her cheeks, to look less fragile and transparent.

'Did your mother ever talk to you about having her fortune told?'

Sonya said, with a glance at her brother that was defensive and challenging at the same time, 'I saw that fortune-telling lady with Aunty Cheryl. They were down the street.'

Chris felt David stiffen. 'When was this?' he asked.

Sonya said, 'Davey wasn't there.'

'Can't you –' David warned.

'No. I want to tell Constable Blackie. You see, Mum wanted Dad to come back, for us to be a family again.'

'And the fortune telling lady offered to help her.'

'That's what Mum said, but I don't think she was really helping.'

'Your father wasn't going to come back?'

'No!' David said with scorn.

'Dave was at a birthday party,' Sonya said.

It was the first time Chris had heard a mention of either of the children having friends in Queenscliff.

'How did you know it was the fortune-telling lady?'

'I went to her house once, with Mum.'

'You went inside?'

'Mum made me wait on the porch. She said she'd only be five minutes. But the fortune-telling lady was nice. She gave me a biscuit and told me her name.'

'It's Mrs Marr, isn't it? Could you hear what your aunt and Mrs Marr were saying that day in the street?'

'Oh no, and Mum didn't see them.'

'Are you sure?'

'She would have gone up to them. She would have wanted to know what they were doing.'

Chris wondered why the two women had met in the street. Why draw attention to themselves? If the meeting had been pre-arranged, then it must have served their purpose to meet openly.

David said suddenly, 'Constable Blackie, do you believe in ghosts?'

Anthea replied for both of them. 'No, we don't.'

'That man, the one who – Mr Hardy – '

'He hasn't come back as a ghost, and he won't.'

Their faces softened, though Sonya glanced anxiously towards her brother.

'Did you meet Mr Hardy when he came to visit your mother?'

'He never came while we were there.'

'But he did come?'

'Mum said – she said he wouldn't want to saddle himself with two brats. But we – '

'You never got in your mother's way,' Anthea said gently.

'We were at school.'

'Did your mother tell you how she felt about Mr Hardy?'

'She liked him, then she was angry with him.'

Chris said, 'You do understand how important it is to tell us everything, even a small detail that doesn't seem important.'

They nodded in unison, grave and self-contained.

David said, 'When we were at Inverleigh, we heard Aunty Cheryl on the phone. I don't know who she was talking to, but she was upset.'

'Was your aunt concerned about you overhearing?'

'We were in my room.'

Chris thought it was unlike Cheryl to take even a small risk. But then she struck him as a combination of caution and recklessness, planning ahead, yet more than capable of acting on impulse.

'Did it sound like a man or a woman?'

'I *think* a woman, but – '

'Not Mum,' Sonya said.

'Who rang who?'

'We heard Aunty Cheryl's phone ring. Then, well, straight away she sounded upset.'

'Aunty Cheryl said, Don't you dare threaten me. Then there was a silence, wasn't there, Son?'

'We thought Aunty Cheryl might have hung up, but then she said, They're not here. They're at their mother's. Do you think she meant us, Constable Blackie?'

'It sounds as though she might have,' Chris said cautiously. 'Are you sure you didn't talk to your aunt about the phone call?'

David looked at Chris as if to say, of course he was sure. 'We waited a little while, after the shouting stopped. Then we heard the front door.'

'We went on waiting after that,' Sonya added. 'Then we wanted to run away. We looked for Aunty Cheryl's phone but we couldn't find it.'

'We saw her in the distance, over by those big cows. Are they cows, Mr Blackie?'

'They're young male cattle, but they're – '

'Never mind about that now,' said Anthea. 'You decided not to follow your aunt. What happened when she came back to the house?'

'She was on the phone again, but she didn't sound angry. She smiled at us. When she'd finished she got out some biscuits and we had afternoon tea.'

After a short silence, Chris asked, 'Did your Mum tell you who she bought the other dressing-gown for, the one that's the same as yours?'

'Mum bought one for herself.'

'Another one.'

'I think it was that man.'

Sonya looked stricken. It was a connection she couldn't ignore – physical, material. Her mother had tried to buy a man's affections and now that man was dead.

Anthea put her arm around the girl and together they walked away from the pier.

THIRTY-FIVE

Cheryl was waiting for them on the front steps of the Mercer Street house. She smiled with cold triumph at Chris and Anthea and said hello to her niece and nephew.

When Chris asked what she was doing there, Cheryl said, 'I've come for Sonya and David,' as though this was the most natural thing in the world. 'They're going to stay with me till they go back to boarding school. Don't worry.' Cheryl turned to Chris, her tone of voice suggesting that worrying was exactly what he should be doing. 'I've spoken to your inspector, and to that other policewoman, from Geelong. They agree that it's best for the children to be with a family member. The policewoman's going to come and talk to the children once they're settled.'

Sonya had retreated behind her brother, who looked white and stricken. It was all Chris could do to stop himself from grabbing both children and hurrying them away.

Anthea took them through to the kitchen, while Chris asked Cheryl to wait in the living-room, 'for a few minutes, please.'

Chris pressed numbers into his phone with shaking fingers.

Masterson answered gruffly. Yes, he'd agreed to the arrangement. Delia's sister had offered, and the neighbour couldn't keep coming in.

'I don't think the children will be safe on the farm.'

'Why not?'

'Cheryl knew that Delia was mistreating Sonya and she did nothing about it.'

'The girl says she fell down some steps, so it's your word against hers and her mother's. It's not as though we're sending them to Bluebeard's castle.' Masterson sounded pleased with the comparison.

'But – '

'No buts, Blackie. The decision's been made. Just get on with it.'

Chris wondered if he'd been entirely mistaken in thinking Masterson had begun to soften towards him; or, if not soften, then to accept some sort of compromise. Talking about his daughter had seemed to offer an opening of sorts. But now the inspector's hostility and dismissive tone were back. It could be that Masterson regretted speaking about his family; it could be that he was angry at having to turn his attention to Delia Robbins when he'd ignored her up till now.

Chris phoned the child protection unit but the officer who'd visited Sonya was unavailable. He left a message.

In the kitchen, Anthea had made a hot drink, but the children were sitting with their mugs untouched in front of them.

Chris shook his head when Anthea looked at him anxiously. He cursed himself for every kind of fool. While he'd been thinking that they might have a few days' grace, Cheryl had moved swiftly behind their backs.

David and Sonya sat as though they were joined at the hip. Sonya wiped away her tears to ask, 'What will happen to Mum? Will she have to stay in hospital a long time?'

Not, what will happen to me, Chris noted. He said gently, 'She might have to stay for a while.'

'I don't want Mum to get into trouble,' David said.

'You're not to blame,' said Anthea. 'You and Sonya. Not for any of it.'

David lifted his chin, while Sonya reached for his hand.

'We're on your side,' Chris said. 'I want you to remember that.'

They turned on him identical blue stares, familiar with the empty promises of adults.

Chris kept expecting Cheryl to appear. They were all

speaking softly, but she wouldn't give them many minutes to themselves. He pulled a phone out of his pocket. 'Here. Take this.'

David stared. 'But what – '

'It's my spare. Don't worry. You won't be getting calls for the police.'

Sonya tried to smile, but David didn't. He reached for the phone and began studying it. 'It's got my number and Anthea's,' Chris said.

He was probably breaking a dozen different rules. To hell with it, he thought.

He added a charger, which David immediately put into his pocket with a resolute expression.

Anthea said, 'I can help you pack.'

Chris stood in the kitchen by the bricked-up cellar door and ran his hands over the clean surface, reminding himself that cellars had outside entrances as well as inside. He'd been over the backyard twice. If the cellar hadn't been used in the last hundred years, why expect to find any trace of its entrance on the ground? Sonya and David knew nothing about it; when he'd asked them, they'd answered simply and directly.

He knew he was trying to distract himself and that distractions were useless and a waste of time.

He spoke to Cheryl briefly, telling her the children would be ready soon.

Cheryl sat composedly, the light from the window behind her. She smiled again, but said nothing more.

David hesitated in his bedroom doorway, a rucksack in his arms.

Sonya came up behind him carrying a smaller bag. On impulse, Chris asked if they'd packed their dressing-gowns.

Sonya nodded. 'It'll be cold on the farm.'

'I'll look after Son,' said David.

His sister's smile was pale, determined. 'And I'll

look after Davey.'

'You're good kids, both of you,' Chris told them. Anthea blinked as she gave them each a hug.

Cheryl looked back at the two constables as she led her niece and nephew to her car. Her expression was triumphant. Don't think you're a match for me, it said.

Chris decided that Cheryl judged people as either for or against her; there was no middle way. The insight brought him back to Delia. When Cheryl lifted her chin and shook back her hair, the gesture of defiance might have been her sister's.

Sonya and David followed their aunt step by step and hand in hand. They did not turn round, and Chris was glad of this. Let Cheryl believe she'd won; let the children support this belief. They were smart enough to allow their aunt to think that they were glad to be going with her, or, if not exactly glad, then accepting of the fact that they should stay with a relative.

The phone was a risk, but Chris trusted David to find a secure hiding place. Cheryl was vigilant, but did not possess a thousand eyes.

He cursed himself again for not anticipating that she'd take them. He reflected that he was wrong about so many things. Every morning he could get up, if he chose to, wondering how many mistakes he was going to make before the sun went down. He was taken over once more by a visceral doubt, a physical slicing and falling away. He understood that the freedom he'd taken for himself and Anthea was the freedom of not being in charge. But you couldn't have your cake and eat it; this had never been an option and it wasn't now. You couldn't play at being a detective, then give up when it got too hard.

He'd failed Bobby. Was he about to fail these two brave children now?

'Couldn't you have done something?' Anthea demanded after they'd watched the car disappear.

'The unit in Geelong okayed it. Masterson agreed. It's policy,' Chris continued bitterly, 'for children to stay with a relative when their custodial parent won't, or can't care for them.'

THIRTY-SIX

The surrounds of the hospital and the building itself looked attractive in the autumn sun. Chris stopped for a moment to admire the slant of light on pale brick. He looked up thinking that behind one of those windows Delia Robbins lay. What was going through her mind?

Chris spoke to the nurse in charge and followed her down one long corridor, then half way along another, noting her aggressive, stumpy walk. It reminded him of Bridget. In other circumstances, he realised that he might have considered such a way of walking evidence of survival against the odds.

Delia did not raise her head when Chris entered her room, which contained nothing but a bed and chair, both bolted to the floor. There were bars across both the inside and outside of the single window, and a glance confirmed that the room contained nothing that might be picked up and thrown, or that the patient might use to injure herself or anybody else.

Chris sat down on the chair and said good afternoon.

Delia looked at him, a swift look full of spite.

He noted how thin she'd become since the first time he'd seen her, and how her hair, showing grey at the roots, stood out in uncombed spikes.

'I've had it up to here with the police,' was Delia's opening remark. 'I've already had that beefy inspector, and some cowgirl from child protection. It was you who sicked them onto me. You know something? I don't give a shit. The kids're better off without me, and I'm better off without them.'

'Better off with your sister?'

'Why not? They'll soon be back at school. My ex is a

scum-bag, but at least he pays their fees.'

'You bought Gerard Hardy an expensive present,' Chris said, thinking he would change the subject, then come back to the children later.

Delia laughed. Chris waited for a flicker of the eyes, a nervous movement that would tell him Delia knew Hardy had been wearing the dressing-gown when he was killed.

'Gerry went away,' she said. 'Just like Justin – when there was nothing more he wanted from me, he vamoosed.'

'Cheryl tried to keep you at the farm at Inverleigh that Thursday night, but once you found out Hardy had come back to the *Royal*, you insisted on going there. What happened then?'

'Oh yes, she was right! My sister's always right!'

'What did Cheryl do?'

'She said if I was determined on such a mad course of action, she'd come with me.'

'What were you going to do when you got to the hotel?'

'Bang on the door. Wake everyone up. Jump off the tower. I don't know!'

'Did you have a front door key?'

'No.'

'Did Cheryl?'

'Why would she?'

The key was important, but Delia was quite capable of standing in the street and shouting for Hardy to come down. He might have too, in order to avoid a scene.

'Did you see anybody in the street?'

'Cheryl thought she heard footsteps behind us.'

'What about you?'

'What do you mean, what about me? I was furious with that jerk! He wanted to see over the house, wanted to talk about the Richardsons, then when he'd got what he wanted, when I had nothing more to tell him, he dumped me! He used me and I didn't – I didn't even – '

'Realise that he was gay?'

'Go on, call me stupid. Everyone else does! My sister would be happy to see me locked up. Don't let her tell you otherwise!'

'It's not your fault if Gerard Hardy used you. If it's any comfort, you're not the only one. Did you go to the hotel's back entrance on Thursday night?'

'No.'

If Delia and Cheryl had been just a few minutes later they would have met Manoli leaving.

'When you showed Hardy over your house, what was he looking for?' Chris asked.

'He wanted to know which room had been hers. How should I know? Why the hell should I care? He said it shouldn't have been renovated. It should have been left as it was. I pretended to be interested. I thought, come on Delia, it isn't every day a lovely young man comes knocking on your door.'

'When you ran your car off the road, you were on your way to your sister's. Did you phone to tell her you were coming?'

'No.'

'Were you expecting her to be at home?'

'Where else would she be?'

That was a good question, Chris thought.

'What does your sister think about the tarot readings?'

As though her muscles had decided to act independently, Delia thrust herself up from the bed and lunged towards Chris.

The door opened.

'Time's up,' the nurse said firmly, grasping Delia by the arms.

'It's okay - ' Chris began.

'Okay for you, Constable Blackie, but this one's given me more than enough trouble already.'

Chris realised he'd lost his chance to talk to Delia about David and Sonya; he'd even been hoping to persuade her that they shouldn't stay with Cheryl, and try to get her cooperation on that.

He had to wait to see the doctor, a young Vietnamese woman obviously rushed off her feet, who responded warily to his questions. She said that Delia was being treated as high risk following her suicide attempt. While in hospital she would be given a thorough psychological assessment.

Chris wasn't sure Delia had tried to kill herself, but he didn't want to argue. He listened without further interruption or comment.

He decided to walk off his worry and frustration. He'd gone all the way to Corio Bay before he took stock and realised he was staring at the water. It seemed to be happening to him a lot lately.

With a shudder, he turned his back and found a bench to sit on.

He tried to think of an excuse for turning up at Inverleigh. When none came to mind, he wrenched his thoughts from David and Sonya and forced himself to concentrate on other matters.

How had Hardy felt returning to Queenscliff, knowing Delia was just down the road from the *Royal*? How had he felt walking past with Charles Nevis and pretending he had never met her? Unless Nevis was lying, and Hardy had told him about his association with the current owner of that blighted house.

His dressing-gown cord had been placed neatly beside his body, folded in half and then again. The cord had been on the side of the body facing away from the entrance to the final chamber and the sandpit. Chris had had to walk right around before he noticed it.

He continued to ponder mental illness as his feet took him up the hill, away from the haunting and seductive sea.

Masterson presented his own visit to Delia in hospital as an accomplishment, and once more brushed aside Chris's fears for the children.

He downplayed Chris's report on the phone conversation David and Sonya had overheard.

'It could have been anyone.'

'I think it was Mrs Marr,' Chris said.

The phone rang on the inspector's desk. He picked it up, said, 'Yes, no,' then, 'Tell them to pull their bloody finger out.'

Suddenly the tension in the front office was unbearable. Chris shut the door quietly behind him.

THIRTY-SEVEN

Anthea brought tea out to her balcony.

She sat with her bare feet on a chair, scrunching her toes in a cushion as she listened to Chris's account of his visit to Delia. She looked up to say, 'Delia's been lying to us from the start.'

'Something's changed,' Chris said. 'Maybe she can't see the point any longer. But I don't believe she killed him. She doesn't have the ability to carry out a complicated plan like that.'

'Her sister might. Do you think Cheryl's a client of Mrs Marr's as well?'

'She denied it. Somehow I believed her.'

Anthea looked thoughtful. 'I did too.'

Sooner or later, everyone who came into contact with Delia Robbins would end up quarrelling with her. The wonder was not that her marriage had ended, but that it had lasted as long as it had.

Hardy had been very good-looking. Would Mrs Marr have been influenced by his looks as well?

Chris poured himself a second cup. He knew his way around Anthea's kitchen, as she did around his. Both preferred 'real' leaves left to steep for the right amount of time in a ceramic pot. Minnie had succumbed to tea bags long ago. Chris had teased her about it, and Minnie, who seldom allowed her annoyance to show, had snapped at him, saying she spent her working life serving food and drink, and all she cared about now was convenience.

Anthea was leaning back, her feet still on the cushion and her toes half buried.

'I should get up and do something.'

'There's no need to rush.'

Chris fetched Anthea's tarot cards and went through them one by one.

He stopped at the Devil. The Devil's beard was fair, beneath a down-turned, greedy mouth. His hands were human, one holding a fiery brand. His feet were taloned; bat wings stretched behind; in front of him stood a pair of lovers, naked and in chains.

The price of sin? Chris pulled out the Lovers card and set it alongside. The figures were recognisably the same. The heart pierced thrice was the Three of Swords. The Lovers meant adultery when that card appeared next to the heart. Chris's eyes returned to the Devil, licking his lips as he contemplated punishment.

If Gerard Hardy had been punished for adultery, was his lover still awaiting punishment? Or had she already been punished, but in a different way? What if that lover were a man? What if Charles Nevis had been, perhaps still was married? It was a question Chris knew he should have asked before.

The Devil signified ravage, violence, force, but also that which is pre-destined, but not necessarily evil. Chris wondered at the distinction, studying the bearded face, focussing this time on the ram's horns sprouting from his head, the pointed, hairy ears, the human man and woman who had, by reason of their lust, become his slaves. In the Lovers card there was temptation – the apples on the tree, the snake – the wages of sin are death. But who believed that literally and had sought to prove it in the basement of the *Royal*?

That night Chris rang Nevis to ask if he'd ever been married. He expecting Nevis to laugh, or at least to be amused.

Instead Nevis was angry. 'I should hope I know myself better than that.'

'Know your sexual orientation, you mean?

Silence on the other end.

'You knew Hardy had stayed in Queenscliff before,' Chris said. 'You knew he was already a client of Mrs Marr's, yet you deliberately withheld that information.'

'I did not.'

The book came back to Chris, with its dark red cover, Hardy flourishing it at Nevis in the restaurant, Nevis deciding to steal it.

'Where did Hardy get his first edition of *Ultima Thule*?'

'He bought it online.'

'Where online?'

'It was before we got to know each other. He might have told me, but I don't recall.'

'Did he show you the receipt?'

'No.'

'Did you ask to see it?'

'Why would I do that?'

'Did he tell you how much he paid for it?'

'I don't remember any of the details.'

'Why did you take it?'

'Because he owed me.'

'What for?'

'I was going to give it back.'

'Did you go into Hardy's room the next morning?'

'What? After I'd been told what happened?'

'Before Matthew came to tell you.'

'No.'

'Afterwards?'

'No.'

'When you were having dinner at *The Chandler* on Thursday night, you said Hardy was excited, pleased.'

'That's right.'

'Think back to what he actually said.'

'I've told you all that I remember.'

'Did he say anything about Mrs Marr, her appearance

or her manner?'

Nevis was silent for a moment before saying in a different, less irritated voice, 'Gerry said something about Dorian Gray. Was that in relation to the psychic? I think it might have been. I didn't take much notice at the time.'

'Dorian Gray?'

'You know the story? Gerry said something about the underneath beginning to wear through.'

'What made you think he was referring to Mrs Marr?'

'He'd just been there.'

'It could mean Hardy had met Mrs Marr before, and was making a comparison.'

Charles Nevis sounded older, as though the story about Dorian Gray might apply to him, not a sudden change from young to old, but a hardening and tightening of his vocal chords.

'Gerard Hardy meant a lot to you,' Chris said. 'You drove him down to Queenscliff in order to spend time with him, even though he'd made no promises.'

'Promises?' Nevis laughed.

'Hardy was good at those. He managed to make Delia Robbins believe he'd promised her a lot.'

'Oh, that cow!'

'So Hardy did talk to you about her.'

'I might as well tell you. You know, it's funny, since coming back home none of it seems real. I keep expecting the phone to ring and for it to be Gerry brown-nosing the way he did when he wanted something. Sorry if that sounds crude to you.'

'But you're relieved he won't.'

'Spoken like a true copper. You want me to say I'm glad he's dead.'

Chris waited, knowing that, now Nevis had begun, he would feel compelled to explain himself.

'I'm relieved not to be humiliated any longer, knowing

I'm too cowardly to insist on a clean break, and Gerry is confident all he needs to do is keep hold of the strings and give a little tug every now and then.'

'What did he tell you about Delia?'

'Apart from her being a manipulative cow? Gerry boasted that he had her crawling after him.'

'What did he intend to do if she became a nuisance?'

'Gerry didn't think like that. He didn't plan ahead in that way. He was used to winning confrontations.'

'Did he have sex with Delia?'

'He said he did. To disgust me. I don't know if it's true.'

'He would have boasted to Mrs Marr as well.'

'She was different. She interested him.'

'Because she communicated with the spirits?'

'I never met her except to say hello to on the porch. But I got the feeling that they were alike in character. And of course there was the spiritualist side of things.'

'What about sex with Mrs Marr?'

'I don't know if Gerry actually went to bed with her.'

'Would he have told you if he had?'

'Probably.'

Chris tried one last question. 'Was there anything else Hardy said that evening, or perhaps on the drive down?'

'Drive down?' Nevis repeated mockingly. 'On the drive down Gerry slept. That's why he was so perky when we got here. Once we were over the Westgate Bridge, he shut his eyes and snored.'

Chris had another bad night, visions overlapping one another, vying with one another for his exhausted attention. The Lovers, the Devil, the World with the bull in the corner, the Four of Swords mixed and mingled, flashing colours at him, mocking, shrieking their laughter yet remaining silent.

Mary Richardson glided in her black dress behind

them, but could not break through.

Chris got up and lay down again, pulled the doona over his head, then tossed it off. At four o'clock he gave up, put on his dressing-gown and made a pot of tea. He sat staring at the darkness through the window, wondering if Cheryl had already found the phone, waiting for the dawn to come.

THIRTY-EIGHT

Normally, Chris enjoyed eating his breakfast and drinking coffee made the way he liked it, with the sun warming his back through the kitchen window, but that morning his coffee tasted gritty and his cereal stuck to the roof of his mouth.

When he opened the door to Minnie, all he could think of to say was, 'Oh, it's you.' And then, 'You'd better come in.'

It had been raining, a swift early morning shower. Minnie carried an umbrella and was dressed in her work clothes.

'There's coffee on,' Chris said.

'I can't stay, but there's something I – well, I think you ought to know.'

'About Louise?'

Minnie shook her head, dislodging silver drops. 'No. About Bridget McGuire.'

'Are you sure you won't have a coffee?'

'Just a quick one then.'

Minnie put down her bag and umbrella, watching Chris carefully, head on one side like a bird that might have to fly away at any moment.

'There's something the matter. Is it the children?'

'Yes. But tell me your news first.'

'You know Bridget's on with that Greek fella?'

Chris nodded.

'She doesn't have a lot of choice, stuck in St Leonards with her Mum.' Minnie's voice was sharp. 'You understand why I'm telling you this – not to get the girl into trouble.'

'Please go on.'

'She went round to that psychic's and they had a big argument.'

'Who told you?'

'Danielle.'

Chris recalled Edwina's phone call that he hadn't followed up. He found it hard to concentrate on what Minnie was telling him.

'You're upset,' Minnie said.

Chris's voice shook as he told her about David and Sonya, how their aunt had been granted care of them while their mother was in hospital. They were stuck with her in an isolated farm house.

Minnie said, 'That's terrible. What can you do?'

'That's what I'm trying to work out.'

'Let me know if I can help.'

'I will, Minnie. Thank you.'

Cheryl would be waiting for him to phone, or turn up at Inverleigh. She would have coached the children, and they would have agreed with what she told them to say. Chris tried to think of a way to persuade Masterson that the children's predicament was urgent.

He wondered whether Delia and Cheryl had fought with one another, growing up. When he rang the hospital, he was told the psychiatrist was with Mrs Robbins and they couldn't be disturbed.

It wasn't like the first press conference – no lights blazing out from the *Royal* to waiting journalists and public fired up by a football win.

It wasn't like the first time, with a crowd avid for the basement, the thrill of a dead body down there, in their town, in an underground space that had once done duty as a morgue.

Chris recalled the bars that still sat across the high, small windows. His throat felt impossibly tight, as though filled with sand.

Inspector Masterson was different too. He still looked

imposing, tall and broad. But the spotlight had shifted. Masterson was no longer under it in the way he'd engineered that first Saturday night, confident that success was in his hands and all he had to do was close them round it.

New information had come to light concerning their chief suspect.

Chris and Anthea exchanged a shocked glance. Ferrier looked smug. Sanders was keeping his head down.

A witness had come forward to say the suspect had been seen digging in the hotel basement on the afternoon Gerard Hardy was killed.

'It was the cook,' Ferrier told Chris and Anthea. 'He didn't say anything to the police because he didn't want to get the Kent girl into trouble. But he told Bridget McGuire, and Bridget rang Inspector Masterson this morning.'

'Where was Sarah digging?' Chris asked.

'In the sandpit. A grave for the sodomite. When she was seen talking to him at the basement entrance on Thursday evening, she arranged to meet him down there. She took him by surprise and strangled him.'

Chris thought it would be impossible for Ferrier to look more pleased with himself than he did at that moment.

'Do you think Bridget is telling the truth?' Anthea asked after Ferrier had left them.

Chris nodded. 'Yes, I do. Bridget might lie on her own behalf, but she wouldn't risk lying about what Manoli saw.'

Chris pictured two wounded creatures helping one another – Manoli struggling with his alcoholism, Sarah with the visions that had blighted her since childhood. But then the picture shifted and instead he saw two opaque and devious individuals.

Anthea sat staring into space.

'Are you alright? You've gone very pale.'

'I don't feel well.'

'You should go home. I'll take you.'

Chris wanted to go home himself and run a bath, something he rarely took the time to do. He wanted to soak until the water cooled, then add more hot water, and then more again, as though his doubts and fears, all the unanswered questions, could soak out from his skin and float away.

In his pocket was the report he'd written on his late night conversation with Charles Nevis. Would Masterson bother to read it now?

After he'd dropped Anthea off, Chris thought he would detour via the *Royal*. He remembered how it had been completely silent in the basement on that Friday morning; there'd been no sound from overhead at all. Gerard Hardy's hands had looked enormous from a distance. In his memory, they took on giant shapes, reaching almost to the low stone ceiling.

He thought again of the raw, new town of Queenscliff, lacking a permanent way to dispose of its dead, of the temporary morgue that had given way to cells for lunatics, and what the guests above had made of that. Such reflections were often close now to the surface of his mind. There appeared to be nobody at all at the hotel. The front door was locked and the back gate as well.

'Constable Blackie.'

Chris swung round.

Manoli was walking towards him along Mercer Street.

'So Bridget finally pulled the plug on Sarah,' Chris said. 'Why did she wait so long?'

Instead of answering, Manoli said, 'Come down to the basement.'

Manoli unlocked the hotel's back door. Standing behind him, Chris was aware of the tight muscles in the cook's neck, how braced and tense he was.

The basement keys were back under the reception counter.

The smell at the bottom of the stairs seemed to be advancing towards them.

The sandpit was empty. Chris realised he'd been frightened of what might be down there.

'What was Bridget arguing with Mrs Marr about?' he asked.

'She – I never agreed with her going to that woman – she wanted help to persuade my wife to agree to a divorce.'

'Did Mrs Marr help her?'

'No. But Bridget kept on hoping that she would.'

'Why did you want to bring me down here?'

'To show you that it – it's just a hole.'

'Why was Sarah digging?'

'She told me she was setting the trapped spirits free.' Manoli's words echoed around the small, closed space. 'Bridget's got a job in Melbourne. They're leaving in two weeks.'

'Maybe you should look for a job in Melbourne too.'

'Who would have me?'

'You don't know till you try,' Chris said.

THIRTY-NINE

On Chris's second visit to Delia in hospital, the nurse paused outside the door to say, 'Might be your last chance. Doctor's making her final assessment today.' She didn't try to hide her relief that Delia would soon be off her hands.

Delia was sitting on the bed with her back to him. Her head was down and she looked thoroughly miserable. Chris walked to the end of the bed, hesitating to place himself between Delia and the window. He noticed that the chair was gone.

When he said hello, Delia didn't look up. Her hands kneaded one another in her lap; her fingers were red and swollen.

'When your sister drove you to the *Royal* on Thursday night, did you park in Mercer Street?'

For a moment, it seemed as though Delia wasn't going to reply. Then she said indifferently, 'Up the other end.'

'Were any of the hotel lights on?'

'I don't remember. I called out. No one came. I waited, then I started blubbing. Typical.'

'What happened then?'

'Cheryl said we'd come back in daylight. She said I could arrange to see Gerry. He wouldn't refuse if he knew how important it was to me. What a laugh!'

'You knew that night was your last chance?'

'Last chance for what? Last chance to make a stupid fool of myself?'

'How far would your sister go in order to protect you?'

'What, you mean she killed him? Now you're being a fool. Cheryl looks after her own interests. She took me back to Inverleigh, locked my car in the garage and kept the key.'

'Did she go out again?'

'Not that I heard.' Chris noticed that energy came in small bursts, then left Delia flat again. 'I didn't hear her car. I was so exhausted that I went to sleep and stayed asleep till morning.'

'How did you find out about the murder?'

'Cheryl made breakfast and we went for a walk. We talked about the meeting, how to plan it, what to do. When we came back, we heard about it on the news.'

'Did Cheryl tell you she met Mrs Marr in Hesse Street?

Delia looked up incredulously. 'Why would she do that?'

'Why do you think?'

'My sister hated me going to her for readings. I mean hated it.'

'Do you think she was trying to persuade Mrs Marr to let you go?'

'Maybe. If she did, she wouldn't have been gentle about it. You may have noticed that my sister doesn't do things by halves.'

'She's taken charge of your children.'

Delia laughed. 'She won't hurt them. She covets them. She's got no kids of her own and she's always wanted mine. She's welcome to them. I don't care!'

Chris knew he ought to grasp the opportunity; but how? How to persuade Delia to act on her children's behalf?

'Sonya and David shouldn't be on the farm alone with Cheryl. They're not safe. You need to - '

'I don't care!' Delia screamed at him.

There was a warning knock on the door.

'Get out! Get out!'

'Constable Blackie?'

'Alright, I'm coming,' Chris told the nurse.

Anthea lay on her couch, not hungry, but feeling she should eat something, conscious of an ache in her lower abdomen.

She went to the toilet and saw a stain on her underpants, a streak of dark matter where they should be clean.

She blinked. She took her pants right off and held them up to the light.

The toilet had only one small window. Outside the sky was overcast, threatening rain. Twilight would come early.

No, she thought, then said aloud, 'Oh, no.'

The doctor didn't keep her waiting for more than a few minutes, and Anthea, tempted to lie down on the waiting room floor, felt grateful for this. There were four other patients in the room. One was Bridget McGuire with an older woman Anthea assumed was her mother.

The doctor took blood for tests and told her to go home and lie down.

'What will – how long – '

She didn't know which questions to ask, and wanted answers to none of them. She longed to go back, wipe the blood out by act of will.

'I should have the results by late tomorrow morning. I've labelled your sample priority.'

'What if – ' Anthea began again.

'Some bleeding's not uncommon, so try not to worry. If it becomes heavier, ring me. Is your husband at home?'

'No. No, he's not.'

'I understand that it's your first time and that it means a lot to you, but if you do miscarry, well, you're young and healthy. There's no reason why you shouldn't conceive again.'

Anthea started to cry as soon as she was out of the surgery. She'd sent Chris a text, but had switched her phone to silent when the doctor called her in. She saw that Chris had sent two messages. The first said, 'I'm so sorry!' and the second, 'Where are you? What do you want me to do?'

Anthea texted, 'I've been to the doctor and I'm on my

way home.' She did not want to call him.

Chris replied immediately. 'I'm on my way.'

He looked more worried than Anthea had ever seen him, his face scrunched into a thousand lines.

Anthea was lying under the doona. She lifted herself on one elbow. She didn't want anything – she had water by her bed – but oh, she was pleased to see him.

Chris took her in his arms and they stayed like that, Anthea leaning, Chris awkward on the edge of the bed.

He pulled back to ask, 'You've phoned Olly?'

'He's on his way. I couldn't, I still can't believe it.'

Chris asked what the doctor had said and she told him. Her cervix had been closed, which was apparently a good sign.

'Are you hungry?'

'Maybe toast? A small piece?'

Chris made toast and boiled the jug for tea.

When he returned to the bedroom, Anthea said, 'Bridget McGuire was in the surgery.'

'You're thinking – '

Anthea stared out the window. Swan Bay was there, in all its glitter and enticement.

'After three months, how much blood and – and tissue?' Anthea turned back to Chris, her face naked and appealing. 'How much blood?' she said.

Olly went to Anthea at once and kissed her, folding her in his arms.

Anthea cried with relief at having him there. Chris quietly took his leave.

He could look up the time of greatest danger for a miscarriage. Was it two hours after the first sign of blood? Six hours? Twelve?

There mightn't be an answer, no figures that were

statistically conclusive; and even if there were, Anthea's case might fall outside the norm. If she got through the night without a sudden loss of blood, she might begin to hope it was a false alarm. She and Olly would count off the hours till they could phone for the test results.

Chris's phone rang when he was half way home. He pulled over to answer it.

'Constable Blackie.'

He drew in a sharp breath.

Mrs Marr's voice sounded very clear, clearer than when they'd last met face to face. She said, 'Your young assistant is in trouble.'

Cars and trucks went by at a steady pace. Chris forced himself to breathe.

'My clients are vulnerable people. I won't have them harassed.'

'I haven't harassed anyone. Neither has Constable Merritt. Threatening a police officer is a serious offence.'

Mrs Marr laughed before breaking the connection.

Chris's first impulse was to dial again, but he knew the psychic would be expecting this, that it was what she wanted him to do.

When he pressed Anthea's number, Olly answered. He sounded surprised.

'Can I have a word with Anthea?'

'You were here only a few minutes ago. What's the matter?'

'Just checking.'

Olly said, 'I'll let you know when we have any news. I have to go now.'

Chris thought, perhaps it's better this way. Anthea would hear the agitation in my voice no matter how I tried to hide it. Better, too, that Olly is screening her phone calls.

Chris's mind ran in wobbly circles, trying to figure out

how Mrs Marr had known Anthea was pregnant, let alone in danger of miscarrying. Who knew, apart from Olly and himself? What about Bridget, waiting in the doctor's surgery? Anthea would have said nothing about her reason for being there, and neither, of course, would the doctor; but the sympathetic receptionist, who'd brought her a glass of water, might have let something slip.

When Bridget opened the door, she frowned and looked about to close it again.

Chris quickly stepped inside.

'Tell me about your mother's visit to Dr Moreland.'

Bridget coloured angrily. 'It's none of your business.'

'You were in the waiting room when Constable Merritt came in.'

'So? That's not a crime. She jumped the queue. Mum and I had already been waiting for twenty minutes.'

'Did the receptionist say anything about why Constable Merritt was there?'

'Why should she?'

'Why are you so angry, Bridget?'

'Angry? Wouldn't you be angry if you were harassed and pestered when you've done nothing wrong? I took my mother to the doctor's. She can't get there on her own!'

A voice called out from the back of the house.

'Oh, God, not again,' Bridget said.

She walked ahead of Chris down the corridor, while Chris studied a patch of knotted hair on the back of her head. She helped her mother use the toilet, then returned her to her chair by the kitchen window.

'You police are all alike. You put words in people's mouths and then condemn them for it.'

Chris said, 'Someone strangled Gerard Hardy, someone who knew he planned to go down to the basement.'

'How would I have known that?'

'Or else heard him and followed him down there.'

'I was here with Mum.'

'Where was Manoli?'

'It's in his statement.'

'I know where Manoli says he was.'

'But of course that's not good enough for you.'

Bridget's mother said in a soft, though perfectly clear voice, 'That nice young man brought me a bunch of flowers.'

Bridget turned on her a look of fury, but she raised her chin defiantly. Her sparse white hair made a halo against the kitchen window. 'Let me tell him. What harm can it do? My daughter's a good girl. She spends her time looking after me, instead of going out and meeting people.'

Chris said, 'There's no harm in two people liking each other and wanting to spend time together.'

Bridget made a noise of mixed fury and disdain.

Chris began walking to the front of the house and motioned Bridget to follow him. When they were out of her mother's earshot, he asked, 'What was your argument with Mrs Marr about?'

'She's that fortune-teller? I wasn't arguing with her. I don't even know her.'

'Oh, I think you do. What's more, I think you found a way to make it up with her.'

'I've no idea what you're talking about.'

'Manoli told you he'd seen Sarah digging in the basement on the afternoon Gerard Hardy died. Why did you wait till yesterday to tell Inspector Masterson?'

'Because I'm fed up!' Bridget cried. 'I know Manoli's talked to you. I know he's told you that we're leaving, me and Mum. I've had enough of this hole. He can stay here and help look after Princess Sarah.'

'What if she's in jail for murder? You'd like that, wouldn't you?'

'If she's guilty, why not? Why the hell not?'

'Manoli cares for you.'

'Does he? He's got a funny way of showing it.'

Chris thought of the flowers, then the long, dragging acrimony over the divorce.

Bridget's voice changed and she cried out, almost pleading, 'We would have been all right if only you'd left us alone!'

Chris knew he should have realised that Bridget would give nothing away about her association with Mrs Marr. Nevertheless, he felt confident that he'd solved the problem of who had told the psychic about Anthea's threatened miscarriage. It might have been a clever guess on Bridget's part, or the receptionist might have said something – the details didn't really matter. What mattered was that Bridget had been there and she'd immediately realised the use Mrs Marr could make of the information.

Chris went home, and was changing into a clean uniform when his phone rang. This time it was good news. The hcG levels were good, consistent with a living foetus.

'That's great. Tell Anthea I'm thrilled.'

'Thanks.' Olly's tone of voice suggested it was too soon to use a word like 'thrilled', but he sounded enormously relieved. 'She has to have another blood test in forty-eight hours. If the hormone levels continue to rise and there's no more bleeding – '

'Tell her I'm thinking of her.'

'I'll do that.'

Now that the immediate threat to Anthea was lessened, Chris's anxiety over David and Sonya returned.

Seeking a distraction, he looked up 'ghoul' online. The word derived from the Arabic 'ghul', an evil spirit or cannibalistic monster that robs graves and feeds on corpses.

Ghouls lured unwary people into abandoned places before killing them.

When they were talking at the fort, Sarah had explained the difference between ghosts and spirits. Ghosts are 'stuck' between this world and the next, sometimes because they've died suddenly and don't understand that they are dead, sometimes because they have unfinished business with a person or a place. Spirits have passed over successfully.

Sarah had understood his fear of the sea without him having to explain it, to tell the story of his father that he hated telling. Chris knew about explanations which immediately brought down anger or incomprehension, frequently a mixture of both. He knew the plunging sense of failure before attempting one, that only deepened as he struggled on.

He gave silent thanks that his young assistant had never required such explanations from him. And he gave thanks to Minnie, who knew all his sorry history and who never spoke of it, just as he never spoke of the young bridegroom who'd crashed his motor bike, leaving her a widow.

Minnie had said once, 'There are things you never get over. But you can get past them.'

She'd done better than he had on that score.

FORTY

Unable to decide on a better course of action, Chris drove to Colac to meet Jim and Maureen Sinclair.

'I understand that you don't want to talk about it,' he said to Emma Sinclair's parents.

Jim grimaced, while Maureen looked down at the floor. She seemed very far away to Chris, as though willing herself not to be there, not to have to answer questions and put up with a policeman in her house.

Jim said, 'We thought – after the funeral, we thought that it would all be over. We thought we'd never have to deal with that woman again.'

'Did Mrs Marr threaten you?'

Maureen raised her head. Forced back into the present, her expression was both sad and determined.

'Mrs Marr expected you to go on paying her,' Chris said gently. 'Gerard Hardy knew that. How did he find out?'

'It's not a lot of money and we can afford it.'

Blackmail is blackmail, Chris felt like telling them.

'What my wife means, Constable,' Jim said through clenched teeth, 'is that we feel we owe our girl. She has nothing left now but her good name.'

'And the good name of the man she was having an affair with? You're protecting him as well.'

'What man?'

'Please tell me what you told Mr Hardy.'

'We told him we were paying the psychic, that's all.'

'Did he know who Emma's lover was?'

Jim winced at the word. Maureen said firmly, 'No.'

'Did Mr Hardy advise you to stop paying?'

'He was kind and sympathetic. I – I'm sorry that he's dead.'

Jim said, 'Please. We want you to leave now.'
Chris did as he was bidden.

He'd just arrived back in Queenscliff when the call came.
'Mr Blackie!'
David's voice was shocked and frightened. 'That psychic lady's here!'
'Are you okay? Where's Sonya?'
'We're in my room.'
'What are Mrs Marr and your aunt doing?'
'They're fighting! It's awful!'
'Can you – ' Chris was about to ask if he could lock the bedroom door from the inside, but he already knew the answer.
'I'll be there as soon as I can.'
David's voice was an urgent whisper. 'I have to go.'

Chris drove Inspector Masterson and the two detective constables to Inverleigh. Though his siren was on the whole time and he drove as fast as he could, the distance seemed interminable.
Cheryl answered the inspector's knock at the farmhouse door.
Mrs Marr was standing just behind her. Sonya and David had ropes around their necks and the psychic held a knife to Sonya's throat.
'If you want these brats to live,' she said, 'you'll do what I say.'
While Masterson phoned for back-up, Chris walked around the house. The blinds were drawn at the front and he could see no movement from inside. The kitchen blinds were half open, but from where he stood Chris couldn't make out whether there was anybody in the room.
He heard the sound of metal scraping against metal. The back door opened a fraction and something was thrown

out. A shout came from inside, followed by laughter. Chris took two paces forward. A small object glittered in the dust. It was the phone he'd given David.

When Chris returned to the front of the house, Sanders told him that a special operations team was on its way in a helicopter.

The DC looked ten years older and was close to panic, all his suave good humour gone.

'She's waiting for a sign, then she says she'll kill the woman and the kids,' the negotiator told Inspector Masterson after they had landed.

'A sign?'

'From the other side, she says.'

Mrs Marr would know what the arrival of the helicopter meant. The team could shoot their way in; they didn't need to wait. But at what cost? At whose?

Chris turned aside and beckoned Sanders with him.

They ran to the paddock. The Highland cattle were where Chris expected them to be, solid and docile just inside their fence. He fixed ropes around their necks while Sanders got the gate open.

'Round the back,' Chris said.

He waved to the negotiator, calling over his shoulder, 'Tell her it's the bull. From the World card. Tell her that.'

Silently, he begged that the distraction would be enough. The cattle stood unblinking, their huge horns centimetres from the window.

'It's the bull from the World card,' the negotiator said. 'He's come at your bidding, Mrs Marr. Tell him what you want him to do.'

Chris heard a girl's scream, followed by a wail of fury.

Mrs Marr was taken to hospital in one ambulance, Sonya, David and Cheryl in another. The children were suffering from shock and minor cuts and bruises, but uninjured apart from that.

The Channel Nine helicopter made an enormous din arriving; TV vans sped up the driveway. For one horrible moment, Chris thought Masterson was going to hold a press conference on the front steps of the farmhouse.

Sanders shook his head. What if the arrest had gone wrong, and the cameras had been there to film a debacle?

Masterson began walking towards Chris in his usual heavy-footed way, each step beating on the earth.

He put out his hand. 'Blackie. Well done.'

'Thank you, Sir.' Chris couldn't believe what he was hearing.

He wished Anthea was there, and thought fleetingly that she might not believe him. Then he grinned.

On their way to return the cattle, the DC congratulated Chris, who, dizzy with two lots of praise in several minutes, took in great gulps of relief. His face was far too hot. When they got to the water trough he'd dip his whole head in it.

Sanders laughed at the sight of him dousing himself and shaking water everywhere. They made sure the gate was secure, the Highland cattle watching them impassively.

'You go back,' Chris said. 'I'll just stay here for a bit.'

Sanders understood and nodded. He stood staring for a moment at the farmhouse and the press vans before walking back.

Chris gathered water in his cupped hands. He let cold, refreshing water run down the back of his neck. He sighed, exhaustion hitting him, and felt his knees give way. Their adventure did not seem to have bothered the cattle. He thanked them for a job well done.

FORTY-ONE

Chris and Anthea waited at the hospital, in a small alcove outside the room where David and Sonya were asleep.

A television screen – they seemed to be everywhere – was replaying the press conference Masterson had held at Cheryl's farm. Chris wished he could turn it off.

'He came up and thanked me. After it was over.'

'He never did!'

'Scouts honour.'

They laughed. Chris took Anthea's hand and held it tight.

His thoughts returned to Mrs Marr, who might revel in a murder trial as a further opportunity for theatrical performance. Chris imagined the psychic looking forward to her time in court. If convicted, she would probably make money and enhance her reputation giving tarot readings from a prison cell.

'What made you think of the cattle?'

'I don't know,' Chris said. 'Desperation?'

'What if it hadn't worked?'

'I think they would have gone in anyway.'

He played the sequence of events over in his mind – the special operations team arriving, Mrs Marr's intransigence, Sonya with a knife at her throat, the Highland cattle at the back window and the armed men bursting in.

They watched a nurse go into the children's room. She returned in less than a minute, mouthing, 'Still asleep.'

'It might be a long wait,' Chris said.

'I'm okay.'

'What about Olly?'

'He knows where I am.'

'Then make yourself comfortable. Here, lean on me.'

Anthea adjusted her position so her head was resting

on his shoulder.

'Why did she go there? Why take Cheryl and the children hostage? Why go to the farm?'

'The children heard their aunt arguing on the phone. Remember how Cheryl said, "Don't threaten me". Mrs Marr was furious with Cheryl for trying to take Delia away from her. She was vindictive and spiteful. Don't forget, she'd already killed a man.'

'I hadn't forgotten,' Anthea said softly. 'What about Louise? Emma Sinclair's parents?'

'There'll be others, too, that we don't know about. The money's important, but just as important, perhaps even more so, is the emotional hold she has on them.'

'Gerard Hardy found out about the blackmail.'

'They didn't see it as blackmail necessarily.'

'Pressuring them, then.'

'Hardy wasn't like the others. I think that was Mrs Marr's first mistake, believing that she had a hold on him, that he'd keep coming back because of Henry Handel Richardson. But really it was the other way around.'

'You mean because she was attracted to him sexually?'

'Hardy came on to her. Charles Nevis was right. It was second nature to him. Especially when he wanted something from a woman. Or a man. I think they quarrelled on that Thursday night. Quarrelled bitterly.'

'But Hardy was supposed to be happy and excited.'

'Ah, but he was, you see. He was going to talk to Henry Handel Richardson on his own, in the basement of the *Royal*. He didn't need a spirit medium any more. He'd already got what he wanted from Mrs Marr. And he wouldn't have let her down gently.'

'But he underestimated her.'

'She was as ruthless as he was. Even more so, once she understood that his rejection of her was complete.'

'Sarah Kent – what did Hardy need her for?'

'I thought at one time that he might have asked Sarah to go down to the basement with him. I was wrong about that. But Hardy needed to know where the key was kept, and he needed to make sure he could find the entrance without fumbling around in the dark.'

'Then why was Sarah digging in the sandpit?'

'She told Manoli she was setting the trapped spirits free.'

Anthea smiled, then shook her head. 'Did Hardy come to Queenscliff planning to break with Mrs Marr?' she asked.

'I don't know that he planned it. It may have been the reading on Thursday that convinced him he didn't need a medium any longer. He may have boasted that Ethel would talk to him without a "fortune-teller's" help. When Mrs Marr objected, he accused her of forcing her clients to keep coming back to her, and said she was a fool if she thought she could treat him like them. But he under-estimated her. Her reaction wasn't to keep trying, like Charles Nevis, or to fly into an impotent rage like Delia Robbins. He was a thoroughgoing egotist and he despised middle-aged women who were flattered by a young man's attention.'

'Henry Handel Richardson?'

'Ah, but she was dead, you see. And I don't know if he thought of her as a woman. As we know, having a man's name was important to her, and she may have been bisexual, in inclination if not in practice. No, I don't think Hardy thought of her as a woman, not in the way he thought of Delia and Mrs Marr, who were repugnant to him. When he'd got what he wanted from them, he let his repugnance show.'

'So it was a double rejection – of her skills as a medium and of her as a woman.'

'Hardy had rendered her of no account, but she wasn't going to have that. Mrs Marr went to the *Royal* that night. I think she got there before Sarah had locked up and found a place to hide. After Sarah had left, she fetched the basement key. Wearing gloves, she opened the basement door and then replaced the key. Then she went to the end of the brick passage and waited. Of course she couldn't know where Hardy would make for, but that didn't matter because she'd hear him. Hardy would have found the basement door unlocked, but that wouldn't have deterred him. He may even have taken it for a welcome sign.'

'The dressing-gown cord?'

'I don't think it was used to strangle him. There was always something odd about that. It was too clean. Hardy's skin was broken. The cord should have had skin fragments embedded in the wool. No, the psychic brought her own weapon.'

'Where is it now?'

'My guess is keeping Hardy's laptop company at the bottom of the bay. Mrs Marr couldn't afford to leave it. She didn't know what he'd written about her and her clients.'

'Why didn't Hardy fight her off?'

'She took him by surprise and from behind. And there's another reason. Hardy knew what he hoped would happen in the basement, but not what to expect.'

'You don't think he – '

'He was in a state of high anticipation, suddenly bewildered, shocked at finding himself unable to breathe – '

'And by then it was too late.'

'Mrs Marr folded the dressing-gown cord neatly and fixed his hands in prayer position on his chest. She took his laptop from his room, then she let herself out the back door and walked home.'

'And neither the honeymoon couple nor Nevis heard her?'

'Nevis slept soundly through it all, just as he claimed to have done.'

'Was it Mrs Marr that Lily saw?'

'Probably.' Chris recalled his mistaken assumption

about a teenager sneaking home after curfew. 'Lily knew Mrs Marr well enough to look at, of course. But my guess is she was wearing a thick coat and a woollen hat. Even in a brighter light, a positive identification would have been difficult, and wisely Lily didn't let herself be bullied into making one.'

'What about the vet's dog?'

'It's unlikely Jasper would have barked at Mrs Marr, because he knew her. On the other hand, he might have. Or he might have barked at a possum, or a rat.'

'Mrs Marr was lucky the vet was kept late.'

'She would have been careful not to turn any lights on. But yes.'

Anthea stared towards the door through which the nurse would come to tell them they could see the children.

'She believed she could make me have a miscarriage.'

'But she couldn't and she didn't.'

Anthea's expression cleared. 'I think I can tell people now,' she said.

'Good, then. That's good.'

'I wouldn't have wanted to fall at the first hurdle.'

'No.'

'But now I'm over it.'

'You are.'

In the end they were only allowed to say a few words to David and Sonya and kiss them goodnight.

Chris was so tired that undressing seemed a herculean task. He fell asleep at once and couldn't remember his dreams.

The next morning he waited with Anthea on the station's back veranda.

Masterson had shaken their hands and said goodbye. So had Ferrier and Sanders. Chris noticed that Anthea had not met Sanders's eyes and thought that, if the DC had been hoping for a last private conversation with her, then he was disappointed.

The computers and other equipment were being moved out of the front office. Chris was counting the minutes until all of the detectives were gone.

He cocked his head at the sound of a car starting up.

Five minutes later, Anthea was wiping window ledges with a damp cloth. They moved the desk so that it was once again facing the window, and stacked the white board in a cupboard.

Chris sat down on his swivel chair and laid both hands, palms downward, on the desk. He sighed and said, 'That's better.'

Anthea lifted her cloth as a kind of salute. 'Will we start on the kitchen?'

'In a minute.'

'I'll miss this view,' said Anthea.

'And I'll miss – '

Chris could not complete his sentence. He stood up.

'The tarot?' Anthea smiled. Chris turned towards her.

'You suspected me, at one time,' she said.

'Of what?'

'Of believing in it.'

'Well – '

'Poking around under Delia's water tank.'

'It wasn't such a bad idea,' Chris said.

He thought of Ethel Richardson making up stories in order to turn her mind away from her family's misfortunes.

He told himself the world was full of people he would never understand. To see that David and Sonya were properly cared for – that was enough to think about for now.

'What did Bridget have against me?'

It took Chris a moment to grasp Anthea's meaning. He said, 'She was a customer of Mrs Marr's as well.'

'So she was earning points?'

'Something like that. She wanted Manoli's wife to

agree to a divorce, but it wasn't working. She argued with the psychic, then tried to make it up to her.'

'Poor Bridget. I wonder if they'll make a go of it, those two.'

'And Sarah and Matthew.'

'I think they'll be okay.'

'They won't stay at the *Royal* though.'

'No, they won't do that. Matthew will find another job in hospitality.'

'And Sarah?'

'Maybe she'll find peace. I hope so.'

'Maybe she'll have a baby,' Anthea said, touching her belly lightly.

After Anthea had left, Chris took his time over moving the rest of his things into the front office. He opened the station's doors and let the clean, cool air blow through.

Anthea still hadn't said whether she was going to apply for maternity leave, or resign. Her remark about missing the view from the front office window could be taken either way.

Chris pictured again the Lovers card, the World card with the bull, the dead young knight with his hands in prayer position. It wasn't the first time that farce and tragedy had proved themselves to be closely linked, nor would it be the last. He made a resolution that, in the time allotted to him, the time that he had left, he'd strive to understand his town better than he had so far. Then he felt – it came upon him suddenly, without warning – an immense, vertiginous frustration with the limits of this, or any other human understanding.

He felt as though he'd been promised a bright and shining light, and then the sun had gone in. But promised by whom, and for what purpose? He felt dizzy and took himself out to the back veranda.

He stared into the distance, which he could do so long as he was not facing the sea. Many clever men and women had asked questions, down the centuries, about the meaning of existence, and would no doubt go on asking. He didn't have to feel let down or cheated that not only answers, but even the right questions eluded him.

Chris sat in the sun and allowed himself the indulgence of a day-dream.

His house and block were tiny, but a third bedroom could be built on the back. He'd sacrifice his vegetable garden. What about an attic room, or two? David and Sonya could have privacy then, their own privacy when they came to stay, which they'd need as they grew into adolescence. They wouldn't want an old fogey like him falling over them every step they took.

Chris recalled how, on the pier, he'd hardly registered the heaving sea beneath them, how all of his attention had been fixed on Sonya's slight, curved figure and her brother's wary eyes. That was the way to deal with your phobia – not through avoidance, which he'd practised unsuccessfully for years – but by having someone else to think of and worry about.

Chris pictured himself ringing around till he found the right builder, chatting about possibilities, talking through the idea and the costs. It was expensive, putting second storeys on, but if he didn't have enough, then he could take out a loan.

Read all of Dorothy Johnston's Sea-change Mysteries:

Through a Camel's Eye
The Swan Island Connection
Gerard Hardy's Misfortune

Upcoming:
The Lodeman

Read on for Chapter One of T*he Lodeman*

ONE

Chris Blackie would have played only a very minor part in the investigation into Captain Delraine's death if Brian Laidlaw hadn't found the body.

It was almost too dark to see where he was going. At this time of year, the rising sun took a long time to penetrate the sandhills. Chris used a torch to walk from the carpark, but when he got to the bottom of the path, he switched it off.

The tide was going out. In the shipping channel, a pilot boat, its lights still on, made for the open water. The heavy pulse of the diesel engines echoed off the dunes.

From humped shadows, a man stood up. Chris knew who it was, but might have recognised him anyway, by the shape of his beanie, the way his hair and beard stood out around it, only ever erratically trimmed, by his long-boned frame and braced, watchful stance.

For a long time, Brian Laidlaw had resisted getting a mobile phone. Only the uncertain health of his friend Camilla Renfrew had persuaded him to do so. The retired sailor was often out beachcombing; he spent most of his time on the beaches and the spongy shores of Swan Bay, and the fact that Camilla might fall, or otherwise hurt herself and need him, had changed his mind.

When Brian rang, Chris had been asleep and dreaming, the way he sometimes did in the hours before dawn. The dream was still with him, though he shook his head to clear it. Brian had told Chris where he was, and the name of the dead man, Captain Frederick Delraine.

Delraine was lying face down on the sand. Chris knelt and felt for a pulse. Brian had moved a few steps away and stood staring after the pilot boat, while dawn turned the horizon green and silver.

The dead man was very cold. Chris estimated that he'd been in the water for at least six hours. He was wearing a shirt and trousers made of heavy cotton, but no jacket, socks or shoes.

Chris pulled on a pair of the latex gloves he always carried with him and felt in the pockets – no keys, wallet, or phone.

There were no obvious signs of injury, but the strengthening sun magnified a fine white froth around his lips. Chris smelt faint traces of vomit and noticed that Delraine's shirt was stained.

'Did you move him?' Chris stood up to ask.

'No,' Brian answered curtly.

Chris phoned the Criminal Investigation Unit in Geelong and then for an ambulance.

Brian began to walk away.

Chris called out his name, anticipating the CIU's questions, the old man's reluctance.

'Come back. Tell me what happened. We don't have much time.'

Twenty-five minutes later, a small procession led by paramedics with a stretcher made its way across the sand from the steps. Chris recognised Dr Hammond and felt pleased. He was pleased, too, that nobody had come by while they waited, no early morning joggers or dog walkers.

Chris gave a brief report. After that, the detective in charge, a Sergeant Dawkins, ignored him. The doctor did as well. Brian answered the sergeant's questions in monosyllables.

Dawkins looked annoyed, as though being got out of bed so early disagreed with him. After asking Brian a few more questions, he told him to go home and wait there. When Chris offered to ring Camilla, Brian dismissed the suggestion with an angry shake of his head.

Chris's first impression on entering Captain Delraine's room was that it had been stripped bare. He felt anxious because Sergeant Dawkins had trusted the pilot dispatch officer on duty to lock the room and not remove anything. He wondered, listening to Dawkins giving orders on the phone, who had already been through the captain's belongings.

He stood in the doorway recalling the sergeant's words.

'Have a look round, Blackie. If there's anything interesting, let me know.'

If Chris had been in charge, he would have wanted to examine the room himself. He would have had a forensic expert there. It seemed Dawkins had already made up his mind that the captain's death was an accident, or possibly suicide.

There was no imprint of personality, less than in an ordinary motel room, where, on opening the door, your nose might pick up after-shave, deodorant, sometimes a furtive cigarette.

Chris reminded himself that it was only a few hours since a man had been sitting on the bed, or single chair next to the window, getting ready for the night. The bed covers were pulled tight, not a crease or rumple. Had Delraine smoothed them before going out? Or had someone else? Perhaps it had been second nature for the pilot captain to set his room in order before leaving it.

Chris pulled his gloves back on and set about looking for a note, already aware that he would be disappointed if he found one. The bedside cabinet was empty except for a packet of anti-histamine tablets and a box of tissues. A reading light stood next to the bed. The waste paper basket had either just been emptied, or Delraine disposed of his small items of refuse somewhere else.

There were two suits hanging in the wardrobe, four shirts, two extra pairs of trousers, a fine wool navy jacket and a three-quarter length raincoat. No jeans or tracksuit, Chris noted. Even off duty, the captain apparently dressed more formally than most people nowadays. The drawers beneath the hanging space held socks, pyjamas and clean, folded underwear. There were no pyjamas underneath the pillow.

Chris went methodically through pockets, starting with the suit coats and jacket. He peered into drawers and probed the backs of them. He lifted the mattress and reached under the bed. What had happened to Delraine's wallet, phone and keys?

Chris's brief conversation with the shocked and white-faced pilot dispatch officer established that Delraine had locked his room before going out the night before. The PDO, Michael Travers, could not say whether Delraine had taken his phone or wallet with him. Delraine had poked his head around the office door at around eleven and said that he was going for a walk.

The PDOs worked twelve hour shifts. Chris wondered why this man, who looked exhausted, hadn't been relieved.

Last night had not been particularly cold, yet Travers was pretty sure that Delraine had been wearing a jacket, and he was hardly likely to have set off in bare feet. He hadn't seen or heard the captain returning.

When Chris asked about CCTV, Travers hesitated before replying. Chris thought, you've been though the footage. You know what's on it. He asked to see the film and Travers, after a brief hesitation, agreed.

The film was poor quality, grey and grainy, yet the man leaving the front door of the operations centre was recognisably Captain Delraine. He wore a jacket, shoes and socks. His face was turned away from the camera. He walked slowly and, to Chris's eye, stumblingly as well.

The time on the screen was 11.03.

Chris turned from the monitor to ask, 'Were you worried?'

'A little.' Travers licked dry lips.

'A little?'

'The captain often went for a walk before going to bed. And I – I couldn't leave my post.'

'I'll take the film,' Chris said. 'How many cameras at the back?'

There was just one, Travers said, covering the courtyard and the door leading to the laundry and kitchen.

'I'd like all of it, please. Let's say from 8 pm last night?'

The captain did not keep a car in Queenscliff. Everything he'd brought with him was either at the operations centre, on the beach, or in the sea somewhere. Except, of course, if someone had cleaned out his pockets and his room.

Chris's phone rang.

'Well?' Sergeant Dawkins barked. 'Have you found it?'

'A note? No.' Chris paused, then said, 'I think – '

'You think, Constable? Just do what you're told.'

Chris sighed as he pulled a plastic bag out of his pocket and placed the packet of hayfever tablets inside it. He stood staring at the label. It wasn't one he recognised. Taking the tablets felt like an automatic reaction to the sergeant's put-down, but he couldn't imagine what good it would do.

His phone rang again. As he answered it, Chris shoved the plastic bag and its contents deep into his pocket.

Port Phillip Sea Pilots died as the result of accidents. Sometimes their crews died with them. Most of Queenscliff knew that Chris's father had drowned attempting to save his master; the town's older inhabitants remembered every drowning that involved pilots, their drivers and their crews.

A pilot who walked into the sea intending never to return was more than an anomaly. It was an event that went against nature. Chris did not believe Delraine had killed himself. He did not believe the pilot had left a note and that someone else, for whatever reason, had removed it.

Accidental death? No, that was illogical as well.

The first in Dorothy Johnston's Sea-change mystery series

Through a Camel's Eye

Still he looked for hoof prints, glad there was nobody there to laugh at him for doing so. He shaded his eyes and squinted at a dark object, half covered in sand, then began to walk towards it. He should have been wearing sunglasses to protect his eyes, but he never thought of things like that. It was a woman's coat, black, or at least it had been.

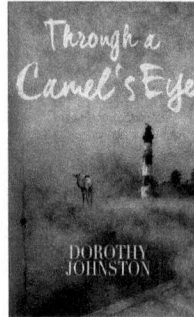

A young camel disappears from its trainer's paddock and the coat of a murdered woman is found abandoned in the sand dunes. These seemingly unrelated events are a far cry from the regular police duties of Constable Chris Blackie and his rookie recruit from Melbourne, Anthea Merritt, in the small seaside town of Queenscliff. Little by little and with a burgeoning sense of menace, these two unlikely detectives carefully navigate the eclectic, often eccentric personalities of the town, as well as the disdain of law enforcement colleagues further afield, to uncover the unsettling truth.

Described as a 'sea-change mystery' *Through a Camel's Eye* deftly juxtaposes the idyllic surroundings of a coastal Victorian town with the gravity of murder.

'Dorothy Johnston stands with the best of Australian crime writers, her exquisite sense of people and place as evocative and compelling as the elegance of the plots.'

Sara Dowse, author of *As the Lonely Fly* and *West Block*

The second in Dorothy Johnston's Sea-change mystery series

The Swan Island Connection

All children were a mixture of innocence and guile, Chris Blackie thought, but the innocence had been squashed out of Bobby McGilvrey unnaturally young.

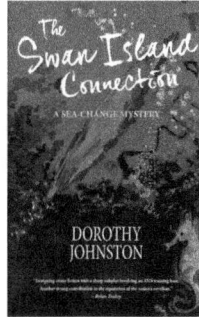

A shocking murder rocks the quiet coastal Victorian town of Queenscliff, a place were police work usually entails minor traffic infringements and the occasional Saturday night drunk.

Local senior constable, Chris Blackie and his deputy Anthea Merritt fully expect a murder investigation to be handled by the Criminal Investigation Unit based in Geelong. But they're blind-sided by the interest shadowy figures from the secret military training base on nearby Swan Island take in the case.

Consigned to the edges of the investigation and fearing an imminent wrongful arrest, Chris and Anthea defy their superiors and follow their own lines of investigation – at great personal risk.

'Dorothy Johnston has delivered an intriguing blend of social observation and crime fiction in her latest novel set in Queenscliff, Victoria. The story is spliced with a sharp sub plot involving the nearby training base for the Australian Secret Intelligence Service. Another strong contribution to the reputation of the nation's novelists.'

Brian Toohey

About the Author

Dorothy Johnston was born in Geelong, Victoria, and lived in Canberra for thirty years before returning to Victoria's Bellarine Peninsula where her 'sea-change mystery' series is set, commencing with *Through a Camel's Eye*, followed by *The Swan Island Connection* and *Gerard Hardy's Misfortune*.

She is the author of twelve novels, including a quartet of mysteries set in Canberra. The first of these, *The Trojan Dog*, was joint winner ACT Book of the Year and runner-up in the inaugural Davitt Award. *The Age* gave it their 'Best of 2000' in the crime section.

Two of Johnston's literary novels, *One for the Master* and *Ruth*, have been shortlisted for the Miles Franklin award.

She has published many short stories in journals and anthologies, along with essays in Australia's major newspapers. For more information about the author, please visit her website: http://dorothyjohnston.com.au